COOKHAM TO CANNES

BRENT TYLER

For Debbie

Chapter 1

Our little business had collapsed and we, that's my wife
Debbie and I, were sitting in our local pub, spending money
that we could ill afford. It somehow seemed the right thing to
do. Being cooped up in a small house all day, worrying about
the future without popping out every now and again for a drink
or two can drive a person insane. Debbie would often say,
'What about the landlord? He keeps phoning.'

'Let him do the worrying for a change,' I would reply.
'We've got enough problems of our own.'

It was December – the snow was falling heavily. Locals in
their wellies, thick jumpers and scarves fought with the door to
get in and then wrestled with it again to stop it from slamming.
Rubbing hands together and with puffed-out, ruddy cheeks
they'd order their drinks. Christmas was upon us and, much
like the turkeys at the farm just down the road, we weren't
looking forward to it. We'd given up trying to analyse where it
had all gone wrong. We just knew that it had and that we must
move on, but to where and to what exactly? We were in our
mid-forties, we had no money, no income and an eviction
notice just around the corner. In the space of a couple of
months we'd gone from just about being able to make ends
meet to having absolutely nothing, and what was worse, we
had no idea how to deal with the situation. Our world had been
turned completely upside down.

We'd sit in the pub a couple of times a week, Debbie with
homemade pâté, toast and a glass of rosé, me with a bowl of
chips and a pint. Then, after a few minutes' silence we began
to sound like the vultures in *The Jungle Book*:

'What are we going to do?'

'I don't know. What do you want to do?' And so it went on.

We'd racked our brains to the point where we really
couldn't think straight anymore. When your bank account is
virtually dry and you're also in the middle of a deep recession,
life is tough. Being unemployed at any time is the worst job in

the world – you've got all of the stress of a normal job but no salary to go with it.

We'd thought of just about everything to get us out of the situation. Debbie was, and still is, a fantastic cook and I'd had a lifetime in sales, but no one was hiring. Restaurants were closing at a rate of ten a day and all the advertised sales jobs were commission only. We scoured the local Job Centre vacancies for work but there was nothing, absolutely nothing, or at least nothing that we could do. There was plenty for engineers, plumbers, electricians, supply teachers, nurses and so on, but very little for us – at least not enough to keep body and soul together. When we weren't looking through the local paper, we were trawling the Internet in the makeshift office at the front of our freezing house.

We'd spent hours, days, searching everywhere to no avail, until one day Debbie, who was sitting at her computer, stumbled across an advert in a magazine which read: *Helpers wanted south of France. Free accommodation in return for a few days' work a week – one day on, one day off.*

'Brent!' she shouted. Moments later I appeared, struggling to walk in my several layers of clothing and checking periodically to see if there was still any movement in my toes.

There was no heating in the house, not because we hadn't paid the bill but, when turned on, there was a terrible smell of gas. As we weren't talking to our increasingly irate landlord, who would have refused to pay for an engineer to come out anyway, we froze – and unfortunately, so did the house. We watched the damp inside the fitted wardrobes in our bedroom make its way rapidly up the walls. Condensation penetrated the double glazing, the wallpaper began to peel off and the plumbing had packed up, which was exactly what *we* wanted to do – pack up. To add insult to injury, a letter arrived that day addressed to our landlord from HMG, detailing his heating allowance for the winter.

'He's in bloody Spain,' I shouted, 'and has been for years! The bastard should be reported.' We later learned it would have made no difference whatsoever because, due to some quirk of British law, it was legal to claim the money if you were

2

a UK citizen of pensionable age, no matter where in Europe you lived.

'Look,' said Debbie excitedly, 'we've always talked about living in the south of France and this might just be our chance. I mean, what have we got to lose?'

'Nothing, actually,' I replied, looking down at the pile of red bills that were on the desk. The phone rang. 'Withheld, don't answer it,' I said. 'Never good news.'

The next morning, she rang the person who'd placed the advert and some time later had secured us board and lodgings at a mobile home park in Mandelieu, a small town not far from Cannes. 'Blimey, that was easy!' I said.

'Apparently, not too many people want to go and work in the winter,' Debbie replied. 'Everyone wants to be there in August, by which time my love, hopefully, we'll have really nice jobs. Come on, we need to get going.' For the first time in a very long while, there was no sadness behind her smile. Debbie had made her mind up and was off to mark our arrival date in France on the calendar on the wall. I put the cynical thought out of my mind that it had happened far too easily and was now looking forward to our arrival date, 21 February 2010.

'What are you doing?' I asked, as Debbie started to write feverishly on a piece of A4 paper.

'Making a list of everything we need to get there. Grab a seat, come on.'

'Are you sure about this?'

'Unless you can think of anything better. Anyway, might do us the world of good. A change is as good as a rest and all that. Get thinking.' For hour upon hour we wrote down everything that we could think of to get us on our way. The first and most obvious hurdle was money. Quite simply, we didn't have any – certainly not enough to get us to the south of France and then, how much would we need just to get by? Poring over our map of France, we calculated, recalculated and calculated again everything from miles per gallon to stop-off points, to a daily food allowance as well as the exact date by which we'd need to find a paying job.

For the first time in what felt like ages, Debbie wasn't just motivated, she was very optimistic, too. She spoke that evening of all of the places she'd visited in France with her family when she was a young girl. Her mother and father had owned an apartment in La Grande Motte, a seaside town just outside Montpellier. She talked with great fondness about the beach, the restaurants and the happy times that she and her brother and sister had spent by the pool at an apartment block called *Le Club*.

'You'll love La Grande Motte,' Debbie said, enthusiastically. 'Literally translates to "The Big Sod"! It's right on the sea and next to the Camargue too,' she added, pointing to a large area of green on the map. 'The Camargue's famous for its wild horses and there are flamingos too,' Debbie explained.

'Flamingos in France? What the hell are flamingos doing in France? That's a bit of a hike!' I said.

'Never really thought of it like that,' Debbie replied. 'You've got to see it to believe it. And look, there's Aigues-Mortes. That's nice. Spent some lovely times there, too. It's a beautiful, old, walled city – full of artisan shops and restaurants on every corner. I can't wait.'

There was still the thorny subject of money, but we surmised that eight weeks was enough time to beg, borrow or steal the three thousand pounds we needed. We put an advert in our local newspaper to sell what we either couldn't take with us or didn't want to put into storage. Bargain hunters came and went until we were left with a huge office desk and a television that didn't work. We had also advertised some of our more expensive items on an online auction site, but there was no joy there. There were bits and pieces that we really didn't want to get rid of but, as we needed the money, we were prepared to let them go at a reasonable price. Unfortunately, our idea of what was reasonable was poles apart from the prospective buyers.' So we began the task of deciding what would fit in our car to take with us, what to put into storage and what to throw out.

The amount of clutter we had accumulated was frightening.

'Bloody hell, Debbie!' I shouted.

'What's up?' she replied.

'Five years of marriage it's taken us to get this lot together and it looks like someone's been fly-tipping in our garage!' Debbie laughed. We went to visit various storage companies to see who would give us the best deal. At the same time, we bought all manner of packing materials, tape guns and marker pens.

Soon enough, what could be packed in cardboard boxes was neatly stacked on one side of the garage along with garden pots of various sizes, a water feature, a bird table and a power drill that, to this day, I have absolutely no idea how to use. There were holes all over the kitchen wall where I'd attempted to put up shelves, but whenever I'd tried to use the drill, the wall just crumbled, leaving messy cavities and an even messier floor. I gave up.

Debbie, however, was in her element. She's an extraordinarily organised person; she's incredibly methodical and has a photographic memory when it comes to where things are in the house, which can be very useful. What is not quite so useful is that although she can pack a box of books with military precision, what she could not grasp then, and still cannot now, is any concept of a box's weight once full. She'd line all the boxes up on the floor like little soldiers, fill one, tape it up, label it and proudly march off to the next without any idea as to who was going to lift it, or how – it simply didn't cross her mind. We packed, unpacked and repacked the car, trying to maximise every inch of available space for the journey ahead.

All this activity must have seemed strange to our retired neighbours, to whom we had said nothing about our plans. It wasn't that we didn't get on with them; in fact, quite the opposite. It was simply that although they were not great friends of our landlord, they had agreed to keep an eye on his property in his absence. Quite how much contact they had with him we didn't know, but we didn't see any point in taking the chance of antagonising him any further. It was obvious that his patience had finally run out as a day or two later we received an email from him saying that he had had enough of the rental market and was putting the house up for sale forthwith. We would be contacted by one of the local estate agents in the very near future and we'd be expected to assist with facilitating any would-be buyers.

True to his word, the next day the estate agent arrived, declaring,

'I can't see much happening before Christmas. Daft time to put a house on the market, if you ask me. Can I smell gas?' and off he marched around the house with his tape measure and Dictaphone. He was right about one thing – not a soul came to see the property until the new year and even then there was a lot of rubbing of chins and scratching of heads.

'There's a lot of work needs doing to this place,' I'd hear them say. 'Doesn't look like much has been done to it since the sixties. Not sure if I've got the time or money for this.' They came, they went, but it didn't seem like anyone was interested.

It was January, bitterly cold. We still hadn't managed to get enough money together for our trip and, like many people, we hadn't been able to afford to buy each other a Christmas present. What little money we made from the sale of our household goods had gone on packing, a deposit for our storage and the late payments that we'd accrued on our car finance. We tried just about every avenue we thought open to us but no one was going to lend to people in our situation. We scoured the Internet, the newspapers, made numerous phone calls but it was becoming abundantly clear that our options had all but run out.

Our families weren't rich and we really wanted to avoid asking friends because it just didn't feel right. We hated the thought of letting them down in the event that it all went wrong but in the end we had no choice.

I'd put off many times making the phone call that was our last hope but it seemed that I simply couldn't delay it any longer. Pete and Jen had become great friends over many years. Pete was a senior manager at an international building firm and was highly respected – so highly that year after year, even though of pensionable age, they wouldn't let him retire. Jen, a highly sought-after seamstress, was contracted to most of the exclusive boutiques in the area. They both knew what it was like to struggle financially and had worked hard for every penny they had. It was tough to make that call.

'I can't believe I'm having to do this,' I said to Debbie. 'Are you sure there's no other way?'

'We've tried everything else,' she replied. 'I don't think we have any choice.'

Reluctantly, I picked up my mobile from the desk.

'Jen, it's Brent. I'm sorry, but....' A few minutes later, I came off the phone. I looked at Debbie and smiled. 'She said yes, they'll lend us the money.' Tears began to roll down Debbie's face as she ran towards the bathroom.

'Don't worry,' I remember Jen saying as she passed me an envelope full of cash a few days later. 'It's not as if you're leaving the country. Oh, actually you are!' She laughed.

An hour later we had said our goodbyes and I returned to our freezing cold house with the final but most important piece of the jigsaw. In a few days' time, thanks to our very dearest friends, we'd be heading to the south of France.

'Look, Debbie,' I said, waving the envelope triumphantly in the air, 'we've got it!'

'I can't believe they lent us all of that money,' said Debbie.

'I can. Pete will have thought it was worth it just to get rid of us.'

The next day we went to say goodbye to Debbie's mother in Henley. We met in Café Rouge where, somewhat ironically, the staff could speak just about any language except French. Marlene had been a real pillar of support for us when we were suffering. She'd get the bus from Henley to Cookham, bringing us food parcels and job adverts that she'd cut out of the local paper. I had thought that our last coffee with her might have been an upsetting one but it was anything but – we were all very positive.

'I'm sure everything's going to be fine,' she said. 'A fresh start is exactly what you need. Besides, if you don't do it now, you'll never do it. Not like you're getting any younger, is it?' She laughed.

'Thanks for that,' I said.

'Oh, shut your noise,' Marlene replied. 'Cheers. *Vive La France!* Oh, and before I forget, here's a card for you but don't open it until you get on the ferry. Now, you'd better get off if you've got an early start in the morning and don't forget to call me when you arrive.'

'Can't we just give you three rings?' I said.

'No you bloody well can't! And look after my daughter. Now, if you don't mind, I've got a crossword to do,' she said, picking up the *Daily Telegraph*. 'Bye-bye my love,' she whispered to Debbie, who leant over to give her a kiss.

Wow, that was easier than I thought, I said to myself as Debbie and I climbed into the car. On the way back we stopped to pick up a pizza and a couple of bottles of wine to raise a toast to not just our last night in Cookham, but also our last night in England for what we hoped to be a long time to come. We sat in our candlelit lounge, staring at the now bare walls and watching the condensation run down the windowpanes. Huddled together and wrapped up in several layers of clothing, we tucked into our four cheese pizza and sipped cheap wine from plastic cups.

'Last night of doing this,' I said through chattering teeth. 'This time tomorrow we'll be somewhere in France.'

'Thank God for that,' replied Debbie. 'I don't think I could face another night in this freezing bloody house. Here's to Pete and Jen. Cheers.'

We'd planned to be out of the house early the next morning, around six-thirty. However, things took a little longer than expected. We were finally ready to go about an hour after we'd hoped. The sun was up and so were our neighbours. We had bought them a card which had a picture of an elderly couple sitting on a park bench. The caption read: *Age really doesn't matter...unless of course you're a cheese*, which I thought they'd find amusing. We liked Harry and Rosie immensely, but thought it best not to say goodbye in person, so although I could see their lights on in the kitchen and cigarette smoke billowing through the small window in their lounge, as Debbie turned the ignition in the car, I quietly slipped the envelope into their letter box, slunk into the passenger seat and gingerly closed the door.

We made our way down the drive, joined the main road and turned right into a small parade of shops. I got out of the car with another envelope containing the keys to our house and a letter explaining that we had left Cookham for good. I put the envelope through the estate agent's door and, soon after, Debbie and I were back on the road, heading away from our sleepy village in rural Berkshire.

Chapter 2

The heavens opened as we made our way along the M25; the windscreen was getting pelted with all kinds of debris thrown up from the tyres of the heavy goods vehicles in front. The sky was dark, headlights were on and we were pootling along at about forty miles an hour. I was glad we hadn't booked a ferry ticket in advance, otherwise I might soon be panicking that we'd be late and, consequently, have to pay twice. OK, it was only thirty-five pounds but every penny was precious. Rather pleased with myself, I put my head back, closed my eyes and tried to drift off, but I couldn't. I was far too excited to sleep. Instead, I opened up the map of France and began to study it intently.

From Calais we'd be coming down the motorway to Reims and carrying on to Dijon, where we hoped to find somewhere to stay overnight. The next day we'd drive past Lyon, Avignon, Aix-en-Provence and eventually we'd arrive in Mandelieu. With a fair wind, we'd estimated that it should take about eleven and a half hours to get from one end of France to the other, so we'd easily make our scheduled time of five o'clock to arrive at our new home and meet our future employers. I couldn't wait.

Just before midday we pulled up at the ferry terminal. I got out of the car and walked over to the P&O ticket office.

'One way to Calais, please,' I said, my thirty-five pounds at the ready.

'Certainly. That's one hundred and five pounds. Cash or card?'

'Excuse me,' I replied. 'It says thirty-five pounds on your website.'

'That's if you book in advance.'

'How far in advance?'

'Twenty-four hours.'

'You're kidding. Hang on, I'll be back in a minute.' I then went and stood in the queue at the Sea France desk, only to be told the same thing. Ten minutes later I went back to the car. 'Maybe we should just check into a cheap hotel for the night and book it from there,' I said.

'By the time we've done that and had something to eat,' reasoned Debbie, 'we'll be no better off. Let's just get on with it.'

Half an hour later we were standing on the deck of the ferry in the face of a biting wind. Gazing for some time at the white cliffs of Dover slowly disappearing into the distance was our way of saying goodbye. I fiddled with my keys and removed the spare one to the front door to Sunnyside that I had forgotten to give to the estate agents. I threw it with great enthusiasm into the sea. A short while later we sat down in the lounge area.

'Shall I open it?' said Debbie, taking the envelope which her mother had given her out of her handbag.

'Why not?' Inside was a good luck card containing a twenty-pound note. Marlene had written,

'Hope this helps. Bon voyage. Love, Mum.'

Within a couple of hours, we'd crossed a fairly choppy channel. We drove down the ramp, out of the port and onto the main road, arriving soon after at our first French roundabout. The only question was, which way to go round? There was a sign that told us that we didn't have priority coming onto the roundabout, contrary to what many people had told us, but nothing was telling us which way to go, clockwise or anti-clockwise.

'I think,' I started, but before I had the chance to get my words out, Debbie had put her foot down and was off, having made the right choice. I'd never driven in Europe before and found it very strange. Being in a right-hand drive vehicle, Debbie was close to the kerb and, as the passenger, I found myself towards the middle of the road, facing the oncoming traffic with no control whatsoever over my destiny. 'Bloody hell!' I shouted as a lorry came hurtling towards us, missing my door by what felt like only millimetres. 'Christ, that was close,' I said, closing my eyes and breathing a sigh of relief.

Debbie said nothing. She'd driven in France before and knew exactly what to expect.

One of the first things I noticed was that the *autoroutes* were as smooth as silk – not a pothole in sight. Whether this confidence in their roads encouraged the French to drive faster, I don't know, but tailgating was rife. We were going along at a mere seventy miles an hour and were being passed, two lanes to our left, by four or five cars, all bumper-to-bumper. One touch of the brakes and there would have been a major pile-up.

With nothing much else to do, I reached for the GPS. I changed the distance we had to travel from miles to kilometres, fiddled around with every option possible, ate almost a complete bag of liquorice allsorts and then spent an hour or so staring blankly at the *Daily Telegraph* crossword. We played the alphabet game. We named as many animals, countries and bands beginning with the letters a,b,c and so on until we ran out of categories. Time went very quickly and before we knew it we were on the outskirts of Dijon.

'Hurrah!' I shouted. 'We're here!'

'We've still got a bit of time before we need to stop,' Debbie said. 'It'll make tomorrow's journey a bit shorter and, besides, I'm not really tired yet. Why don't you see where the next biggest town is after Dijon?'

I grabbed the map, opened it up and laughed.

'What's so funny?' asked Debbie.

'You couldn't make it up.'

'Couldn't make what up?'

'The next biggest town is a place called Dole!'

That was it. There was no other place we could possibly stay. Sniggering like a small schoolboy every time I saw the sign, we eventually came off the motorway.

Out of the corner of my eye I saw, on the sloped roof of a rather large building and in very big neon lights, a sign that read 'Buffalo Grill'. Opposite, there was an Etap hotel offering rooms for only forty-five euros per night, so we were rather pleased to have found a hopefully cheap meal and room for the night. Moments later we had booked into a non-smoking room that reeked of smoke and were soon making our way arm-in-arm to the restaurant. We received a warm welcome from the front-of-house manager, who politely asked us to wait by a statue of a six-foot Indian chief. This also turned out to be the place where all the diners' children would come to collect a balloon before going home. Shortly afterwards we were sitting in a comfy leather-seated booth, usually reserved for four people, and gazing at the menu.

'Ribs, they've got ribs!' said Debbie, excitedly. 'What are you going to have?'

'Looks like either burger or horse,' I said, trying to keep a straight face.

'You wouldn't!'

'Eat a burger? Has been known.' We ordered a *pichet* of rosé and waited for our food to arrive.

Over dinner we sat and talked about the day's events and how we were glad to have left Sunnyside behind. We wondered what the faces would have been like at the estate agent's when they opened the envelope and found our keys. We had a pretty good idea; we also imagined how our landlord would have reacted when he heard the news of our sudden departure.

At the same time, we were eagerly anticipating what was waiting for us when we arrived in Mandelieu. Just before we finished eating, Debbie said,

'We have done the right thing, haven't we? I mean, we're not going to regret this?'

'Regret swapping a freezing cold house and a load of nasty phone calls for the south of France? I wouldn't have thought so, would you? That burger was delicious,' I said, looking at my empty plate. '*Monsieur, encore un pichet, s'il vous plaît.*'

An hour or so later and feeling fully replenished, we strolled back to the hotel, stopping at the car on the way to make sure that anything that looked remotely valuable was covered by our duvet.

The next morning came around sooner than I had imagined. We'd managed to get a good night's sleep, so much so that ours was one of the last cars to leave the car park. The sun had burst through the clouds on a crisp February morning and once again we were in the car heading south. Debbie drove us past Lyon and Avignon and I drove her mad with my random outbursts of *Sur le Pont D'Avignon*. Only knowing the first four words, I made the rest up as I went along. Soon, we started to see signs to places that we recognised – Cannes, Nice, Marseille to the left and Montpellier to the right.

'I wish we were heading towards Montpellier,' said Debbie, ruefully. 'La Grande Motte's just down the road from there.'

'Won't be long,' I replied. 'We'll be there sooner than you know it.'

As we continued, I remember thinking that there was a great deal of snow around for this part of the world. The mountains in the distance were, of course, capped but that was to be expected. What wasn't quite so expected was that the fields surrounding the motorway were white. The sun, however, was just beginning to thaw everything out and it felt warm. The temperature gauge on the car's dashboard read 20°C, not something I was accustomed to in early February. I could get used to this, I thought.

An hour further into the journey we took the exit to Cannes and were heading along the coastal road towards Mandelieu. It was getting dark and there was nobody about. A few spots of rain were beginning to fall on the windscreen and we were both getting quite tired. The long drive was finally catching up with us. We were very much looking forward to sitting down with a glass of wine in what we hoped would be a warm house.

Chapter 3

'It's somewhere along here,' said Debbie as we pulled over on a quiet, isolated country lane, 'and if she tells me one more time that I have reached my final destination SHE is going through the window where she'll meet hers. Turn that bloody thing off!'

We drove up and down the road several times, turning into many different driveways, apologising as we shone our headlights through various lounge windows. Eventually we came to an unmarked long drive with a wooden hut either side of an open barrier. I got out of the car. As I peered through the darkness, there it was – a faded sticker, no larger than a playing card, peeling away from a window in of one of the huts. 'Cannes Vacances,' the barely-legible sign read.

'This is it,' I said to Debbie, who had wound down her window. 'Can you put the headlamps on full?'

'Sure. Wait a minute, I'll join you,' she replied, opening the car door.

For a few moments, we stood next to each other and said nothing. We stared along a concrete road lined with mobile homes. We were at the main entrance but could see more rows to our left and right. Some looked quite well looked after with cream exteriors, sloping roofs, solid windows and wooden terraces. There were others of a similar style but not so well cared for and then there were the two-tone beige and brown corrugated iron shacks, belonging to a bygone age. There were a couple of cars that we could see, one of which had its windscreen caved in but not completely shattered, as well as a massive groove that ran along its bonnet where something very heavy had obviously fallen on it. Twenty-foot-high cypress trees swayed in the breeze, guttering rattled off the sides of some of the homes and the odd see-through green plastic carrier bag tumbled past our feet. We tried to look inside the windows of the huts, but they were lined with thick, stained, floral curtains. In the distance we watched the flickering street lamps from the main road and heard cars driving through the rain, which was then coming down quite steadily.

I glanced towards Debbie, trying not to look at her directly. I knew exactly how she was feeling.

'Let's do it,' I said, picking up the phone. 'It's Brent and Debbie. We're here.'

We continued to study our surroundings, still saying nothing to each other and then, out of the darkness, we heard a woman's husky voice say,

'So you found us all right then? Sorry about the weather. Not usually like this. It's the first time we've had snow in seven years. Never mind, follow me. I see you've got a carful, so I'll walk in front.' We had just met Pauline, the owner's wife.

As the headlights reflected on her bright-yellow plastic coat, wellies and matching hat, we were beginning to get a much clearer picture of where we were going to be living for, at least, the next couple of months. Driving very slowly, we passed between a row of mobile homes and then a shower block, some toilets and a small plot of land, no doubt waiting for the next home to arrive. Randomly placed standpipes added to the landscape. Some of the homes were enclosed by small hedges, others had decking, but most just had a car port. As we approached the end of the central drive, Pauline motioned to us to park outside one of the older-looking beige and brown homes. 'I'll just go and get Paul,' she said, and not long after we were being given the briefest of tours of our new home by a friendly-looking Yorkshireman, around twenty years our senior.

'Either of you smoke?' he asked, licking the paper of a cigarette that he'd just rolled.

'No,' Debbie replied. 'Sorry.'

'Don't blame you,' Paul replied. 'Filthy habit.' He chuckled. 'I'd give it up myself but there's a really cheap *tabac* in the village. That's my excuse anyway,' he said, putting the cigarette behind his ear. 'Look, we're all going for a pizza about seven – be a good chance for you to meet everybody. See you in about an hour. We'll come and knock for you. In the meantime, if you've got any problems, give us a shout.'

He smiled, put his coat over his head and went out into the darkness.

Debbie grinned. 'You won't get lost in here,' she said. She was referring to my appalling sense of direction when in new places. We'd rented two or three houses in the time that we'd been together and in each one I'd proudly announce that I was off to the kitchen and would then land up in the bedroom or the lounge, anywhere in fact but where I had intended going. This used to amuse Debbie greatly. Here, however, it was impossible, even for me. There were only three rooms. Immediately inside the front door was one space comprising the kitchen, dining and sitting area. To the right was the bedroom, complete with double bed and wardrobe, and to the right of that there was a shower and toilet, housed in the smallest space imaginable. I put our impossibly heavy suitcase on the bed and, while waiting for further instructions, I went to check out what appliances there were. There was a click, click, click, click as I tried to light the small gas fire mounted on the wall.

'Have we got any matches?'

'No. Try the kitchen drawer. If there are any, that's where they'll be!' Debbie shouted from the bedroom.

'Don't you just hate being right all the time?' I said as I opened the drawer. A few minutes later we were warm. I'd got the cooker working and had managed to get a signal on the portable TV – until it started to spit with rain, and then there was no TV at all. The shower was even worse – there was no pressure at all. The water came out at no more than a dribble.

'Don't worry,' said Debbie, 'I'm sure Paul can fix it.' I wasn't so convinced.

Just before seven there was a knock at the door and soon after we were walking towards the site exit, accompanied by Paul and Ruth.

'That's a lovely dress,' said Debbie.

'Thank you,' replied Ruth. 'Still had the original ticket on it when I bought it. The thing is, I get all my clothes from charity shops. I can't remember the last time I bought a new dress. This one, a fiver. You wouldn't know, would you? I'll tell you something, if I'd met Paul years ago, he'd be a millionaire by now.'

Paul laughed. 'She's probably right,' he said.

'Do you come here every year?' I asked.

'Been coming here for the last three,' he replied. 'Don't get paid anything but Bob pays for our golf, which is really expensive here. Seventy euros per person. We play at least once a week, so works out at about five hundred euros a month, which is OK.'

'Paul,' said Debbie, 'I know we've only just got here but there's a problem with our shower. It just dribbles.'

'The pressure to these vans is terrible, love, but don't worry,' he said. 'In a few weeks they'll put the water on in the shower block for when the new visitors arrive. Until then, there's not much I can do about it. Sorry.'

As we crossed the road, we glimpsed, hidden behind some overgrown bushes, a very run-down-looking restaurant. The grubby windows, though large and potentially inviting to passers-by, were covered in posters advertising events long since gone. Christmas menus, details of summer barbecues, as well as many other scraps of paper advertising local events were still displayed and old pieces of sellotape that had turned yellow with age had not been scraped away.

The unoiled front door squeaked loudly as it was opened and sprang back sharply when let go. Being the last of the four of us to enter, I just managed to get my hand out of the way before losing my fingers.

'Forgot to mention that,' said Paul with a smile. 'Everything's a bit like that round here. At least you'll know for next time.'

Inside, standing in a circle next to the bar, was a small group of people awaiting our arrival.

'Hello, I'm Bob,' boomed a rotund and jolly character who we took to be the owner of the site. He introduced us to his wife, Pauline, who we'd met earlier when we arrived, and also to the other people who would be joining us for dinner, some of whom were helpers, some family and others who we were never to see again. Such was their interest in us and tales of back home that Debbie and I found ourselves being quizzed in two separate groups. Occasionally we'd glance through the small crowd and give each other a reassuring smile. Our new-found friends were doing everything they could to make us feel welcome. It was such a change from the barrage of unfriendly phone calls and letters to which we had become accustomed when we were in the UK.

Half an hour or so later, our group of around sixteen sat down next to the window at a long, wobbly wooden table. Debbie was at one end and I the other. Those sat next to a leg tried to steady it with a folded napkin or an empty Rizla packet. The waiter then brought tatty menus, cutlery that didn't match and an assortment of well-used and now almost opaque wine glasses. As I looked around, it occurred to me that money hadn't been spent on the place in years. The black-and-white-checked lino was heavily stained and cracked and the tired walls hadn't been washed, let alone repainted, in a very long time.

At the far end of the restaurant was a small bar, a glass-fronted fridge containing soft drinks and an extremely old chest freezer with Wall's Ice-cream emblazoned on the front. The only source of heating was a portable Calor gas fire which, as the evening progressed, made its way closer towards the bar, where the owner's wife was dispensing drinks. In front of our table was a counter, behind which a young man, dressed in a white, food-stained t-shirt and tatty jeans, was busily rolling out dough that he sprinkled with different toppings, ready for the pizza oven.

Towards the middle of the restaurant there was a large table covered with all manner of paperwork, a calculator, a copy of the local newspaper and a packet of cigarettes. Sitting at that table was a tall, pot-bellied man wearing a pair of tracksuit bottoms, some heavy duty flip-flops and a faded rugby shirt that just covered his navel – until he reached up to adjust the dial on the television that was suspended above where he was sitting.

Bob turned to me. 'Do you drink rosé, Brent?'

'I've been known to have the odd glass or two, Bob – usually in the summer, though.'

'It's always summer here, boy.' Bob smiled. 'I'll tell you something else, the rosé in this region is fantastic, amongst the best in France. And there's nowhere better to get it than in this place. You wouldn't think so, would you? Love to know where they get it from. Won't tell me, though, will they? Very secretive, the Frenchies. Now, what are you going to have to eat?'

'Haven't really made my mind up. Any suggestions?'

'The calzone for me – every time. You should try it. Don't mind a bit of spice, do you?'

'I quite like it actually.'

'Did you hear that, Paul? Brent's going for the calzone. He's not like you, you big girl!'

And so the banter went back and forth with the volume of laughter increasing steadily with the amount of alcohol consumed. Eventually, dragging himself away from the TV screen, the owner took our order, which included Bob's request to make his and mine extra hot. I had no idea what a calzone was and my wife, who could have told me in an instant what Bob had just convinced me to eat, was at the other end of the table. As I had no way of asking her subtly, and I didn't want to show my ignorance to the rest of the group, I sat there hoping that whatever came out of the kitchen would be mild enough to be edible.

I was just beginning to really unwind after what felt like a very long few days, when suddenly there was a loud bang from somewhere behind me, followed by an ear-piercing scream from one of the lady diners. As I turned round, the biggest ginger cat I'd ever seen, who had somehow managed to clamp all four of his paws to the window, was looking angrily into the restaurant. This was clearly not something new to the regular customers, who were very soon shouting 'Psssht!' and waving menus furiously at the window.

'You all right, Brent? You've gone a bit pale. I'm Brian, by the way,' said a kind-looking chap in his sixties. 'We get a lot of feral cats around here. Don't feed them, mind, you'll only encourage them. They're not dangerous. They can't harm you as long as you've had your jabs. You have had your jabs, haven't you?'

I nodded back politely, wondering what jabs he meant exactly. Had rabies been eradicated in France? I had no idea.

'That's all right then,' he said and then carried on his conversation with the others.

'You'll be seeing a lot of him,' Bob told me. 'He only comes down here in the winter. It's far too hot for him in the summer at his age. He's worked with me for years. You'll like him, and his wife, Janice, is lovely, too.'

As I was getting hungry, I was glad to see the food arrive. I don't know exactly what I was expecting, but it certainly wasn't a giant pizza folded into the shape of a Cornish pasty. Not only was it big, it was also hot – very hot. I really like spicy food and I'm no stranger to the occasional vindaloo but this was hotter, much hotter. When Bob said they made calzones especially for him, there seemed to be a good reason for it – very few people would be able to eat it. I took one bite and my eyes began to water, my nose started to run and my tongue was on fire.

'Great, isn't it, Brent?' Bob said. 'I knew you'd like it. Do us a favour. Before you get stuck in, go and get a couple more *pichets* of rosé and tell Marie-Anne it's for me. Good lad.' I took a huge glug of water, got up and headed towards the bar. '*Deux pichets de rosé, s'il vous plaît, madame, pour Bob.*'

'*D'accord.*' Marie-Anne winked at me and stooped below the bar, where she turned the tap on a five-litre box of rosé labelled 'Pays du Languedoc' and filled two medium-sized, glass *pichets*. My knowledge of France wasn't great, though I felt fairly certain that the region was somewhere over towards the west and not around the corner from where we were, as Bob had suggested, but it really didn't matter. As long as Bob felt that he was being properly looked after, that was really all he or his fellow diners wanted.

'Good boy,' said our host before continuing to shout his conversation towards the other end of the table. We hadn't been sitting down long and not only had I not managed to eat another bite of the calzone but I was also struggling to keep my eyes open.

'You haven't eaten much, Brent. Not hungry?'

'Just really tired, Bob, do you think I could finish this later?'

'Of course. No problem. Michel, can I have a box for Brent? Looks as though Debbie's done all right,' he said, peering across the table at Debbie's empty plate. 'You go and get your heads down. See you in the morning. If there's anything you need, give Paul a shout. They're off now, everybody!' Bob said, announcing our departure. We left to the cheery sounds of our new friends saying, 'Nice to meet you,' and 'See you in the morning. Bye.'

Outside, it was tipping down. With coats over our heads, we steadily made our way back to our van.

'What are you looking for?' Debbie asked, as I began to rummage through the kitchen cupboards as soon as we got in.

'Something to eat. I'm starving.'

'Shame. Do you want me to make you something to eat? I can do you an omelette. Won't take a minute.'

'No, you're OK,' I said, picking up a loaf of bread. 'Tell you what though, that man is not human. I'd hate to be his insides – must be torture. I bet you won't see him much before coffee-time, tomorrow.' I'd just finished a ham sandwich and was about to go to bed when there was a light tap, tap, tap on the door.

'Hello, you two. Did you have a good evening?'

'Yes, thank you, Ruth, great,' I replied. I heard Debbie yawn from the bedroom.

'Paul and I just thought we'd pop in for a quick glass of wine. Didn't get much chance to talk to you at dinner. He forgot the corkscrew. Won't be a minute. Not too late, is it?'

'Of course not,' I said. Debbie came out the bedroom and forced a smile.

When Paul arrived, we all sat around the table and listened to his army stories, which he repeated. When he'd finished those he talked about his cleaning company that he had sold and after that I didn't remember much.

Both time and alcohol evaporated very quickly and at some point in the early hours we said goodnight to our new neighbours. As Debbie locked the front door I collapsed face down on our bed and slipped into a very welcome, drunken sleep.

Chapter 4

The next morning, I woke to the sound of a golf buggy passing our bedroom window at five-minute intervals. Debbie was already reading her book.

'Morning. Been awake long?' I said.

'About half an hour. That's Paul,' she replied as the buggy went by again. 'He's delivering gas bottles. The walls aren't very thick here. I heard them clanking on the back. Anyway, surprised the rain didn't wake you up earlier. Sounded like a thousand budgies running across the roof.'

'Don't know about budgies. I think I've got a herd of wildebeest trampling their way through my head. What time is it, anyway?'

'Eight o'clock.'

'Oh God, really? Half an hour to go then. Ouch, my head. What have I done?'

'That'll be the Armagnac.'

'Armagnac? I don't remember drinking any Armagnac.'

'I think, my love, therein lies the problem. Fancy a fried egg?' Debbie laughed.

'Oh, don't. Stick the kettle on, would you? I hope I don't look as bad as I feel.'

Just as I was finishing my coffee and Debbie was sitting quietly with her book, there was a light knock on the door.

'Hello, Brent,' said an all-too-chirpy Ruth. 'Just off to the *boulangerie* to get some baguettes. Would you like one?'

'Yes, please.'

'You look a bit rough this morning. You OK?'

'I'm fine. Yes, thanks. Bye.'

'How can people be that cheery first thing in the morning? Do I look that bad?'

'Well....' Debbie started.

Seconds later, I clumsily began to rummage around the bathroom cabinet, looking for some aspirin.

'Do you need a hammer to go with that?' asked Debbie, her reading having been disturbed by me clattering around.

'No thanks, already got one.'

'What are you looking for?'

'Anti-bangers.'

'Plastic medicine bag, bottom shelf,' came the reply.

Twenty minutes later, with eyes bulging out of my head, we crossed the drive to Paul and Ruth's home, or Mission Control as they liked to call it.

The entrance to the property was a trellised arch with several terracotta pots dotted around the outside. Some had cracks running along them, others had a few chips, but all were full of soil, most with moss on top. Dead brown leaves from the summer's roses and lilies spread across the small patch of grass which met the trellis. Under the arch, to the left, there was a large shed secured by a small padlock with a combination. Holding the lock was a small latch and plate, secured with four tiny Phillips screws. Heaven help any would-be thief trying to break into this lot, I thought. A note was taped to the outside door saying, *Helpers' washing, Wednesdays and Sundays only. Thank you, the management.*

In front of the shed was a large area of decking with a washing line tied to the beams that supported the roof. Towels, underwear, sheets and pillow cases swayed in the wind. Surrounding the plot was dark wooden fencing. There was a gate at the back leading on to one of the main aisles, and empty white plastic hanging baskets, sporadically placed, dangled from the tall fence supports. Yellow and green garden hoses were neatly coiled on the floor or hung from hooks in the corner by the shed. An old rusty sack barrow was lying on its back in the middle of the decking and there was a large wooden table with five white unmatched, stained plastic chairs pushed up against the side of the home. On the table were several used coffee cups with a few cigarette ends floating inside, an ashtray and a 2008 tourist guide to Grasse and the surrounding areas.

As the gate at the back swung gently in the breeze, I glanced over to the windows of Paul and Ruth's home. There seemed to be no movement from inside and the big, heavy curtain which covered the front door was still drawn. 'Perhaps not back from the shops yet,' I said. 'Shall we....'

'Hello again!' interrupted Ruth, who suddenly appeared from around the corner, her arms laden with baguettes. 'Hasn't Paul answered? You can always try banging on the door, but you'll have to knock quite loud. He's a bit deaf. Doesn't like to admit it – same as his mother. There you go. That's ninety cents, but you can give it to me later. I'll get the coffees. Sit yourselves down.' Moments later, Paul poked his head around the front door.

'Hello, campers, did you sleep all right?' he said with an enormous grin. 'Comfy old beds, those. Just like Army beds. Did I tell you I was in the Army? Can't remember. Can't remember much about last night at all actually.' He laughed. 'Can get a bit like that round here. Come as a friend and leave as an alcoholic is what I say.'

'Oh, just ignore him,' replied Ruth, placing a tray of coffees on the table.

'So, you're looking for work 'round here then?' said Paul, picking up his mug. 'We see a lot like you every year. Not many succeed. Forgot me fags. Be right back.'

Debbie and I looked at each other.

'Sorry about that,' apologised Ruth. 'He doesn't really think. A bit too honest for his own good sometimes. I'm sure you'll be fine,' she said awkwardly. A few minutes later, Paul reappeared with his tobacco, cigarette papers and some A4 paper. 'You'll have to sign these because you're not insured here. I take it Pauline told you that?'

'No, actually she didn't,' replied Debbie, who was beginning to feel a bit unsettled. The thought of needing to be insured hadn't previously occurred to us.

'It's just a little disclaimer,' continued Paul, 'in case something goes wrong. You'll have to pay your own medical costs but I'm sure you've got all of that covered already – just a precaution, that's all. I've designed a work detail,' he said, handing us a sheet of A4 paper, 'which I'll give to you every morning on the days that you're working, so you know what's got to be done. Keeps it simple, and besides, my memory's a shocker.' He laughed. 'We've got four vans to clean today and not sure if I told you this either, but I'm going tomorrow to get Dave and Elodie from the airport, so you won't be alone. Morning, Marc.'

'All right, Paully?' said a good-looking chap in his thirties, who walked past us and into the shed. Moments later he reappeared with a piece of copper pipe. 'Sorry, can't stop. Problem with the boiler in forty-seven,' he explained, before walking out through the gate.

'That's Marc,' said Ruth. 'He's Bob's son. Nice enough lad, but he'll drink you out of house and home if you're not careful. Just turns up at people's places in the evening and sits himself down, uninvited. Never brings anything with him. We've tried telling him, but it makes no difference whatsoever. Even tried telling his dad. He went mad. There's nothing that boy can do wrong. Nearly didn't come back this year because of it, so careful what you say.'

'You finished your coffee?' Paul asked. 'Great. Come on, let me show you what you'll need.'

Debbie and I followed him to the shed. He showed us the combination and proudly opened the door to what Paul called his Aladdin's cave. 'Alakazam!' he shouted gleefully as he revealed the cave's contents. My initial reaction was that it was a room full of old clutter that most people would have long since thrown out, yet here it was prized enough to be kept under lock and key.

There were salt and pepper pots, all mismatched, as well as glass and plastic jugs from coffee machines that had been discarded some time before. Cups and saucers, cutlery, plastic draining-boards and chipped mugs filled plenty of shelf space, while small trophies and engraved cups took up more room. There were small trays full of nuts, bolts and screws. Mops, brooms, broom heads and broken handles leant against the walls. Buckets of rags littered the floor space and hanging up on the metal racking, which held many of the cleaning products, was a huge pair of presumably once white, now grey, Y-fronts. Paul caught the wry smile running across my face.

'Nothing goes to waste here,' he said. 'They'll be cut up later. We'll get a van's worth of cleaning of them, maybe even two as they were Bob's!'

Two rusty washing machines whirred away in the background. A twin-tub with a wheel missing was jammed in beside them and a huge notice, written in red ink on a tumble dryer, read *Only to be used in emergencies*. I spent a good few minutes trying to imagine a situation in which a tumble dryer had been deployed in an emergency but couldn't so I made a mental note to ask another time.

Moments later we were carrying as many buckets, brooms, cleaning products and old rags as we could manage and were heading off to begin our day's work.'

'You'll need some greenies,' Paul said. I looked puzzled.

'Scouring pads to get all the green stuff off the side of the walls,' he explained. 'It's been a belter of a winter. I'll bring the ladders for the guttering. Be careful. It's slippery. You did say you've got insurance, didn't you?' Debbie glanced at me, gently shook her head and shrugged her shoulders.

And so, we began to work on the first of the three hundred or so mobile homes in the park. We scrubbed the cream outsides of the newer homes until they were sparkling. We also began to vigorously scrub the older beige and brown tin huts, which turned out to be a bit of a mistake. The paintwork fell away like snowflakes.

'Forgot to tell you to just use a hose on them,' Ruth said cheerily as she drove past in a golf buggy, piled high at the back with sheets, pillowcases and an array of cleaning products.

The gutters on the roofs of the homes were full of leaves and other debris that had fallen from the trees and, despite being given a crowbar to scrape along the insides, I found it much easier to use my hands.

'We'll finish about twelve,' said Paul, who was trimming a hedge opposite. 'Then we'll have an FLFL.'

'We'll have a what?' Debbie asked.

'The last three words are Long French Lunch. I'm sure you can work the first word out for yourself!' He laughed.

At coffee break and with no food in the cupboard, we downed tools and went to visit our first French supermarket, only a mile or so away. We'd figured we'd only be ten minutes and that we'd be back in plenty of time to finish the morning's work.

From the outside the supermarket was very similar to any in the UK – but the inside, however, was a different story. I chose to scoot round first of all to see what was there, while Debbie was happy to take a trolley and go methodically up and down each aisle. It was obvious, quite quickly, that French people's shopping habits and the way we used to shop were very different. Although there was a large section that displayed fresh produce, I was surprised to see so many shelves filled with canned vegetables. Row upon row of tins of haricots verts, Brussels sprouts, carrots, onions, spinach, beans and even mushrooms filled every inch of available space. Surely, I thought, this was a mistake? But no, the supermarket bosses knew their customers very well. As I glanced into some of the trollies that passed me, I saw that not only were they piled high with tins, but many also contained six-packs of UHT milk, to which a complete aisle in the shop had been dedicated. Opposite that aisle was a very small section allotted to bottles of fresh milk.

Hundreds of different cheeses were beautifully displayed on the deli counter and a very proud butcher showed off an array of meats, poultry and sausages. I turned the corner and, much to my delight, I arrived at the English section. It surprised me that my diet, according to the French, would be likely to consist of a packet of water biscuits, crackers, Marmite, mint sauce, tomato soup and a tin of baked beans with sausages.

The freezer section was very similar to what I had been used to, except on this occasion something happened that I'd never seen before anywhere – ever. Filling his basket with frozen lasagnes, spaghetti Bolognese, ravioli and pizzas was a man wearing chef's whites. For a few moments, I stood there, not able to believe what I was seeing. I went over to where he was standing, asked which restaurant he worked for and vowed to avoid the place like the plague.

Meeting up with Debbie in the wine section, I was amazed to see bottles of red wine starting from as little as one euro, thirty cents. We bought a box of six, surmising that, if the worst came to the worst, we could put it in gravy – or Marc.

The French are very sociable people and where better to meet up and have a chat than in a queue while waiting to pay? This didn't seem to apply just to the customers as the cashiers also had their part to play. The line in which Debbie and I were standing went all the way to the back of the shop but no one batted an eyelid, or even noticed for that matter. There was just no sense of urgency. Looking at our watches, sighing and tapping our feet made no difference. The elderly lady and the cashier trying to take her money were having a great time, so much so that the only sound we could hear was the two of them laughing. Once her shopping was packed, the customer spent an age rummaging around her handbag, finally producing a chequebook, and took what felt like a lifetime to write out the cheque.

Returning half an hour late from our scheduled fifteen-minute break, we drove back through the barrier and put away our shopping as fast as we could.

'You should have waited till later,' Paul said, seeing that we were a bit flustered. 'Best time to go is lunchtime. They're empty. It's not like in the UK, you know. As soon as the clock strikes twelve, they're off home. Roads are packed, but there's no one in the supermarkets. Nothing comes between the French and their lunch. Anyway, not to worry.'

Feeling as though we should try and make up for some of the time lost, we had a shortened FLFL and returned to Mission Control a bit early.

'Great job this morning, thanks,' said Ruth. 'Just another two to do and then finish. Doesn't matter what time. Oh, and we might be all at the restaurant again tomorrow night for Dave and Elodie. I'll let you know.'

Armed with more cleaning materials and a pair of large pink Marigolds that I'd found in the shed, we began the afternoon session. Brian would, every now and again, drive past in his tractor, pulling a trailer full of greenery, waving as he went. Ruth dropped by with cups of coffee and the French would drive past, nodding politely with the occasional '*Bonjour*'. Bob, accompanied by his dog, made the odd appearance. Bella, a tan boxer, was running alongside the car, the only way she ever got any exercise.

Five o'clock came around quite quickly and, happy with the thought that we'd have the chance of a good rest the following day, we went back to our van and watched some TV until the rain came. We replaced watching TV with a game of Scrabble that we decided would be good to play using only French words. That lasted a full fifteen minutes before Debbie announced that it was time to cook dinner while I went in search of a corkscrew.

A few hours later we went to bed, thoroughly replenished and very pleased with our decision to come to Mandelieu.

Chapter 5

I was woken the next morning by the smell of cooked bacon and tomatoes drifting its way into the bedroom. Through the gap in the door I could see Debbie standing over the frying pan and getting out some plates.

'Morning,' I yawned.

'Morning, sweetie,' Debbie replied. 'Be about five minutes.'

'You're up early.'

'I know. Today we start.'

'Start what?' I replied, wearily taking a mouthful of coffee.

'Looking for a job. We've got six weeks here, max, and our money's not going to last forever. We've got to get going.'

After breakfast, I sat at the table with my phone and searched for the campsite's wi-fi signal. 'How's it going?' asked Debbie, who was doing the washing-up.

'No signal.' I sighed. 'Looks like we'll have to go and see Pauline.'

After a quick shower and ready to be at the office for when it opened at ten o'clock, we made the short walk down the drive.

'I hope these places are secure,' I said to Debbie.

'Why do you say that?'

'Well, all the money we have in the world is in my raincoat pocket and if....'

'Don't worry,' replied Debbie, reassuringly. 'I'm sure we'll be fine. Come on.'

'Hello, I'm Sharon, the receptionist. You must be Debbie and Brett,' said a tall, skinny woman in her early thirties as we walked into the office. Pulling tightly on a roll-up, out of the corner of her mouth she said, 'I understand you're looking for a job? Not really the time of year, is it? Never mind, I'm sure you'll find something. If there's anything I can do....' If it wasn't for her London accent, I would have felt confident that Sharon was related to Paul.

'Actually, there is,' I replied. 'The Internet.'

'Oh that. Not very reliable. Bob won't spend the money. Charges the clients a fortune, though. Tenner a day and then blames the amount of people trying to use it when it goes down. Nice work if you can get it. I'll try and help. Where's your computer?'

Proudly, I produced our phone, complete with two-inch-square screen, out of my trouser pocket.

'Is that it? Wow!' She laughed.

'Our proper ones are in storage,' I said, disappointedly.

'Look, you can use Pauline's PC when she's not here.'

'Are you sure?' asked Debbie.

'Of course. She won't mind. Come on. That's her desk over there. She won't be in for an hour or so, so you'll be all right until then. I'll just sign you in. Coffee anyone?' As Sharon went to fill the kettle at the back of the office, Debbie sat in front of the computer and I pulled up a chair next to her.

'That's a good likeness,' I said, pointing towards a painting of Bob Marley.

'That's Marc. He's pretty good. The tiger's his, too. Have you met him yet?'

'Briefly,' I replied.

'You won't see him much before eleven. He's Bob's son. I get on with him really well. They want me to marry him but I keep telling them I've got Terry, works on the boats. We're engaged, you know.'

'Congratulations,' I said, turning to Debbie. 'You OK?'

'Apart from the fact that it's all in French and this is an Azerty keyboard, just fine.'

'Have you managed to get our CV up yet?' I asked.

'No, don't think this computer's recognising the phone.'

'Fucking hell!' shouted Sharon. 'Excuse my language but the sodding Internet's down again. Oh, and here's Pauline now. Sorry, guys. Maybe, you could come back at lunchtime when there's no one here. Internet might be working then. Hi, Pauline.'

'What are we going to do, Debbie?' I said, by now thoroughly frustrated as we walked back down the drive.

'What can we do? Come back at lunchtime, I suppose.'

'We could try an Internet café in Cannes,' I suggested. 'Good idea Sherlock, except how are we going to find one of those without the Internet?' She had a point.

As we walked, Marc came towards us.

'Nice paintings,' I said.

'Thanks for that, yeah. Look, I haven't got time to stop now, but I'll pop round yours for a beer a bit later, introduce myself properly, if that's all right. I'll ask Sharon if she wants to come along. About six-thirty OK? See ya then.'

'He'd better bring some beer with him,' I said to Debbie.

'I'm sure it'll be fine, as long as he doesn't touch my rosé! Anyway, they've got some really cheap beer in the shop.'

We made a further trip to the supermarket and as well as some beer and a further six bottles of wine, we bought some of the finest pork ribs I'd seen in a long time, big racks and really meaty. I adore spicy tomato and garlic ribs and, as is usually the case with Debbie, there would be enough to feed a small army. The three hours cooking time would be worth the wait.

At lunchtime we went back to the office. 'Sorry, guys,' said Sharon. Foiled once again by the lack of any Internet access, we left. We munched our way through a ham and salad baguette, polished off a bottle and a half of rosé and went for a snooze.

At about five o'clock I took myself off around the campsite and got back just as Debbie was putting the ribs on. At six-thirty, true to his word, Marc arrived, arm in arm with Sharon.

'See, I said she might come,' he said, pulling up a seat at the terrace table.

'Beer, Marc?'

'You haven't got a rosé by any chance, have you, Brent?' he said, rubbing his tummy and grimacing. 'The thing is, I've been at Paul's all week and he only ever gets in beer, so I'm a bit beered out.' Through the window, he noticed that there were three bottles of rosé on the kitchen work surface. 'See you've got a few bottles in. You'll get along well here.'

Even though it was February, the evening was warm enough to sit outside on the terrace. Marc and Sharon told tales of the strange happenings on the campsite and the even stranger holiday-makers. There was one woman in her mid-sixties they'd nicknamed Floppy, who was the head of one of the government's committees responsible for dealing with alcohol abuse. She would spend all of August on the park, paralytic. From the minute she arrived to the minute she left she couldn't stand up. There was a group of Polish builders who would also drink themselves senseless and go banging on residents' doors at two in the morning in search of more vodka.

'And,' said Sharon, 'a Peeping Tom.'

'No, really?' said Debbie.

'Really. Haven't seen him this year but last summer I was getting ready for bed and I saw a pair of eyes staring through the gap in the curtains. At first I thought it was you, Marc, do you remember?' She laughed.

'I remember all right but don't know what I'd want to do that for,' he replied. 'I've normally just had my dinner by about then. Ouch, that hurt!' he said, holding his shin.

'Did you report it?' asked Debbie.

'Well, I told Bob, if that's what you mean,' said Sharon.

'What did he do?'

'He laughed and told me to call Crimestoppers. Sad bastard. Next time I'm just going to leave the curtains wide open. That should put him off for life. I think he's pretty harmless really. Just be careful, that's all. Ooh, something smells nice, Debbie,' she said, sniffing the air. 'What are you having?'

'Spicy spare ribs,' Debbie replied, and before I had chance to say anything she asked, 'Would you like some? We've got plenty.'

'Lovely, Debbie,' jumped in Marc, quick as a flash. 'You sure that's OK?'

'Brent, give me a hand. More wine anybody?'

Having left our guests and standing next to Debbie in the kitchen, I said 'What did you do that for?' as she took the ribs out of the oven.

'Don't be so mean. We've only just met them. You never know, they might be able to help us one day, and besides, I'm sure we'll get an invite back.'

'Oh, you're such an optimist.'

A few moments later, Debbie and I were back at the table.

'This is absolutely delicious,' said Sharon, who was licking her lips. 'You're a very lucky boy, Brent, very lucky. I've never tasted ribs like this. Pass me your glass, Marc. Yours, too, Brent,' she continued, at the same time draining our third bottle of rosé. 'A toast: here's to Debbie. Brent, I think you're nearly out of wine,' she said, glancing through the window. 'Marc, go and get,' my eyes lit up, 'your guitar.' My eyes dimmed again. For a moment I was convinced Marc was going for more wine.

'I dunno, Shazz. I'm not sure.' At which point Sharon grabbed Marc and wrestled him over the wooden barrier that surrounded the decking.

'Don't suppose he'll bring back any wine?' I said optimistically.

'Doubt it,' said Sharon. 'Been in his van many times – never seen any.'

Minutes later Marc reappeared, guitar in hand, and broke into a rendition of *Wonderwall*, which was very good. Unfortunately, it soon became apparent that Marc only knew two tunes – one was *Wonderwall* and the other one wasn't. Taking a break every now and then, we sang the same two tunes until late into the night, or perhaps more accurately, until the last drop of rosé was gone.

Debbie and I sat outside for a little longer enjoying the silence, which was broken shortly afterwards by the, now unmistakeable, voice of Marc shouting 'Aaaaaargh!' That was followed by a heavy thud and 'Fucking stupid bush! Bastard,' which, in turn, was followed by Sharon's raucous laughter. Somewhat worse for wear, but smiling nonetheless, we closed our front door and retreated to the sanctuary of the bedroom.

Chapter 6

'Have a good a good time last night, did you? We could hear you across the road. Warned you about Marc, didn't I? Won't see him much before midday. Can do as he likes, and usually does.' Smiling, Ruth came down the steps of Mission Control with a tray of coffees. 'You seem to be settling in OK then. Oh, hiya,' she said to a couple who had come in just behind us. 'Brent and Debbie, this is Dave and Elodie. They arrived last night. Help yourselves to coffee.'

Dave, a diminutive man in his late thirties, was wearing a sweatshirt, jeans, gardening jacket and baseball cap. 'Hello,' he said, giggling nervously. Standing next to him was a shy, slender woman dressed in a white embroidered denim trouser suit and high-heeled shoes. 'I'm not really quite sure what she was expecting to be doing but it doesn't look like it was cleaning.' He laughed.

Elodie was South African and had, only a few weeks before their arrival, met Dave at a bar in Reading. From being a successful businesswoman in Johannesburg, she had some months later found herself homeless in the UK. How she had managed to make that transition nobody quite knew, but her story was perhaps not that dissimilar from our own.

Paul came out of the van and handed us the work detail. Debbie, our two new co-workers and I set off.

'I've never cleaned before,' said Elodie sheepishly. 'I've always had cleaners. Don't know where to start really.' She gazed helplessly at the cleaning equipment.

'Do you want to change into something that you don't mind getting ruined?' Debbie suggested.

'I'll be fine. Don't worry.' And off she walked in her suit, high heels and pink Marigolds.

'That's the slobbiest thing she's got,' Dave chipped in.

We worked side by side for the rest of the day, with Debbie and I showing them the ropes. Elodie was painfully slow but did her best, while Dave ran around at a hundred miles an hour trying to compensate.

'So, what's your background then, Dave?' I asked.

'Landscape gardening really. Not a lot of that around this time of year, so we thought we'd come out here. See what happens. You never know.'

'Been with Elodie long?'

'About a year. Can't believe I'm with her. I'm only here until she finds someone better.' That's an extraordinarily odd thing to say, I thought. 'She used to be somebody. She was a top interior designer in South Africa. Had loads of money until some bastard stole it. Did Nelson Mandela's house,' he said proudly. 'Yeah, she's very talented.'

At first we thought that there was something not quite right with Elodie. Dave often said to her, 'Sweetheart, you've missed a bit,' and off she'd trot back to the same spot armed with every cleaning product known to man and triumphantly return five minutes later without having made any difference whatsoever. It was only when I saw her secretively taking a pair of glasses out of her top pocket that I realised the problem: her eyesight was very poor and she didn't want anyone to know.

Dave had his own set of unique skills. He was as clumsy as they come, particularly with the power washer. 'Oh, bollocks!' I'd hear him shout as he tripped over the mains cable or the hose. 'Be back in a minute,' he'd say, having broken the plastic nozzle connector. Half an hour later he'd return; 'Got another one.'

I remember one morning he was up a ladder, cleaning the leaves out of the gutter, when there was a very loud 'Aaaaaargh!' followed by a crash. As I went round the side of the van, there was Dave lying on the ground. 'Just slipped.'

'You OK?' I asked.

'Yeah, fine. Not so sure about the side of the van, though.' Dave laughed. I glanced over. As the ladder came down it had taken most of the paintwork with it. 'Got any more white paint, Brent?' As he tried to untangle himself from the ladder, Dave stood on a piece of moss and down he went again. Tears of laughter streamed down his face as once again he tried to free himself.

The following day, Paul and Ruth decided that Dave and I should continue to work on the outside of the vans, while Debbie and Elodie would clean the insides. Not only would they clean, the girls would also have to check the inventory for all the kitchen equipment, as well as make sure that there was enough bed linen, blankets and towels. I would see them coming back from the Aladdin's cave with trays of slightly chipped mugs, glasses that you'd be loath to keep your toothbrush in, cutlery, plates of different sizes with barely visible patterns, percolator jugs – and one particular pair of faded Y-fronts that Debbie waved triumphantly in the air as she walked past. As each room was completed, including dusting, polishing and mopping, the idea was to close the door and not to return. In principle this was a sound plan, but unfortunately Elodie had trouble with remembering where she had been five minutes previously. This seemed to greatly amuse both Debbie and Elodie, who would walk arm in arm past Dave and me, laughing and waving as they went.

On our days off we continued to trawl the Internet for work. We registered with the few English-speaking employment agencies that were local to us, as well as those in the UK, and kept our eyes on the websites that carried jobs in France.

The advice from the people we spoke to was the same: with Debbie's cooking experience and with no children, no pets, and no dependants (or to put it another way, 'no life' as they saw it), we should look for a 'couples job'. If things went our way, we could soon be working and living in a very expensive villa for someone super-rich. The money was good and all of our utilities would be paid for. There would be no rent and if we were really lucky, the owners would only be in residence for a few months of the year, usually over the summer. When they were there the work would be very full-on, but when they were away it was a lot more relaxed and our time would be pretty much our own.

We quickly learned what a 'couples job' entailed. Debbie would manage the inside of what would typically be an eight-to-ten-bedroom villa. She would prepare the breakfast, make the beds in the morning, cook for up to twenty people for lunch or dinner, sometimes both, and generally make sure that the guests were well looked after.

It would be my lot to look after the outside of the property. This would mean gardening, maintaining the pool, cleaning and taking care of the cars, as well as picking up guests from the airport. This was all very well, except that I knew nothing about cars, pools or gardening. I had no idea what 'planting out in the spring' meant. I hadn't got the foggiest about 'over-wintering', and perennials, annuals and bi-annuals were a complete mystery.

The thought of living in a posh villa, on the other hand, sounded extremely attractive. It soon dawned on me that this was going to be a very steep learning curve, one which I was going to have to climb very quickly if we had any chance of making a new life in France.

With some helpful advice from one of the agencies, we wrote, rewrote and wrote again our CV until it read as if we were a combination of Alan Titchmarsh and Delia Smith. What we didn't know wasn't worth knowing. We spent hour upon hour in the office tweaking this and tweaking that. We wrote a character profile for each of us and in the evenings Debbie sat in our van writing out menus which we hoped would give us a bit of an advantage.

We used our phone to take photos of each other and, with the help of Pauline's computer, pasted them on to our CV. I was wearing a casual cotton suit and Debbie looked very elegant in her roll-necked jumper, but when we saw the results it came as quite a shock. How had we managed to put on so much weight? When we first met I was about twelve and a half stone. I was now fourteen and a half. I didn't recognise myself. Debbie had also put on a few pounds.

'You look lovely,' I said.

'I look like a bloody chipmunk,' she replied. 'How did I let myself go so badly?' She started welling up. 'Christ, Brent, look at the state of me. Bloody hell.'

During our second week at the site two more helpers arrived. Billy and Brenda were Liverpudlians in their late sixties and, like Paul and Ruth, had been coming to Mandelieu for years. Every morning they'd sit outside their van, which was opposite ours, with a pot of tea. Billy would nibble away at a Rich Tea biscuit.

'I'd offer you one, Brent, but I've only got two left.' Billy took the lid off and gazed inside the teapot. 'Is that the first time we've used this tea bag, love? Doesn't taste very strong to me. Always a bit weaker on the second day, Brent.' I thought he was joking – he wasn't. Billy and Brenda hated spending money in a way that other people hate going to the dentist.

They would come down to Mandelieu for February and March, not because they particularly liked the south of France, but because it meant not having to spend money on heating their five-bedroom house in Liverpool during the cold months. Had help been needed on the site in December and January, they would have been there, too.

'Surely the airfares cost more than your heating?' I said.

'Ah well, I suppose,' replied Brenda, who was about to elaborate, but Billy, quite unsubtly, nudged her.

'Listen, Brent,' he said, keen to change the subject. 'You can get to Cannes for a euro. Bus stops just outside here. You have to change once, but Cannes for a euro and the buses are clean. I see you've got a nice car, but you don't have to pay for parking if you go on the bus. Think of the money you'd save. And take a picnic, Brent, you don't want to be going into any of those fancy restaurants.'

We quite often chatted between the two vans but, more often than not, it was the backsides of Billy and Brenda that we'd see. They had become the self-appointed park gardeners and were usually to be found pulling up weeds from under the vans. For some people this might have been quite therapeutic. Not for them.

'You don't want to do it like that, Brenda, you'll do your back in.'

'Oh, piss off, you silly old sod,' was the usual response.

I was cleaning out a gutter one day where they were working, when Billy called out, 'Hey, Brent, what you doing up that ladder? There's no compo here I tell you, no compo. He'll not pay you anything if you fall off. Always remember that, Brent, no compo. Brenda, pass me that fork, will ya?'

'Glad I've got you all together,' said Ruth as we drank our coffee, later that morning. 'Bob's having a bit of a do round his place tonight. It's Pauline's birthday. You've not been there yet, have you, Debbie? It's just across the road, through the gate next to the restaurant. We're going over about seven-thirty. We'll come for you.'

As the four of us walked down the drive that evening, Ruth said, 'Got any interviews yet?'

'We've sent off for four or five jobs now. Just waiting to hear back,' Debbie replied.

'What about Dave and Elodie? How are they getting on?'

'They want some help with their CVs and I have a feeling they're going to need it.'

'Why's that then?' asked Paul.

'Well,' said Debbie, 'I had a quick look at Dave's and next to *September 2009 to date*, he's written the word *Nothing*.' Ruth and Paul laughed.

'At least he's honest,' said Ruth.

'True,' replied Debbie, 'but I can't see that's going to get him very far – can you?'

'And how about Elodie?' asked Paul.

'She hasn't got one at all,' said Debbie. 'Never needed one. Brent and I are going round theirs tomorrow.'

'Good luck,' said Ruth.

Chapter 7

As we went through the gate over the road there was a pathway lined with oleander bushes, all neatly trimmed, behind which was a very nice bungalow.

'That's not his,' said Paul. 'Bit too posh for him.'

We walked round to the right along a gravel path, and soon found ourselves at the entrance of a large mobile home. Outside was an old motorboat on a trailer, Bob's 4x4, a golf buggy and a Volkswagen camper van, much of which had been re-built with fibreglass. To get to the house we walked under a trellised arch, in front of which were some straggly rose bushes, a few terracotta pots of varying sizes and a gnome apparently called Wilfred. Opposite the front door was a drinks bar with lights running around the edges. Bob, dressed in a Hawaiian shirt, beige shorts and flip-flops, welcomed us. Billy and Brenda, who had arrived before us, were sitting on bar stools and tucking into the peanuts and crisps.

'Good evening, Brent. You any good with barbecues?' asked our host as he reached into the fridge and brought out some trays of meat. 'If you could see to the sausages, pork chops and burgers, I'll look after the booze. Careful with Bella, though,' he said, looking down at his dog who was sniffing the air in eager anticipation. 'Turn your back for one minute and there'll be nothing left. Debbie, could you give Pauline a hand with the salads?'

Slowly, people began to arrive. Sharon's fiancé, Terry, who I met for the first time that evening, sat at the bar all night and said nothing to anyone. He watched Sharon fling her arms round Marc's neck, kissing and cuddling him, but it didn't seem to bother him at all. At about ten o'clock Marc disappeared and materialised again half an hour later. Soon after I could hear the faint sounds of an acoustic guitar, followed by 'Today is gonna be the day that they're gonna throw it back to you.' As I gazed into the distance I could see Marc walking towards us and the sound getting steadily louder. It was time to go.

'Let's get out of here, Debbie,' I said. Before she had a chance to answer there was some commotion involving Bella. This usually placid and well-behaved dog had cornered Billy and was growling and raising her paw.

'I don't know what's wrong with your damn dog, Bob. Must be on heat or something.'

'No, she's not, Billy,' he replied. 'Look at her paw. She's after whatever you've got in your pocket. What have you got in your pocket, Billy?'

'Nothing much.'

'Billy, what's in your pocket?' Bob said, firmly.

'All right, all right – there's no need to shout,' he said; and with that, out of his trouser pocket Billy produced some kitchen roll, inside which were the two biggest pork chops that had been on the table earlier. 'Didn't want them going to waste. Thought me and Brenda could have them for our tea tomorrow.'

'No problem,' Bob replied, genially. He smiled and shook his head. 'See you tomorrow. Goodnight. Tighter than cramp, those two. Another beer?' asked Bob as we watched Billy and Brenda disappear into the night.

A few more glasses of wine and several renditions of *Wonderwall* later we followed suit.

The following morning the site was like a ghost town. Debbie and I had showers in the block that was now fully functioning; although it felt a bit strange to be walking up the road in dressing gown and slippers, hot and cold running water that came out at more than a just a dribble was very welcome.

At eight-thirty we walked over to Mission Control. The curtains were drawn, the front door was locked and the only sign of life was a paper bag being blown around in the gentle breeze. Parties at Mandelieu had a reputation for going on well into the early hours and we had no reason to believe that the previous night's get-together had been any exception. On the table outside their van, Paul had left two sets of instructions – one for Debbie and Elodie and the other for Dave and me.

There was also another note tucked under a rain-filled ashtray which read '3.30am. Just got back. See you for coffee, P & R.'

We gave it ten minutes for Dave and Elodie to arrive and then, when they didn't, laden with our cleaning materials, we went to work. We said good morning to Billy and Brenda, who were walking towards the site exit, complete with rucksacks.

'Off to Cannes,' said Billy, beaming. 'Got our picnic and you know what, Brent? It's only a euro.'

'You've already told him that, you daft old fool!' snapped Brenda.

'Come on. We'll miss the bus. See you later.' We made a detour past Dave and Elodie's. There was no sign of life there either.

The weather was beginning to warm up quite nicely and by ten o'clock I'd been back to our van and changed into shorts and a t-shirt. When I went to find Debbie at eleven o'clock I found that she'd done the same. At last, it was beginning to feel like the south of France.

'Morning, campers. You all right?' asked Paul. 'You missed a good night last night. You should have stayed.'

'Oh, it was so funny, I've got to tell you,' said Ruth as she brought out a tray of coffees.

'Go on,' I said.

'Bob bought Pauline a red basque for her birthday and spent all evening trying to persuade her to put it on. Obviously, she refused. She kept saying, "There's a time and a place, Bob, and this isn't it. Besides, I've already tried it and it makes me look like a sausage bursting out of its skin. God knows what you bought me that for." In the end, Bob got so frustrated he went and put it on himself.'

'No!' I said, in disbelief.

'You've not heard the best bit yet,' said Paul. He laughed. 'The daft beggar was so pissed he didn't put any pants on.'

'You're joking,' said Debbie, nearly falling off her chair.

'I wish he was,' said Ruth. 'Pauline didn't know where to look. In fact, none of us did. Not much to look at, to be honest with you.

'Seen bigger things crawl out of apples,' added Paul.
'It was a good night, though, or should I say, morning?' said Ruth, letting out a weary sigh. 'We left at about three. Bob fell fast asleep outside in a chair and Pauline covered him up.

'No idea what happened to Marc,' said Paul, 'but wouldn't be the first time he's woken up in a bush somewhere. It's all right in the summer but you don't want to be doing it this time of year. It can get seriously cold.'

'What about Billy and the pork chops?' I asked. 'What was that all about? Bob says he's not exactly broke.'

'He's right!' replied Paul. 'The bugger's as tight as a camel's arse in a sandstorm. I reckon he's a secret millionaire. Bags of money. And I don't know if they told you, but Bob pays their airfare to get here too, so it's not like he's had to shell out for anything.'

'No, they didn't tell us,' I said, glancing across at Debbie. 'They definitely didn't tell us that. Interesting.'

'We'd better…' I started, and then the phone rang. I wandered outside and a few minutes later came back and announced that we had an interview in Fréjus the next day. 'Remember the bloke at that campsite who we phoned when we were in England? He wants to see us tomorrow. It's only for the summer but the pay's pretty good.' The phone rang again. 'Wow, I said, after hanging up a few minutes later, 'we've got another one.'

'Really? Where?' asked Debbie.

'Here actually. The chap's going to call us from the Cayman Islands.'

'Not short of a bob or two then,' Paul said.

'Wouldn't have thought so.'

It was amazing how much lighter the work seemed that afternoon, having received a bit of good news. Time seemed to evaporate as our thoughts turned to the possibility of making a real start in France.

The next morning, we jumped in the car and set off to Fréjus. We followed the coast road through La Napoule and headed west. The scenery was simply breath-taking. Palm trees lined the main road. The sea was calm and there was hardly a cloud in the sky. I looked at the temperature gauge in the car which read 17°C.

'This is the life, Debbie. It's February and look at it! Just look at it! I could get used to this.'

We passed through Saint Raphaël, where we promised we'd stop and treat ourselves to lunch on the way back if the interview went well. The journey took about an hour – an hour that had gone very quickly. We arrived twenty minutes early, which gave us enough time to have a look around the site.

'Good lord,' said Debbie. 'It's a lot bigger than where we are now.'

'And it's all on different levels,' I replied. 'Some of that looks really steep. Wish we'd managed to stay fit.' It felt as if we were in a massive goldfish bowl. The vans went as high and as far as the eye could see.

At eleven o'clock we walked up to the office where Graham, the site manager, was waiting to greet us. 'Nice to meet you at last,' he said. 'Let me show you round. You can leave your things in the office. We'll start up the top.'

There must have been a thousand vans on the park and, like Mandelieu, they were all of differing quality. There was a large restaurant, an Irish-themed pub called Paddy McGinty's, a swimming pool with two giant slides, a stage, a playground with swings, climbing frames and a sandpit the size of a small beach.

As we climbed the steep concrete steps, I said to Debbie, 'Bit different this.' She nodded in agreement but, struggling for breath, was unable to reply. We sat in a van similar to ours, where Graham told us that this was where we would be staying, should we be successful. We'd be working six days a week. We wouldn't always have the same day off, but there was an opportunity to earn a bit of money on the side by doing some additional washing and ironing, if we wanted it.

We could also make some extra cash by hiring out spare blankets and pool towels from the storeroom.

'Is that all right with you, Debbie?' Graham asked.

'Great,' she wheezed.

'You both speak French, don't you? That's really important. We've only got one other couple to see, but neither of them speaks French, so you've got a really good chance. He's got more handyman skills than you, Brent, but that's not what's important.' I smiled. 'It used to be that we had a lot of Brits holidaying here in the summer, but not now. Due to the recession they're all staying at home. The French aren't travelling far, either, so it's mainly French here. I can't tell you how important the language is. You might also be asked to help out with some of the entertainment. Either of you like karaoke?'

'Brent loves it,' enthused Debbie, normal voice resumed.

'That's great. So, what do you think?'

'Really looking forward to it,' I said.

'Me, too,' agreed Debbie.

'I'm sorry to keep this short, but I'm on my own at the moment and I've got all sorts of contractors on site. If you don't nail them down they've got a habit of disappearing. That's the thing about the French, they take on five jobs at the same time, promise the earth and then don't turn up. Once you've got them you hang onto them while you can. Have you got any questions?'

'No, I don't think so,' said Debbie. 'If you let us know when you would like us to start, that would be great.'

'I need to sort that out with the boss but we need to move quickly. We're seeing the other couple tomorrow and we really want to make a decision by the weekend. I'll phone you either way on Monday and let you know. I'll just see you down. Thanks for coming. Can you manage, Debbie?'

Soon we were back in the car and on the coast road, feeling that we'd done well enough to stop in Saint Raphael for lunch. We chose a restaurant in one of the pretty side streets. The waitress led us to a table by the window and then ignored us for a full twenty minutes, so we left. I was very glad we did as five minutes later we found a restaurant where we were able to sit at a table, right on the beach. We gazed out to sea while enjoying two enormous bowls of mussels that we washed down with a *pichet* of crisp rosé.

'If I go now,' I declared, 'I'll be a very happy man.'

'I won't,' replied Debbie. 'You're not insured.'

'Oh, you can be so romantic! I thought that went really well,' I continued, raising my glass.

'Apart from me wheezing all the way round. God, I am so unfit. Do you think he noticed?'

'Hope not. Anyway, by the time we get there you'll be as fit as a butcher's dog. Double work detail for you tomorrow, my girl.'

We sat in the restaurant for a good hour and a half watching the world go by and soaking up the atmosphere.

'Your bill, sir,' said a friendly waiter as he continued to clear tables around us. Such was our enjoyment of the afternoon we hadn't noticed that the restaurant had emptied.

'Blimey, think we'll be coming back here again,' I said, reaching into my pocket. 'Thirty euros for all that and what a view!' Fully re-invigorated, and taking our time, we slowly drove back to Mandelieu.

A few yards along the main aisle of the park we saw Bob, who was walking towards us. He motioned for me to wind down the window.

'How did it go?' he asked.

'Great thanks,' I replied.

'Good lad. I've got a little job for you, Brent, if you fancy it. Some owners are coming into Nice on Saturday. All you've got to do is pick them up from the airport and get them back here. There's sixty-five euros in it for you. I was going to ask Paul but his car stinks of fags. Floor's like an ashtray. Have you seen it? A right shit tip. Besides, thought you could use the money.'

'Thanks, Bob, that's great,' said Debbie.

That'd be nice, I thought. And he was right: we really needed the money. Our envelope containing the little bit of cash we had was getting thinner and thinner. We hadn't been at all extravagant, but it was a lot more expensive in the south of France than we had realised. Sure, we didn't have rent to pay, but we weren't getting any income either, and it wouldn't be long before we were down to our last few hundred euros.

'I'll come and have a cup of tea with you after work and fill you in. You can tell me about the site in Fréjus. Might be able to do some business with them. Who knows? See ya.'

As promised, Bob popped by that evening for the briefest of visits. He handed me a piece of paper with a scribbled note and a flight number and disappeared again.

The next morning, he was back. It was our day off and I was sitting on our terrace having a coffee.

'Morning, Brent,' Bob said, cheerily. 'Is Debbie about by any chance?'

'Sorry, Bob, she's still in bed.'

'Still in bed?' he said, looking at his watch and frowning.

'With Philippa Gregory, actually.'

'With Philippa…?' he said, quite confused.

'Yeah, Philippa Gregory. And Debbie's left strict instructions that they're not to be disturbed until at least lunchtime.'

'Oh, oh, I see,' replied Bob, who had turned red and was looking decidedly uncomfortable. 'This happen quite often, does it, her and…?'

'Yes, quite often.'

'And what do you do when all this is going on?'

'I keep out of the way, Bob. You know how it is. Live and let live, that's what I say.'

Desperate to change the subject, Bob said, 'The thing is, Brent, I'm told Debbie can cook. It's Billy's seventieth birthday on Saturday and we're going to have a bit of a do at Paul and Ruth's. I was wondering if she could knock up a few nibbles and maybe a cake? Nothing fancy. I'll pay for all of the food and not a word to Billy – or Brenda, for that matter. You can both take the day off if that would help. I'll square it with Paul. Will you ask Debbie to come and see me when she's finished, with erm, thingy?'

'Yeah sure.'

'Now, this pick-up, Brent. Did you understand my note?'

'No problem.'

'Good, because it's dead easy. They're going back in a couple of weeks' time so you might as well do that one as well. I won't be here. Don't know if I've mentioned it before, but I've just bought a house in Normandy.'

'No, you didn't actually. Congratulations.'

'I'll be on my way there when they go. In fact, I'll tell you what, Brent. You've got a nice car – you might as well do all the airport runs as long as you're here. Can build up quite nicely. Easily get two or three a week. Anyway, got to dash.'

'Thanks, Bob.'

'Who was that at the door? I could hear you talking,' said Debbie as I went to rinse out my mug.

'Bob.'

'What did he want?'

'You, actually. Not urgent.'

'Oh, you should have come and got me. Not like I was doing anything important. What did you tell him?'

'I told him you were reading your book.'

'He didn't mind?'

'No, of course not. Look, he said could you go and see him when you've got a minute? He wants you to do some cooking for Billy's birthday.'

'Oh, OK, great. I'll just jump in the shower.'

'I'm off to the *boulangerie*. I'll see you a bit later. Bye.'

When I got back, Debbie was writing at the table. 'Bob all right was he?' I asked.

'Yes, fine. Though, perhaps it was my imagination but I did think he was looking me up and down a bit strangely when I first arrived. Are you sure he was OK this morning?'

'Positive. Good as gold.'

'Must be me. Anyway, look,' Debbie said, producing a wad of notes. 'He's given us two hundred and fifty euros. Think that'll be enough?'

'Would have thought so.'

'He said if I needed more, I can always go back. Come on, give me a hand, I'm making a list,' she said, shuffling along the banquette to make room for me.

Chapter 8

After lunch, we went to Mission Control and into the shed, where Debbie began to sort baking trays, cake tins, crockery, cutlery and tablecloths. Realising that I wasn't going to be very helpful with that task, I decided to go round the site, where I looked for spare plastic tables and chairs that could be used to accommodate the guests. About three o'clock Paul and Ruth, who had got just back from golf, found Debbie and me in the shed, talking about the party.

'Hello, you two. What are you doing here?'

'Just looking to see what we can cobble together for Billy's birthday party on Saturday,' I said.

'Billy's what?' asked Ruth.

'Birthday party.'

'First I've heard of it,' said Paul. 'Where's he having it?'

'At yours, Bob said. He came round and told us about it an hour or so ago.'

'Cheeky bastard. Oh, and I suppose he'll want me to do the cooking as well, will he?' snapped Ruth.

'No, he's asked me actually – hope that's OK,' replied Debbie, who was making her way out of the shed with an armful of plates.

'Has he now?' Ruth said, glaring at Paul.

Just then, Bella poked her head round the corner and that only ever meant one thing – Bob was not far behind.

'Filled them in have you, Brent? Great. Stick the kettle on, would you, Ruth? Do you need a hand with those, Debbie?'

'I'm fine, thanks. Just taking them over to ours to be washed.'

Debbie spent Friday morning in the office, trawling the Internet for canapé recipes, while I went through the crockery, washing up what wasn't chipped or cracked. I soaked the cutlery, scrubbed it until it was gleaming, matched salt and pepper pots, and laid everything out on the table. At lunchtime we went to the supermarket and came back with more shopping than we'd been able to afford in a very long time. Debbie made the mixture for a chocolate sponge which she put into the oven. After only ten minutes the gas bottle ran out.

'Bloody hell!' shouted Debbie, 'Quick, the cake's going to be ruined. Go and get Paul, will you?' He wasn't at home but a decidedly frosty Ruth was.

'You'll have to wait. We've run out,' she said.

'Oh no,' I started. 'When's the new…?'

'Don't know. You'll have to go and see Paul. He's fixing a boiler in number twenty-seven. Doubt there's much he can do. Bye-bye,' she said, firmly closing the door.

Paul, thankfully, was much more accommodating than his wife and was soon outside our van with a bottle of gas that he'd borrowed from one of the absent owners. The cake was saved, although it hadn't fully risen and had started to set on top.

At around six o'clock on Saturday evening Debbie started assembling the canapés. She'd made Welsh rarebit on slices of baguette topped with our homemade chutney that we'd brought with us from the UK, sweet potato stackers, blinis with smoked salmon, crème fraîche and chives, devilled quails eggs and prawn and chorizo skewers. There were also some baked figs stuffed with Roquefort, wrapped in prosciutto as well as mini Thai fishcakes with sweet chilli dipping sauce.

At seven o'clock we went back over to Mission Control where we were greeted by a much more mellow Ruth. At seven-thirty, everyone who was staying or working on the site arrived. Everybody brought at least one bottle of something with them, except Marc.

Inside, all of the food had been beautifully laid out and somehow thirty people managed to squeeze inside. Peering through a crack in the curtain, Bob asked everyone to keep quiet as we could hear voices and footsteps drawing closer.

'Don't know why the hell we've got to come over here for, Brenda,' we heard Billy moan. 'Raising a glass to some new helpers? I don't even soddin' drink. And another thing….'
Before he could say another word, the front door was flung

open and Billy was greeted with a rousing chorus of *Happy Birthday*. Billy, clearly moved, wiped a tear from his eye.

'I think I need a sit down. Pass me that stool, will ya? You could have warned me, Brenda. You could at least have warned me. Bloody rotten that is, Brenda. Bloody rotten.'

'What makes you think I knew, you silly old sod?' She laughed. 'No one tells me anything round here. Have one of these before they all go, you daft bugger,' she went on, looking at the food that was fast disappearing.

Debbie, who was basking in the wave of compliments about her cooking, looked very happy.

'Three cheers for Debbie!' shouted Bob. 'Hip, hip!'

I glanced over to Ruth, who had slunk back into her chair and was looking quite uncomfortable. After half an hour or so, Bob signalled to Debbie, who went to our home and brought back the chocolate cake covered with candles that she lit before coming in. She was followed by the dozen or so people who had made their way outside during the course of the evening. There was another rendition of *Happy Birthday*; Billy wiped his eyes once more and the usual jokes were made about the amount of candles and the potential fire hazard.

'Love this cake, Debbie,' beamed Billy. 'How did you manage to get the crusty bit running through the middle? Fantastic that. Here, Brenda, have you seen this?' I felt a wry smile run across my face.

As the food disappeared, so did many of the guests. By nine o'clock the temperature had dropped considerably and although we were warm on the inside due to the copious amounts of alcohol, it was decided that it would be a good idea for the fifteen or so of us still remaining, to continue the festivities indoors. Bob and Pauline sat on a banquette that ran along the back wall of the sitting room, behind which was a drawn curtain. Debbie, Ruth, Paul and I sat at a table in front of them.

'Tomorrow,' Bob said to me, producing a bottle of Calvados from his coat pocket, 'you, me, Dave and Marc need to go and pick up a golf buggy from Cannes. We'll stick it on the back of the trailer. Where is Dave anyway?'

'I'm not sure. He was here a second ago. Elodie's still here. Can't be far,' replied Debbie.

'Oh, well. All the more for us then,' said Bob. 'Pass the Calvados round, Brent, there's a good lad. Cheers everybody. Bottoms up.'

There were several more toasts to Billy, toasts to Debbie's cooking, toasts to Mandelieu, in fact toasts to anything anybody could think of as long as it involved drinking more Calvados. As the evening progressed so did Bob's slurring until, eventually, he announced he was off.

As he started to stand up he fell backwards against the window and brought down the curtain complete with curtain pole, much to the amusement of everyone in the room. Everyone apart from Elodie that is, who, while we were seeing the funny side of what had just happened, had seen something completely different. She picked up a napkin and gently began to wipe away some of the condensation on the window that, thanks to Bob, was now uncovered. Putting aside her previous inhibitions, Elodie put on her glasses and stared intently outside. For a few moments she knelt motionless on the banquette, not noticing the crowd that was gathering behind her. With the help of a distant street lamp I could just make out the silhouette of Dave, who was engaged in a passionate embrace with someone – and that someone was Floppy, the somewhat worse-for-wear government's head of alcohol abuse guru. She and Dave were on the lawn right outside Paul and Ruth's home. So engrossed in each other were they that they hadn't noticed that they were now in full view of everybody.

'Excuse me,' said Elodie, pushing her way through the small crowd and heading towards the front door.

Ruth, who up until then had looked decidedly miserable, rubbed her hands together and said gleefully, 'Think there's going to be fireworks,' and rushed to take Elodie's place on the banquette, pressing her nose up against the window.

However, there were no fireworks. Wherever Elodie had gone, it wasn't to confront Dave and Floppy.

'It all happens here,' said Brian. 'I tell you, you get to see all life here. You couldn't make it up.'

'Do you think I should go and see if she is all right?' asked Debbie.

'No,' replied Bob. 'Best leave them to it. One for the road, Brent?'

'Oh, go on then, why not?' I replied as Bob poured the last of the Calvados into my glass.

'Can't see me getting much work out of those two in the future,' he said. 'Paul, how much longer are they due to be here?'

Bob was right – the following day there was no sign of either Dave or Elodie. Dave hadn't gone back to their van that night. Elodie was hardly seen at all for the remainder of the two weeks that she was due to stay in Mandelieu. She substituted Dave for Jack Daniels and emerged on the day of her and her former partner's departure wearing a pair of dark sunglasses and looking a shadow of the happy-go-lucky woman who had arrived a few weeks previously. As Dave and Elodie got into Bob's car to make the trip to the airport, I felt, somewhat cowardly, extremely glad that it wasn't me driving them. Dave had stayed at Floppy's the whole time, doing odd bits of gardening and painting. He and Elodie had avoided each other until the day they left. As I watched them go I thought to myself that it was going to be one very awkward journey.

Sunday, the day of our telephone interview, arrived and Debbie and I banned each other from talking about the previous night's events until the call was over – we needed to be fully focused on what we were going to say to the man from the Cayman Islands. Nothing was going to distract us – or so we thought.

'Bastard! Fucking bastard!' shouted Debbie as she came back from the shower.

'Bastard? Who's a bastard? What's happened?' I asked.

57

'Bloody Peeping Tom. I was in the shower, minding my own business, turned round, looked up and saw a pair of eyes staring at me through the gap at the top.'

'Oh my God! What did you do?'

'I screamed at him to get out, what do you think I did?'

'You going to report it?'

'Of course not, what good will it do? Just next time, you'll have to come and stand guard – fucking pervert. Right, I need to dry my hair. What time is it? I tell you sweetie, I can't wait to get out of this place, I've just about had enough.'

We waited in the office and at exactly eleven o'clock the phone rang.

'You first,' I said, 'I'll put the kettle on.'

'What are you, a man or a mouse?'

'Pass the cheese.'

As I sat looking through some old magazines, Debbie giggled her way through an hour's worth of conversation, at the end of which she put the phone down and her thumbs up.

'He's very funny,' she said with a huge grin. 'Absolutely charming.'

'That's nice. I hope you'll be very happy together. Did he say anything about me?'

'He's phoning back to talk to you in about ten minutes. He said a couple of peasants had just arrived at the gates and he had to go and shoot them. It's de rigueur, don't you know?' Debbie said, putting on a gentrified accent.

'Posh is he?' I asked, slinking back down on to the comfy sofa.

'No, not at all, but when he imitates someone who is, he's very funny.'

'Anything else?'

'He said you don't look much like a gardener.'

'Meaning?'

'In your photo, you're wearing a suit. He may have a point.' Debbie laughed.

'Sorry about that,' apologised Xander Smythe as I answered the phone. 'One must have a cull of the local artisans every now and then – good for morale, don't you know. Breed like rabbits if one's not careful and then where would we be? Now then, young Brent, what do you know about gardening in the south of France?'

'Only what I've picked up since I've been here,' I replied hesitantly.

'And you've been here all of six weeks, not what you'd call a great deal of experience, is it? What do you know about swimming pools? Nothing…I see. I'm sure you can learn but the current guardians won't be with you long. I take it you've never driven a tractor. Can you prune an olive tree? Looking at your CV I doubt you've ever had to deal with an *arrosage* system?'

'An arrow what?' I asked, turning towards Debbie and shaking my head. I was beginning to feel that whatever confidence I had at the start of the conversation was fast being eroded.

'*Arrosage*, dear boy. Sprinkler system.'

'Not much call for those in Cookham,' I replied.

'Hmmmm, don't suppose there is.'

Debbie could see that I was getting a bit frustrated with the way the call was going and put a piece of blank paper in front of me and passed me a pen. On and on he went, pointing out what I couldn't do. *The man's a wanker*, I wrote in big block capitals. Debbie shrugged her shoulders – there was nothing she could do to help.

'What do you know about wild boar? Can you set a mole trap? Have you ever grown variegated alstroemeria?' It soon became clear that Alexander Smythe wasn't interviewing me at all – he just wanted to show off his knowledge at the same time as belittle mine.

An hour later, I put the phone down.

'That sounded like hard work,' said Debbie as I let out a huge sigh and started pacing up and down the room.

'That man is a bastard. He spent the last hour trying to bully me. He knows what I know and what I don't – it's all on the CV for fuck's sake and yet he just kept picking away. I don't know why he bothered,' I said, throwing my notes on the table.

'How was it left?' asked Debbie.

'He said that he'd call back tomorrow, same time. You can speak to the twat.'

'Look, he told me that he'd received ninety-seven CVs and he'd narrowed it down to just two couples, so we've got a chance,' reasoned Debbie.

'Whoopy doopy do. Anyway, who the hell does this guy think he is?' I said, picking up the office keys.

'Possibly the guy who holds the key to our future in France,' replied Debbie as we walked back down the drive.

'God I hope not. Fancy a glass or two? I could sure do with one,' I said.

Unfortunately, I had to admit, Debbie was right. Money was very tight. If this didn't work out, we could soon find ourselves on the ferry back to Dover. In our eyes, we would have failed. Going back to England at that stage was a prospect we just didn't want to contemplate.

Chapter 9

The next day we went back down to the office and, true to his word, Smythe phoned. Debbie listened intently while I riffled nervously again through the pages of most of the magazines in the office and then, out of the blue, a huge smile ran across her face. She put one thumb up in the air, glanced at me briefly and then began to write feverishly on her notepad. I went outside and paced up and down the main aisle for what felt like ages. There was no point me being in the office. I'd only interrupt or worse still, blow it.

'All right, Brent?' said Bob, his 4x4 screeching to a halt, inches away from me. 'Just the man I'm looking for. I completely forgot I've got a family coming into Nice, they land in half an hour. Pauline's got me running around for bloody curtains. Can you pick them up for me? I've written all the details, good lad. How did the interview go by the way?'

Before I had the chance to reply, his phone rang and Bob was wheel-spinning down the road, narrowly missing Bella, who he hadn't realised had jumped out of his car.

I went back into the office. Debbie raised her hand and mouthed the words 'Five minutes'. I wrote on the pad in front of me, *Airport run now – call me when you're done*. Debbie nodded and I ran back down the main drive to get the car.

I got half way to Nice before I realised that I'd forgotten the phone and I was soon getting some very strange looks from other drivers who could see me shouting and swearing at absolutely nothing.

I arrived at Terminal 2, ran to Arrivals and glanced at the screen, only to find that my passengers' flight had been delayed by an hour; so I went to the bar, ordered a coffee and swore some more. After an hour and a half, which felt like a week, they arrived. Liz and James, now retired, had been coming to Mandelieu for the past ten years. Like many of the mobile home owners who used to spend the summer at the site, they'd come down for a week in the spring to give their home a good airing and tidy up outside. James would cut the hedge, weed the gravel path, creosote the decking and fix anything that had broken due to old age or had taken a battering from the elements. There were leaves to rake, gutters to empty and moss to be cleared from between the paving slabs. Liz would fling open the windows to blow away the musty smell of winter, rewash all of the bed linen and curtains, scrub the floors and run the crockery and cutlery through the dishwasher. In the afternoons, when it was sunny, which was most days then, as I passed by their van James would be lying in his hammock sipping a small bottle of beer.

'How are you doing, Brent? You got time for a quick drink, laddie?' he'd ask.

It was the same wherever Debbie and I went in the park – everybody was very polite and hospitable. Liz and James, like many others, took a great deal of pride in their little corner of France and among the French the whole thing had become quite competitive. They'd come down from Paris with timber, saws, roof tiles, shutters, decking, front gates and shiny new gas barbecues, as well as anything else they could think of to rival their neighbours.

When I got back, Debbie was standing at the cooker. 'Something smells nice, what have we got?' I asked.

'Spanish chicken. Pass me the salt, would you?'

'Sorry I'm a bit late, plane was delayed and….'

'You forgot the phone,' Debbie interrupted.

'I know,' I grumbled, pouring myself a glass of rosé. 'Well?'

'Well, he wants us to go over there on Thursday. He'll pay our expenses. If it all works out, we can stay. We can start the following day.'

'The following day? Blimey, that's fast. And if things don't work out?'

'He'll pay for us to get back again. We've got nothing to lose my love,' Debbie reasoned.

'He hates me.'

'No he doesn't. Why else would he be asking?'

'Maybe he fancies you.'

'Oh, for God's sake, he doesn't know me. Come on, this could be our ticket – taste that for me, would you?

'There's more good news too. I've had two phone calls while you've been out. That lady in Mouans-Sartoux, half an hour down the road, wants to see us tomorrow morning and someone's replied to our ad that we put on the website. A really nice woman called Suzy phoned. She and her husband, Charlie, are guardians working in Aix-en-Provence, which it just so happens is on the way to Smythe's villa in Castres. There's been a death in her family and they've got no choice but to go back to England. There's a lot to sort out apparently so they can't keep their jobs. They've asked us for lunch and a chat. I declined the lunch, we won't have time. But look, this morning we had nothing and now we've got three possibilities, things are looking up.'

'I should go out more often.'

The next morning, we took the road to Mouans Sartoux, passing through the small village of Pégomas. Although the first half of the trip was quite uneventful, what we weren't aware of at the time was that the second part was going to develop into the journey from hell. The road, to begin with, seemed like any other but suddenly, without warning, it became one of the scariest places that I had ever driven. To our left was a steep cliff that jutted out, with many of the rocks now multi-coloured where several cars had been scraped. The road was windy and it was impossible to see what was coming round the bend in the opposite direction. To our right was a sheer drop, so sheer that we couldn't see the bottom. To add to the stress, there were several bunches of flowers placed along the edge of the precipice. There were a few tight passing places but once on this stretch of mountain track it was impossible to turn round. Debbie was soon as white as a sheet and became so frightened that she screamed,

'Get me out of here. Brent, just get me out of here!'
Unfortunately, there was nothing I could do.

By the time we got to the outskirts of Mouans Sartoux, Debbie was no longer the calm, self-assured woman that had left Mandelieu a short time before. She was desperately nervous, stressed beyond belief and shaking. We stopped at the entrance to some woodland where Debbie got out and wandered around, sipping her bottle of water and saying nothing for several minutes.

'I can't believe we just did that,' she said. 'That has to be the worst journey of my life. Did you see the trucks going down there? I thought we'd had it, I really thought we'd had it,' she said, tears now running down her face. 'I was so frightened. God, I was so frightened,' she said, struggling to hold back the tears. After Debbie had applied the finishing touches to her makeup, I said, 'That's better.'

'Are you sure my eyes don't look too puffy?' she replied, staring into her compact mirror.

'No, you look absolutely fine,' I said reassuringly. 'How are you feeling?'

'Much better now thanks. I'm OK but there's no way I'm doing that bastard journey again.'

'I'm sure we can find another way back. Can't be that difficult.'

'Too right. I don't care if it's via Timbuktu, I'm not doing that again,' Debbie insisted.

'Ready?' I asked, reaching for the doorbell on the stone pillar.

'Yes. Let's get it over with,' replied Debbie, who by then, had already had enough stress for one day.

Having waited a few minutes and rung several times with no response, we chose to peer through the iron gates. In the distance we could see a big house with pale-blue shutters that was surrounded by a lush meadow, an avenue of magnolias in full bloom, row upon row of olive, citrus, cherry and fig trees and a babbling river with a small footbridge going across it.

We were just about to give up and head back when out of a side door a chocolate-brown Labrador came bounding up to greet us, pursued by a portly, red-faced gentleman in his sixties. He was running along with his feet pointed at ten to two and his bright-yellow waistcoat gleaming in the sunshine. We thought we were about to be introduced to Toad. Waving his car keys in the air and puffing all the while, he said, 'She's not here, had to go to the doctors. Can you come back later? I've got to go to Pégomas – groceries. She said she's really sorry but can she call you to rearrange? Look, I'm in a bit of a rush. You can turn your car round in here, while I get mine out. Thanks a lot,' and off he scuttled back down the drive. Soon after, he passed us in an old, white BMW that had so many small dents in its bodywork that it was beginning to look more like a giant golf ball than a car. It occurred to us that Toad was very familiar with the journey that we had just made. He sped out of the drive, waving enthusiastically and tooting his horn at the same time. As he disappeared round the first bend there was a loud screech of tyres. The BMW reversed back past the gates, while a furious-looking man, in a red Renault Mégane came flashing by in the opposite direction, shaking his fist and glaring at Toad, who was not only oblivious to the situation, he was still waving at us. 'Told you. They're all bloody lunatics round here,' I said as we got back into our car.

We drove down the very busy main street in Mouans-Sartoux and found somewhere to park. There seemed to be a good choice of small bistros that we'd noticed along the road, so we felt that we'd be spoilt for choice in finding somewhere to stop and have a light lunch after the traumas of the morning. Sadly, most of those bistros turned out to be pizzerias and the busiest restaurant, by far, was McDonald's. In the short time that we had been in this part of France I'd begun to wonder what had happened to all of the quaint little places that we'd heard so much about, where we could get a freshly cooked, homemade, three-course meal for fifteen euros. Wherever they were, we hadn't managed to find any. No matter which menu we looked at, it appeared that, pizza, Salade Niçoise or entrecôte was all that was on offer.

'She must've known that she'd got an appointment this morning,' said Debbie who was cutting into her half of the four-cheese pizza that had just arrived.

'You never know, might have had a cancellation. Might have been an emergency, who knows?' I replied.

'It's just after what we went through to get there, I could…hang on a minute, phone.' Debbie listened intently while I continued to tuck in. 'She's apologised about this morning and wants to see us at three. Not a completely wasted day after all,' said Debbie, whose colour was starting to return to her cheeks.

Again, we were met by the exuberant Labrador who followed us down to the villa, leaping up and bounding along as he went. Unfortunately, Debbie had chosen to wear a white outfit and by the time we'd reached the front door it was covered in muddy paw prints. We were about to knock when a woman in her early sixties, wearing jodhpurs, riding boots and a hunting jacket burst through the front door. 'Hello,' she said, thrusting her right hand at us. 'I am Frau Schmidt, you can call me Heike if you like, only not in front of the guests.' She briefly looked Debbie up and down and said, 'I see you've already met Max, sorry about that. Come this way. We will have coffee, I will tell you about the job, you ask me questions. Then we see.'

She led us into a stately, marble-floored, drawing room and motioned for us to sit down. Frau Schmidt chose a comfy chair next to the fireplace which ran the length of one wall, while we were on a high-backed sofa, a good twenty feet away. Such was the size of the room and the height of the ceiling, that although the fire was lit, it only just took the edge off what I imagined to be one of the coldest places in the house. Just as she was about to speak, Frau Schmidt's phone rang. For a few seconds she stared at the handset, debating whether or not to take the call. Having decided to answer it, she launched into an angry rant in German at the poor person who had plucked up enough courage to phone her. No wonder Toad was always in a hurry to get away, I thought.

'Sorry about that,' she said. 'Bloody architects. I've had twenty-seven of them come here to redesign this ceiling and do you know what, I've fired them all? Ja, that's right, I've fired them all. They're all bastards. I've spent all my life designing the interior of buildings and they think I know fucking nothing about architecture but let me tell you now, I know fuck all about architecture. That's right, fuck all. I keep telling them this and what do they do? They just laugh. Can you believe it? Maybe I write it on my gravestone – *Heike Schmidt knows fuck all about architecture*. What do you think about that then? What's wrong with people? They just want your money and they want to do nothing. Look at this fireplace – it's still out of line. They're all useless, useless.' Frau Schmidt's phone rang again. I gazed around the room, trying to look at anything apart from Heike. I was worried that if I caught her eye, I'd too would just burst out laughing. 'Another useless bastard. He can fuck off as well,' she said scornfully, cutting off the caller at the second ring. 'Where was I? Oh, yes. As I was saying, I am an interior architect with very high standards. I have to admit sometimes you will hear me shouting but that's just the way I am. It's nothing to do with you so don't worry, unless of course you really piss me or one of my guests off, then it can be a bit tricky but you seem like nice people so I don't expect that to happen. Right, I show you the house.'

As we followed Frau Schmidt around the villa she made her expectations very clear. Debbie was to have all of the cleaning, dusting and polishing completed by eleven o'clock each morning, after which, she would be expected to prepare lunch. At the end of service, she would get an hour off before returning to prepare dinner. Although not always required to serve in the evenings, there was a turn down service for Heike and Toad, who slept in separate rooms. This was also to be part of Debbie's role. Normally, Debbie's day would be finished by around nine o'clock and she would get Sundays off, unless there was a lunch or dinner party, in which case she'd be given a day in lieu during the week. I wasn't sure exactly what my role was going to be at this stage, but it soon became apparent that Debbie's was one not so much about housekeeping and cooking as about being a hot and cold running slave.

'What happened to your previous guardians?' I asked.

'They were bastards too – Belgian. I went to see where they were one morning and they had gone. Not a word, nothing. Don't they want to work? Two million people unemployed in this country and what do I land up with? A couple of lazy bastards. Actually, thinking about it, now would be a good time for me to show you your apartment. We can walk through the gardens. Follow me.'

The grounds were as beautiful as they were extensive and, not surprisingly, Frau Schmidt knew every square inch of them. She stopped to examine part of the box hedge that lined one side of the drive. Cutting back a straggly twig, about four inches long, she turned to me, 'You see my husband, Brent? Rubbish driver. He drives way too fast and catches things. I think, in his time, he's probably dragged half of this garden with him to Pégomas.' As we walked, Heike's mood lightened. She talked enthusiastically about her garden, naming all of the plants along the way – each one had a story. She told us how she had invested a great deal of her time and money in getting everything 'just so' as she put it. Everything in the house and garden had to be 'just so'.

At the end of the drive was the guardian's apartment. Although it was due to be decorated soon, at the time, it was just a shell. The walls were unpainted with bare wires dangling from them. There were no carpets, curtains, furniture or white goods. The corridor was stacked with bags of cement, thirty-metre lengths of thick, black plastic pipe and there was dust everywhere. 'Should have all been done by now but guess what? The bastards don't show up. I phone them every day, they cut me off. Do you believe it? I sometimes think I'm the only person doing any work in this bloody country! So, you're available immediately? It's going to take a few weeks to get this place sorted out which will take us to the end of the month. Let's both have a think about it and perhaps you can come over again next week and we can discuss money. I hate talking about money, especially when I have to spend it,' she said with a sigh. 'Now, I must get on. Wasted too much time at that English doctor of yours. All he can do is write prescriptions. Another useless bastard. I'll open the gate for you. See you again. Bye.'

'She's blisteringly bloody mad,' I said as we drove out of the gates.

'She seems to have a good command of the English language though.' Debbie laughed. 'That's just reminded me,' she said, 'can you phone the doctor in Grasse that she was talking about? We're just down the road and I really need to get some stronger travel sickness tablets, especially after what happened this morning. You never know.'

I made the call.

'He'll be there in an hour – might have to wait a bit but he'll see you.'

We only had to wait about half an hour but what surprised us was how polite the French were, even in a doctor's surgery. Every person without exception who came into the waiting room, and there must have been at least a dozen, greeted us by saying, '*Bonjour monsieur, dame.*'

'So what do you two do then?' asked the doctor.

'We're working on a mobile home site in Mandelieu at the moment but we're looking for a housekeeper/gardener job. In fact, we've just been for an interview down the road in Mouans Sartoux,' Debbie said.

'Oh, really, who was that with?'

'A Frau Schmidt,' I replied.

'Heike Schmidt?' the doctor responded, looking a little concerned.

'I take it you know her then?' I asked.

'Know her? Indeed, I do – she's a friend of mine,' he said, looking over his horn-rimmed glasses. 'I go to her house every now and again for dinner parties. Socially, she's very nice although I have to admit that a little of her goes a long way,' he added. 'Unfortunately, she has a habit of upsetting almost everybody she comes into contact with. I don't know if she told you but over the past five years she's employed over thirty architects – sacked them all, not paid them a penny.'

'She did say that she was having one or two problems,' I said.

'One or two!' The doctor laughed. 'She's got court cases coming out of her ears, leaking money from every orifice and I suspect is about to go pop any minute. Bet that guardian's apartment's still not ready?' I shook my head. 'Thought not. My advice to you is not to touch her with a ten-foot barge pole, sorry,' he said, while writing out a prescription. Unsurprised, but a bit disappointed, we left the surgery.

'So far then,' I concluded, 'we've got one nasty bastard intent on bullying me, a mentally unstable German woman who's on the brink of going broke, a temporary job down the road and the one in Aix-en-Provence.'

'Aix sounds our best bet if you ask me,' said Debbie. 'Seems a pity we're only seeing the guardians. The owner doesn't get there for another week.'

'Oh well, at least if it does all go wrong, Bob's promised me the airport runs. Come on.'

When we got back to the site I went to the office to check emails and found out that we hadn't got the job in Fréjus. There was no explanation – just one line, thanking us for our time. By the time I got back to our home, Debbie was asleep on the bed, holding her book. I put up a lounger on our small terrace and was about to drift off myself when Ruth wandered by with a mop and bucket full of cleaning materials.

'How did you get on?' she asked.

'Great thanks, went really well,' I replied.

'You got the job?'

'Pretty much. There's still some work to do on our apartment so it could be a couple of weeks.'

'But I thought you were off to the south west tomorrow?'

'We are but if that doesn't work out we'll have to come back, which won't be so bad.'

'Oh really? How's that then?' asked Ruth, somewhat bemused by my answer.

'Even if it takes us a while to move in down the road, Bob's said I can do all of the airport runs. Keep the wolf from the door a bit.'

'You don't want to believe what he tells you,' replied Ruth. 'And besides, if that's what he's said I'm going to have a word with him – he can't do that. All of the other helpers will be jealous,' she said angrily.

'None of the other helpers have cars,' I replied, beginning to feel my temperature rise.

'I don't care, I know people,' glared Ruth.

Each time I tried to explain to her that, firstly, it was none of her business and, secondly, as no one else had a car the whole thing was academic anyway, she kept repeating, 'I know people, I know people.' It didn't matter what I said, over and over again, she came out with the same mantra, 'I know people, I know people.' In the end I left her to it and went back inside. Seething with anger, I explained what had just happened to Debbie, who had not long been awake.

'Jealously, pure jealousy,' she said.

'But why? I don't understand it. None of the other helpers have cars.'

'Nothing to do with them my love.'

'What then?' I asked.

'She wants the money for herself. They've got a car.'

'Yeah, a right shit tip according to Bob,' I replied.

'And you think that makes any difference to Ruth? All she sees is sixty-five euros with her name on it. She's greedy. Doesn't need the money. It's greed, that's all, sheer greed.'

'She might change her mind if she knew how little we have.'

'I doubt it. Take the chops out the fridge for me, would you? Last meal before we go, and quite frankly, I can't wait. People, bloody people!'

Later that evening we packed up our belongings in readiness for our five-hour journey to Castres. Bob dropped by saying 'I'll see you tomorrow before you go. Thanks for all of your hard work – it's been great having you here. I'm sure you'll leave your van nice and tidy,' he said quite firmly. 'Got new helpers coming in when you go. See ya.'

'Was that a gentle warning?' I said to Debbie.

'I wouldn't have thought so. Just the way he is. Probably wasn't happy about having to clean Dave and Elodie's when they went. Besides, he knows us better than that.'

The next day, just before twelve, Bob and most of the other helpers came to say goodbye. Paul and Ruth had, at the last minute, decided to squeeze in a quick round of golf and were nowhere to be seen. Bob made a brief speech, thanking us for our help and how he felt certain that with Debbie's cooking we would have no problem making it in France. He handed us an envelope containing a card, which he told us to open once we were on our way.

'Sorry, Marc,' said Debbie, 'but I left the keys on the kitchen table and shut the front door as we came out. You'll have to get the spare set from the office.'

'Don't worry about that, Debbie,' he replied, producing an unwound metal coat hanger from the golf buggy. Putting a hook either side of the lounge window, Marc was in the house and dangling the keys in front of us within seconds. 'Nothing to it,' he said, giving Debbie a big hug and smiling. 'Come back and see us won't you?'

Soon after, Debbie got into the driver's seat and we drove back down the main aisle of the campsite where we had arrived, one drizzly afternoon, only ten weeks previously. We watched our van slowly disappear from view, turned right onto the main road and followed signs to the A8 and headed towards Aix-en-Provence. I opened the envelope – inside was a card signed by Bob, Pauline, Marc, Sharon and all of the helpers. There was also a crisp fifty-euro note which I added to the two hundred euros in my wallet – all the money we had left in the world.

Chapter 10

'Welcome,' enthused a bubbly, silver-haired, petite woman in her sixties. 'I'm Suzy and this is my husband, Charlie. Hope you found us OK. We're a bit out of the way and the roads can be a bit wiggly piggly but I hope that won't put you off. It's a truly beautiful spot here – we're really sad to be going. Now then, I'll go and get us something to drink. Charlie, be a dear and show Brent and Debbie round the outside, would you? I'll be back in a minute,' and off she scuttled through a small door that presumably led to their apartment.

Charlie gave us a tour of the beautifully kept gardens and told us about the villa's owners, of whom he and Suzy had become extremely fond.

'Mrs David really likes her roses,' he explained, 'spends hours tending them. She can be out here the whole day. I think it's her way of relaxing. She's really nice. The only thing is, if she asks you to do something, do it straightaway, otherwise she gets a bit anxious. She does have a great sense of humour though. I'll never forget my first day here. She asked if I could drive a sit-down mower. Of course, I said yes. What did I do? I reversed it straight into the barn door and fell off. She couldn't stop laughing.'

Charlie guided us through a small orchard with cherry, apple, plum and pear trees – there was an abundance of figs as well as a small vegetable patch that he was about to dig over in preparation for the spring planting. 'Shame I won't get to see the results,' he said. 'Hope you'll enjoy them. Any special requests? You can grow just about anything here.'

On each of the four terraces that made up the garden was a brick-built barbecue, and very expensive-looking garden furniture had been neatly stacked inside a conservatory. The twenty-metre swimming pool glistened in the spring sunshine and six or seven citrus trees in large pots had been brought outside after being protected against the winter frost.

Just inside the main gates some foundations had been laid in readiness for the building of the guardian's cottage that was due to be completed by September.

'It's a bit cramped where you'll be staying at the moment, Debbie,' Charlie said, 'but I've seen the plans for the new cottage and it looks brilliant. Mrs David really has spared no expense.'

'Do you get much trouble round here?' I asked, looking up at the numerous security cameras that lined the perimeter walls.

'No, not at all,' replied Charlie. 'It's all for the insurance. There's some proper antiques in here, including me and Suzy,' he said with a smile. 'They're not out now but Mrs David likes to have them around her in the summer. No point having them if you can't admire them, I guess. Oh, and here's another thing you don't get too often in this job – when Mrs D comes down in the summer, she brings an entourage with her. She comes with two chefs, a butler, two nannies and a chauffeur. She doesn't want you working too hard. Ever heard of that before?' I shook my head. 'No, me neither. She really looks after her staff. Hope you can hang on,' he said enthusiastically.

'Come on, everybody, let's eat,' said Suzy, who was walking towards us with a tray of delicious-looking food. 'Charlie, be a darling and bring the plates, would you?'

'Can we...' began Debbie, who was sitting at the table and enjoying the midday sunshine.

'No, no, you sit there. I'm sorry, Debbie, I know what you said about lunch but I really couldn't let you go without giving you something to eat. You've had a long enough journey as it is and you've still got some way to go. I so hope you don't mind. Come on, we can show you the inside of the house afterwards.'

This wasn't an ordinary lunch – it was fabulous. There was a huge tray of roasted red peppers, courgettes, new potatoes, onions, garlic and fennel. Suzy brought out a mountain of chicken drumsticks, sausages and hams. She had gone to an enormous amount of effort on our behalf, something that we just weren't expecting – it was one of the nicest things that had happened to us since we'd arrived in France. Charlie brought out a couple of bottles of rosé and four gleaming wine glasses – we were being properly spoiled. The sun shone down, we ate, we drank, we talked about the job but most of all we laughed.

After lunch Suzy showed us around the house, which was modernly and beautifully decorated. There were eight bedrooms and a Nanny's quarters, as well as four basic but comfortable bedrooms in the basement for the entourage. There was also a kitchen big enough to land a small jet in. Debbie's eyes lit up.

'What I'd give to cook in here.'

'You never know,' replied Suzy. 'Mrs David loves to try new things and, I hope you don't mind, but I've sent her the menus that you sent over – they look positively delicious. Oh, I do hope you'll take this job – it'll be absolutely perfect for you. I'm sorry, I know we're keeping you but let me just show you quickly round where you'll be staying. Won't take long,' she giggled.

She was right – it was no bigger than where we had been staying in Mandelieu but it was cosy and besides it would only be until September.

'Promise me you'll come back if you get the chance. I think you're lovely people. I'm going to write such a nice letter to Mrs David about you. Please, please, please say you'll think about it.'

'Of course we will. Thanks so much for looking after us, we'll keep in touch.'

Moments later we were turning out of the drive and continuing our journey towards Castres.

'What a delightful couple,' Debbie said, her mood much lightened.

'Yes, and what a delicious lunch too – wasn't expecting that.'

'Me neither, it's put us behind a bit but there was no way we could've refused. Anyway it might put you in a better frame of mind for meeting his nibs.'

'We'll see. Bloody hell, these roads are awful,' I said as we drove round bend after bend.

'Well, we were warned they could be a bit wiggly piggly,' said Debbie. 'Besides, we are in the mountains, what did you expect?'

'Wiggly piggly? Don't know where they got that from, I can't remember the last time I saw a straight bit and the drivers here are nuts. Didn't think you were supposed to overtake on bends – not even in France. Just hope we don't see any coming the other way.'

Having survived the treacherous mountain roads, two hours later a woman's voice proudly announced, 'You have reached your destination,' which was all very well except that we found ourselves in a car park right next to a playing field.

'Doesn't look much like a château,' I quipped. 'Do you reckon we'll have to sleep under the goalposts?'

'We'll have to phone him. We're already half an hour late. You do it, I need to put a bit of makeup on.'

'Did you bother to read the instructions I sent you, Brent?' Smythe asked. 'There were four pages of them – people don't normally get lost.'

'Well, we headed for Carcassonne and then....'

'Why on earth would you want to do that?' Smythe interrupted.

'It said in the ad that the villa was in Carcassonne.'

'Oh dear,' he replied, the disappointment clear in his voice. 'That's just to put off the tax man.'

'I see.'

'Now, where did you say you were exactly?'

'On the ten-metre line,' I replied.

'Pass me to Debbie, would you?'

We turned off the main road and drove down a very narrow lane, at the end of which was a small church. In front of it there was a twenty-foot-tall metal Christmas tree which, despite being the beginning of April, was lit up. The church acted as the centre of a roundabout and as we went round to our right we passed along an even narrower road with terraced houses either side. Shutters of different colours and in various states of disrepair swayed back and forth in the wind. Several houses had Father Christmases dangling from the upper windows. Broken old flower pots lined the pathways and several of the buildings were derelict and boarded up. Most cars that we passed had at least one dent. A bow-legged, elderly gentleman smiled and wafted his walking stick in the air as we slowed down to pass him.

'That's it.'

'That's what?' replied Debbie.

'Smythe's. That's definitely it. *La Rose des Vents*,' I said, pointing to a small plaque to the side of the gate. 'Look at the size of those walls. I bet he pours boiling hot tar from the top when the locals come round.' We parked outside what we thought to be the main gate. 'I'll ring the buzzer. Hello, is that Xander?' I said, speaking into the intercom. 'We're at the gate.'

'Which one?' he asked.

'How many have you got?' There was no reply. After several minutes of shouting 'Hello!' at the intercom and tapping it, I went back to the car. 'He's showing off now, the bugger's got more than one gate.' I walked up and down the lane studying the walls very closely. It wasn't getting dark so how could I miss another set of gates?

Then I saw it. Only several yards away from the main entrance, and covered in moss, was a tiny personnel gate with a buzzer. 'The idiot's had me running up and down the bloody lane looking for the sodding Borrowers' entrance. And look, that's the house just there,' I said, peering through the gates. 'He's sitting in the kitchen. He can see there's a car outside. What is he on?'

'So you're at the main gates then, Brent? Jolly good. I'll be out in a minute.' Wearing a green and white hooped polo shirt, firmly tucked into a pair of pale-blue jeans with razor edge creases, Xander Smythe walked out of the kitchen door.

Forcing a grin, he reached for a switch on the wall that opened the electric gates. 'Park next to the *remorque*, would you?'

'Park next to the what?'

'The *remorque*,' Smythe replied, clearly disappointed at having to repeat himself.

'What's a *remorque*?'

Smythe sighed. 'A trailer. I thought you said you could speak French, Brent,' he said. 'Follow me. Bring your bags with you.'

We walked through the paved courtyard and up a steep path which led to the back of the villa. I dragged our impossibly heavy suitcase behind me, while Debbie, who was trying to keep up, could just about see over the duvet and the other bedding she was carrying. Smythe brought nothing.

'This is the Hillside apartment,' he said, pushing open an imposing oak door. Just then a scruffy-looking, black and brown Norfolk terrier came hurtling past. 'That's Herbie, must've smelled something – you probably! He's a right little character, very intelligent you know. Probably brighter than most of my guests.'

Showing us into the living room and turning the handle of a door at the far end, he continued, 'This set of stairs leads down to the main kitchen. See you there in about half an hour. Please make sure your outside door is locked before you come down – you never can tell. Tutty bye.'

The apartment lounge was full of furniture that looked very impressive but there was nothing that suggested either warmth or comfort. The centrepiece was an enormous, yellow and gold, corduroy-covered sofa. Although it looked very grand it was like sitting on a rock. There was no give whatsoever in either the seats or the back, but it looked expensive and I guessed that was what was important. There was a pair of black table lamps with giraffes painted on the outside, a writing bureau and a very unsteady occasional table. Twee English countryside landscapes decorated the walls. I opened the glass doors which led onto a small balcony.

Opposite there was another long shuttered building. On the right hand side of that building there was an open entrance where I could make out a few bicycles, some wooden loungers, outside tables and chairs, as well as a rusty old barbecue. To the far right was a stone staircase leading up to an apartment which, from the photographs that we had been sent, would be where we'd eventually be staying if we were to be offered and accepted the job.

Chapter 11

'Hello, I'm Pippa, Xander's girlfriend. Do sit down,' said a slim, diminutive, silver-haired woman as we walked into the kitchen. 'Did you have a good trip? I believe you've already met Herbie. That's Thyme,' she continued, pointing to a small tan and white dog with a matted coat, which was snoring in a basket in the far corner. 'She doesn't do a lot. She's old, blind and a bit deaf. Don't think she's got long to go now. I've already got my order in for another one,' she said quite enthusiastically. 'There's a two-year waiting list you know. Very popular, Norfolk terriers. Coffee, anyone?' she asked nervously.

'I love your kitchen,' said Debbie, admiring the range cooker and the array of copper pots and pans that was suspended from the ceiling. Underneath was a large centre console that was used for food preparation. Several china French cockerels as well as Provençale pottery filled the shelves. There were two doors leading onto a small terrace, and on the back wall was something as surprising as it was hideous – so hideous that I couldn't help but stare at it.

'Impressive, isn't it, Brent?' Pippa beamed. 'Xander had it commissioned a few years ago. It was the talk of the town.'

'I bet it was,' I replied, unable to take my eyes away from the mural depicting a few tulips and a very badly painted landscape of rolling hills and meadows.

'The idea is that we can sit here in our kitchen and look out into the French countryside without having to move. How clever is that?'

'The artist's got an incredible imagination Pippa. Never seen anything like it. It's certainly different.'

'You could be right – I've never seen another one. Glad you like it. You have to be very careful when you're washing it down – it's incredibly delicate. It's not painted straight onto the wall. Underneath there's crepi, a type of plaster particular to this part of France and it's very delicate. I'm sure Xander will tell you all about it.'

'Sounds interesting,' I replied, all too unconvincingly. Debbie glared in my direction. Pippa, who wasn't sure whether I'd just been rude to her, began sifting through some paperwork that was on the kitchen console.

'He'll be down in a minute. We're taking you out for dinner if that's OK, and then we can ask you some more questions. So much easier face-to-face, don't you think?'

'I'd better go and freshen up then,' said Debbie, taken unawares.

'I'll come with you,' I added, and off we scurried back up the stairs.

'Did you notice her eyes?' Debbie asked.

'Not particularly. What about them?'

'Black, like a shark's. Nothing behind them. Cold as you like.'

'I hope that's not ominous.'

A quarter of an hour later we were back, sitting at the kitchen table. Pippa was pacing around and tapping her fingers on the work surfaces, stopping every now and again to look at her watch. Gone was the smile. In its place was a furrowed brow and a scowl. We surmised in the little time we had known Smythe that he was probably the sort of person who liked to make people wait – something that Pippa had never got used to. Debbie and I sat in silence watching the hands of the big wall-mounted clock tick painfully by.

Pippa stopped tapping and began to rummage through the kitchen cupboards in a vain attempt to try and take her mind off things and then, all of a sudden, the swing doors that led into the rest of the house opened. Xander Smythe, reeking of deodorant and aftershave, marched into the kitchen. His grey hair, with a perfectly straight side parting, seemed glued to his head.

'What time's the restaurant booked for, Pippa?' said our host in his affected, pompous voice.

'Eight o'clock.'

'Jolly good. What time is it now?'

'Ten past,' replied his frustrated partner, snatching her bag from the table.

'Suggest we get a move on then,' he said.

'We'll lose our table one of these days,' snapped Pippa, her patience having finally run out.

'Oh, I doubt that very much,' replied Smythe, very calmly. 'I've got money, don't you know. Pippa, where are the keys to the Beamer?'

Not being able to open the back windows of the soft top BMW, and barely able to breathe clean air due to the overpowering stench of Smythe's aftershave, we choked our way at great speed down the Toulouse road. He'd slow down every now and again at bus stops along the way to point out advertising posters depicting scantily clad, young models in their lingerie.

'Very, very nice,' he said. 'They get cheekier every year. Tomorrow, Brent, I'll show you the other way into Castres. We'll go past the girls' college. Some incredible lovelies in really minute skirts.'

'He misses them sometimes,' said Pippa, 'so I have to point them out for him. Must be an age thing.' They both laughed.

Debbie and I looked out of our respective windows. This was certainly different from the south of France. Instead of palm trees and mimosa lining the promenade, plane trees ran along both sides of the road for as far as the eye could see. There were signs for industrial zones at every roundabout and enormous prefabricated buildings loomed large, metres from the highway. Shoe, clothing, toy and electrical shops sat alongside car dealerships, tyre centres and DIY stores. Plumbers, builders' merchants, garden centres, pharmacies and bakeries all nestled in amongst each other.

'This is very much a working town, Brent,' explained Smythe. 'Not sure if that's what you're used to where you've come from,' he continued, turning off the main road and into a cobbled street. Did he mean that as an insult? I wasn't sure but it had been a long day. I was beginning to flag and at the time I really wasn't in the mood to be rattling sabres with Alexander Smythe.

'Oh look darling, a place right outside. They must have reserved it specially,' enthused Pippa.

'I do spend rather a lot of money here. One has to support the local economy. Don't want another revolution you know.'

Smythe had taken us to a quaint, dimly lit bistro in the town centre. Old wine bottles with candles and candle wax running down the sides graced the wooden tables. Above the entrance door there was a rugby game being shown on television. Castres Olympique scarves, signed team photos and shirts covered the walls. There were a few locals sitting at the bar and a young couple at a table to our right were toying with their food and sending text messages. The waitress, wearing a black skirt, white blouse and pinafore led us to a table at the far end of the restaurant. Through the open window to the back of me I could hear the sound of a fast-running river and the chatter of passers-by.

'They do some of the best pizzas in France here, Debbie. Do you like pizza?' asked Smythe.

'Every now and again.'

'How about you, Brent?'

'A bit pizzaed out, to be honest with you, Alexander. That's all they do in the south. A change might be nice.'

'I see – oh,' came the both disappointed and disapproving reply. 'You'd better have the duck then. They don't do much else around here. What would you like to drink? I think I could manage a bottle of red,' he said, putting on his posh voice. 'You could have a glass of that if you like, Pippa, just one glass though. Don't want you showing yourself up in front of our guests.

'Now then, Brent, I've written a few notes, quite a few actually,' he said, pulling out several sheets of paper from his trouser pocket. 'I thought we could go through them while we wait for our food to arrive,' added Smythe. 'Don't mind, do you? Now, then, what do you know about systemic weed killers? Thought not. From your experience, I doubt you know much about companion planting? And what would you say were the five most important ingredients for a compost heap? Tell me, how would you go about getting rid of greenfly? Are snails good or bad for a garden?'

And so it went on. The more I didn't know, the greater the satisfaction he was deriving from the experience. By this time, I was beyond caring but suddenly out of the blue and very out of character, Debbie, who up until now had been quietly listening, snapped. My usually mild-mannered and slow-to-anger wife rounded on Smythe.

'Why are you doing this Xander? You know what Brent can and can't do. You've read our CV, you've spoken to him for a long time on the phone and yet you still keep trying to point out his weaknesses. What's the point in that? Exactly why are you persisting in undermining his confidence?'

'I'm merely trying to work out how steep Brent's learning curve might be, that's all. I've been gardening for most of my life – some sixty odd years now – and I still don't know everything. Oh good, the food's arrived. We'll carry on with this later.'

The duck was delicious and Smythe's mood seemed to improve with his intake of wine. He ordered himself another bottle and Pippa tried, in vain, to rein him in.

'The thing is, Brent, I've been stopped before – two years ago. The breathalyser turned red – surprised it didn't blow up,' he said with a smile, 'but they still let me go. They can't be bothered to do the paperwork, you see. They set up roadblocks, usually at the supermarket roundabout. Unlike in England, they don't need a reason to stop you, they just do. Lovely drop of wine this. Cheers everybody.'

He chattered on, all the while congratulating himself as to how he'd managed to get one over on the local police. He talked about the French people, the constant battles he'd had with the local *Mairie* when he was building his villa and the swingeing French taxes but most of all he talked about himself. When he wasn't talking in his affected posh voice it was all very monotone so it became easy for my thoughts to drift elsewhere. Debbie nudged me.

'Brent, would you like some dessert?' asked Smythe.

'No thanks, couldn't eat another thing.'

'That's a shame. They do the best crêpes in the region,' said our host. 'And they always give me extra Grand Marnier,' he added. 'Positively swimming in it, don't you know. Pippa, you going to have one?'

'You bet,' replied his partner, smiling for the first time since we'd left the villa. For once Smythe wasn't exaggerating. Underneath a large pool of amber liquid, the crêpe was barely visible. For a few heavenly moments Xander was unable to speak. His piston-like jaws were savouring every mouthful. After a few moments of blissful silence, he said,

'I seem to have asked all the questions, do you have any for me?'

'I have got one actually,' I began. 'Why are your current guardians leaving? We haven't really had a chance to speak to them.'

'Ah, Sam and Daniel,' Smythe said, with an air of disappointment. 'They want to work closer to the town apparently. They have friends there and they've told us that they're going to be opening a restaurant. Can't see that working at all, quite frankly. They've never brought over anything for us to try and the French are very fussy eaters you know. I'll give it five minutes.'

'That long, dear?' said Pippa.

A good forty minutes later, having given us a full and detailed explanation as to how he could make a restaurant successful, Smythe brought the evening and my interrogation to a close. 'I think that'll do for now,' he yawned. 'Let's reconvene tomorrow morning. Say about eleven o'clock? Give you the chance to have a look around the grounds and then you can ask any questions you like. I'm sure you'll have plenty. I expect you'll bump into Sam and Daniel then. Probably best not to say too much to them at this stage. Don't want you getting into any of their bad habits. I'll just go and settle up.'

Soon after we were back in the car. We drove along the three-lane carriageway which was virtually empty – empty except for one car which Smythe cut across. Had his hearing aid been working properly he would have heard the sound of a horn and several French expletives but he was oblivious. Debbie held on to her seatbelt as tightly as she could while Pippa glared accusingly out of the window in the direction of the offended driver.

Relieved not to have been involved in a horrific car accident on our first day in Castres we sat on our very uncomfortable sofa, opened a bottle of rosé and stared at the television, which was behaving very oddly. I tried several times to put on the film channel and each time I did, it changed back to *Newsnight*. I wrestled with the remote control for a good ten minutes before announcing, 'Even the TV in this house hates me!' Just as I'd given up and was about to go to bed there was a knock on the door that led to the kitchen.

'What does that old bastard want now?' I muttered.

'Quiet, he'll hear you,' said Debbie.

Without waiting for a reply, Smythe opened the door and stood in the frame. 'Sorry, I forgot to mention that the TV in our kitchen and your living room share the same satellite box. Although you may wish to watch something that requires absolutely no cerebral input whatsoever, I rather like to keep my eye on world events, so if you wouldn't mind waiting until *Newsnight* has finished I'd be most grateful. Goodnight.' And, with that, he slithered back down the stairs.

Chapter 12

The following morning, I was woken by a scratching noise coming from somewhere in the apartment.

'I think we've got mice,' I said, nudging Debbie, who was hardly awake.

'What?' she replied, suddenly coming to her senses and leaping off the mattress, at the same time ripping back the duvet.

'No, not in here.'

'Bloody hell, you nearly gave me a heart attack. What time is it anyway?'

'Listen.' I got up, put on my dressing gown and tiptoed around the apartment looking for the source of the scratching. 'It's near the door to the kitchen,' I whispered.

'Don't open it then.'

I went to the broom cupboard, took out a mop and sneaked back to where I had heard the noise. Chance to earn some brownie points, I thought. I waited and waited and then the scratching started again. I opened the door quickly, mop at the ready, and through the door burst the culprit. 'Herbie, you little shit!' I said as he stood on his back legs, wagging his tail excitedly. He then jumped up on the couch, ran dementedly round the apartment and disappeared as quickly down the stairs as he had arrived.

'So we're agreed then?' said Debbie, who was putting on her makeup.

'Yes, agreed,' I replied. 'I'll phone Bob this morning and tell him we're coming back. There's no point hanging around here. The man's a miserable bastard and is just going to make my life hell. Might as well have a look around while we're waiting. What time did he say?'

'Eleven.'

We walked back down the path to the front of the house. Opposite the front door was a small building. Peering through the window we saw a large office desk, a high-backed leather chair, computers, a fax machine, several phones and a mountain of cables. This was obviously where Smythe would hide himself away. To the right of the office, and running parallel to the main house, was a perfectly cut lawn with a flower bed full of roses stretching from one end of the garden to the other. In the middle of the lawn was a sundial mounted on a stone plinth. There was an inscription which read *My darling Xander June 1998 Love Always, Pippa.* I turned to face the front of the house.

'Impressive, isn't it?'

'Shame we're not going to be here,' replied Debbie, 'could be quite nice working here for the right person.'

As we got to the end of the villa, I noticed out of the corner of my eye someone standing in a flower bed, holding a gardening fork. He was a good-looking chap, about six feet tall with shoulder-length hair. There wasn't an ounce of fat on him – straight out of a bodice-ripper I thought. I, on the other hand, looked like the Pillsbury Doughboy.

'Hi, I'm Daniel,' he said, offering his hand. 'You here about the job?' he asked in a broad Yorkshire accent. I was about to reply when I saw two black, shark-like eyes staring at me through a large set of patio doors. I wanted to ask a load of questions just to reassure myself that we'd made the right decision but instead asked if it was OK to carry on along the path. 'Go ahead. It winds all the way round up to the top where there's a big field, or the meadow as Mister Smythe likes to call it. You can wander through the woods to the main road if you like but be careful, there are six beehives up there. Normally they're pretty calm but you don't want to disturb them.'

We made our way up the track which was surrounded by scrubland, stopping every few yards to catch our breaths. Daniel was right: once we got to the top we found ourselves in a field and an overgrown one at that – it didn't seem to us much like a meadow at all. I wondered if Xander Smythe was always this prone to exaggeration.

We sat patiently in the kitchen, the only sound coming from the clock. Thyme lay almost motionless in her basket. There was no sign of Herbie. At eleven-fifteen Pippa came through the swing doors with a tray in her hand, closely followed by Herbie.

'Sorry we're running a bit late, we've just been having tea and biscuits upstairs. Xander will be down in a minute, he's just getting ready. Coffee anyone? Oh, poor old Thyme,' she said, looking at her old dog, who was snoring in the background. 'I really must get hold of that dealer again.'

'So have you had any further thoughts since yesterday?' asked Smythe, leaning back in his chair and clasping his hands behind his head.

'Yes, we've decided that it's not for us, I'm sorry.' Our answer seemed to take him quite by surprise. He raised his eyebrows, leant forward, scratched his forehead and after a few uncomfortable moments replied,

'May I ask why you've decided you don't want the job?'

'To be honest with you Xander, every time you've spoken to Brent,' said Debbie, 'all you've done is comment on what he can't do. We can't work like that, what's the point? It's very demotivating.'

'I see,' replied Smythe, 'the point is, Debbie, Pippa and I were discussing this last night and it could be that Brent might learn a lot. I was only trying to find out how much he did know. Perhaps we can teach him. You see, I've got the opposite problem with Daniel. It doesn't matter what I tell him to do, he does none of it – should've sacked him years ago. For example, before we went away in October I gave him a winter list of jobs to do. When I came back, guess how many jobs had been done? Not a single one, not a single one. So, we were thinking that at least with Brent we'd have a bit of a blank canvas to work on, actually a complete blank canvas from what I've heard so far, ha, ha, ha. Anyway, look, we think it might be worth giving it a try – after all you're here now. We go back to the UK on Wednesday for three weeks. Sam and Daniel can stay with you for another two weeks to help you, no more than that, we don't want to be paying both of you. See how you get on. Have a think about it.'

'So, what do you reckon?' I said, as we paced up and down the lawn.

'Your call really, my love. It's you that he's been horrible to. What really worries me is that one day you'll just explode at him. He likes to wind people up and I know you – you'll smoulder for a while and then one day you'll lose it. Just worries me, that's all.'

'I know but this is all we've got at the moment apart from taking the Fergusons to the airport on Sunday that is. And that's only sixty-five euros.'

'I doubt you've even got that?'

'Eh?'

'I was listening to the radio last night and a cloud of volcanic ash from Iceland has covered most of the sky in Europe. Nothing's taking off. Could last at least another week or so.'

'Oh good. What about this job in Aix? We could still go for that.'

'They've already told us, she's not here for another few weeks and anyway there are no guarantees.'

'I know, it's just the thought of working with this idiot.'

'Look, I've been thinking. He goes back to the UK next week and we won't see him for a while. By the time he gets back we'll have two and a half thousand euros in our pocket. Gives us a bit of breathing space.'

'I suppose. How much have we got left?'

'Fifty euros.'

'Is that it?'

'Yep. That and our expenses to get back to Mandelieu if we don't stay.'

I sighed. 'I guess that's that then.'

'So, have you reached a decision?' asked Smythe, tapping his fingers on the table. Pippa had her head cocked to one side and was listening intently at the kitchen console, while pretending to sort through some paperwork.

I nodded at Debbie, 'OK, all right then. As you say, I could learn a lot from Daniel.'

'What?' said Smythe. 'I didn't say that at all. I doubt very much you'll learn anything from Daniel – hardly says a word. You'll learn much more from me, I'm a far better gardener. I just don't have the time. I'd do it myself but I spent all of last year in the office working on my court case, which as you're going to be working for me I need to tell you about very briefly. Don't want to bore you with the details. Not sure you'd understand even if I did. Look, the thing is I sold a large piece of land some years ago but retained a small but very significant part of it. The only way to get on to the bigger piece is by crossing the small bit that I retained and without my permission the developers have no legal access and therefore can't build on it. Clever, don't you think?'

'Devious is the word I'd use,' I replied.

'I like that,' said Smythe, taking what I'd said to be a compliment. 'The thing is, Brent, my deviousness, as you so delightfully put it, could be worth about two million quid so you can see why I'm keen to hang on to this 'ransom strip', as they call it in legal circles.'

'You said you were appealing, what happened the first time?'

'Oh, the judge didn't understand the case at all – he just dismissed it out of hand. I thought he was an idiot.'

'From what I remember, the feeling was mutual there, dear,' joked Pippa, caught up in the relief of the moment.

'Indeed,' replied Smythe, who was looking none too happy with Pippa's comment. Just as he was finishing his explanation, a lady in her early fifties, dressed in a long red and black hooped cardigan, yellow trainers with fluorescent green laces and trendy black rectangular glasses opened the kitchen door.

'Hello Samantha, meet Brent and Debbie. They're going to be your replacements,' said Smythe, very pleased with himself.

'Congratulations,' she replied, a beautiful smile running across her face. 'I hope you'll be very happy here. Is it all right if I tell Daniel? We're just off to Castres.'

'Of course,' said Smythe. 'It'll give me a chance to show Brent and Debbie round the estate. TTFN.' As Samantha closed the door behind her, he continued, 'That's rather splendid timing, I can show you your new house first. Haven't been in there for years. If it's anything like Sam keeps this place, it'll be spotless.'

Very much looking forward to what was going to become our new home for at least the next month, Debbie and I followed Smythe across the courtyard and up the stone staircase. To the right of the front door were some wind chimes, and a sign that read '*Attention au chien*', which was held on to the wall by a single screw, flapped gently in the breeze. For a few moments, Smythe stood motionless, hands on hips, in the middle of the parquet-floored living room. As I peered to the right, I saw there was an unmade double bed which took up most of the bedroom. A precarious-looking rail with a small tapestry dangled eighteen inches or so above the pillows and two lamps with skewed lampshades sat on the bedside tables. In the tiny en suite bathroom, a man's waterproof jacket and trousers were abandoned in one corner and a clothes horse sat proudly in the bath, full of the morning's washing. Next to the bathroom was a broom cupboard which had been turned into an office. As we walked back into the lounge Smythe sighed.

'If I didn't know better, I'd say they'd been burgled,' he said. There was a very old television set with cables that at some point had been broken and were now joined with gaffer tape. There was also a fire, to the left of which was a basket of logs. A beer mat covered a vent just below the fireplace. An air conditioning unit was positioned above the window that looked out onto the main road and numerous electric cables awaiting light fittings dangled from the walls.

Debbie and I followed Smythe into the kitchen where he was struggling to do something with the cooker hood.

Two or three days' worth of washing up filled the work surfaces and the soles of our shoes stuck to the stained lino underfoot.

'No wonder there's so many flies around here,' said Smythe as he peered at the cooker hood. 'Just pass me those pliers, would you, Brent? I don't know how they've managed it but they've somehow broken the glass off the bulbs. There's just the fittings left. If I can just screw…think that's it. Should be able to undo the rest with my fingers. Ow, shit, bollocks!' shouted Smythe, who'd just got an electric shock. 'Pippa, you can show them the rest,' he said, making his way speedily towards the front door, which he slammed behind him.

'I'd better go after him,' said Pippa, scuttling her way to the exit. 'He'll be all right after a cup of coffee. Don't forget to lock up after you. You never know.' And off she went.

'Serves the old sod right,' I said. 'What kind of an idiot sticks their fingers in an electric socket? Clearly got more money than sense.'

So, we continued the rest of the tour by ourselves. Debbie looked in every cupboard and drawer, working out exactly what would need to go where. She designed colour schemes for the walls and took measurements for the curtains. To the side of the kitchen a spiral staircase led down to a shower room and a second bedroom which was empty. It had its own separate entrance - across from this was the gym which we surmised was just below our bedroom.

The apartment was quite small but there was, at least, a terrace that overlooked the swimming pool. A large black metal rack lined with candles and spent matches stood against the back wall. Empty wine bottles, a metal bed frame, a cast iron circular table with four chairs and a free standing wood burner completed the look. More electric cables protruded from the walls and a redstart came back and forth to build a nest in the beams above. The view over the countryside was spectacular. The sight of rolling hills and valleys as far as the eye could see, peppered with rustic buildings, was quite breath-taking.

At lunch Debbie and I went to the local supermarket and triumphantly returned with a baguette, some ham and several bottles of wine. We talked enthusiastically about the changes that we could make to the apartment – maybe we could be happy here after all. Perhaps Smythe wasn't such a nasty person. Debbie tried to convince me that he was as he was, possibly due to nerves. After lunch, and beginning to feel a lot happier about our situation, we went to look for Sam and Daniel. Along the way we bumped into Smythe, who was walking across the courtyard from his office to the kitchen. In an attempt to get off to a good start I smiled and offered my hand, which he ignored.

'I take it you've finished unpacking your things? I don't see how you can't have – it's not as if you brought much.'

'Just a car full,' I nodded.

'In which case, would you mind parking your car over the road, next to the greenhouse? After all, you are below stairs,' he said. 'A bit later Pippa will show you round the house, and then we can meet up about six to discuss bank accounts and all that type of thing. Must get on.'

'This is the kitchen *arrière*...' began Pippa, opening some swing doors into a small room to our left.

'The kitchen what?' I interrupted.

'The kitchen *arrière*, you know.' I shook my head. 'The back kitchen. Are you sure you speak French, Brent? Debbie, this is where you'll do all of the washing and ironing. It's also where Herbie and Thyme get fed. Meal times can be fun. Neither of them will shut up. Xander hates it.'

We walked through the kitchen via another set of swing doors and into the hallway by the front door that was never used. Just inside the door was a grandfather clock, a wooden chest, a chandelier, several tawdry ornaments and a sweeping wooden staircase leading up to the bedrooms. Through the hallway was a dining room, which was also never used. 'Everyone who comes here either spends their life in the kitchen or outside – this really is a summer property,' said Pippa. To the side of the dining room was a snug with another uncomfortable-looking sofa and a television.

At the far end of the house was the *salon* with a huge fireplace, shelves full of classic books and an enormous, pristine sofa with matching armchairs. On the upper landing was a full-length mirror, a red and black mosaic carpet and a poorly-cast bust of Mozart. Leading from the landing were four self-contained apartments and the master bedroom, in which was a four-poster bed, two large oil paintings, several vases and a small staircase leading up to the *pigeonnier*.

'When we'd finished the tour,' Pippa said, 'why don't you, Debbie, hook up with Sam, and Brent can help Daniel do whatever he's doing – God alone knows what that'll be. I need to help Xander in the office. Any problems you can get hold of either of us there. In the meantime, feel free to explore.'

With Sam and Daniel not back from Castres, I'd decided it a good idea to take Herbie for a walk up to the big field.

'Ah, bastard, fuck, bitch!' I shouted as I flailed my shirt around my head. I'd wandered a bit too close to the beehives, where there was a man in a white suit waving a gun with white smoke coming out of it. The more I ran, the more comical the man in the white suit found it. As I turned round at the bottom of the hill he was doubled up with laughter. Unfortunately, in amongst the chaos, I appeared to have lost Herbie.

As I clambered through the brush and back down towards the house, I became aware that the commotion had obviously been heard. Standing outside his office, with his hands on his hips, was a concerned-looking Smythe.

'Are you OK, Brent? I did hear rather a lot of Anglo-Saxon coming from your direction.'

'Sorry about that, Xander – just been stung by a load of bees and I'm very sorry but I think I've lost Herbie.'

'Herbie? Lost? He's here.'

Treacherous little so and so, I thought.

'We've got some stuff in the kitchen. You're not allergic to bee stings are you? No? OK. Come and see me when you're done.'

'Bloody hell, Brent, you look like you've got German measles,' giggled Debbie, as she applied the last squeeze of a tube of antiseptic cream to my wounds. 'Better go and see Smythe, he looked quite concerned.'

Resisting desperately the temptation to scratch underneath my shirt I opened the door to Smythe's office, only to be greeted by a faceful of the contents of an aerosol.

'What the fuck...Aaargh!'

'Sorry about that, Brent, I didn't hear you knock,' Smythe apologised. 'Pippa, you'd better take him across to the kitchen quick, wash his eyes out.'

'Three years ago,' Pippa explained, while grabbing my arm and leading me to the kitchen, 'Xander nearly died because he'd eaten something with fly excrement on it. He was hospitalised for weeks and for a while it was touch and go. Since then, he never goes anywhere without a tin of fly spray.'

'You OK now?' asked Smythe, without looking up from the document in front of him. 'Jolly good. Carry on.'

The following day, being a Saturday and market day, Smythe and Pippa offered to show us Castres. As the market shut at midday it was decided that we would have to leave by eleven o'clock, latest, if we were to have any chance of a good look around. Naturally, Smythe arrived in the kitchen at eleven-thirty, announcing that we'd have to get a move on. Ten minutes later, after some stupidly erratic and fast driving, a very shaken Debbie and I clambered our way out of the back of the BMW and across the bridge where the market traders were already beginning to pack up. Smythe decided that, as he had seen it all before, he'd go and find a table in a large café that he pointed out to us.

'Off you go, I'll see you there,' said Pippa, who was rooting through her handbag for some disposable gloves. 'You choose your moments,' she scolded Herbie, who had just christened the pavement, leaving a very red-faced owner to deal with the consequences.

In the time that we had left, Debbie and I rattled our way round the market, filling carrier bags with peppers, courgettes, cherry tomatoes and all manner of fresh vegetables. We hurriedly bought some coriander seeds, cardamom pods, curry powder and Moroccan spices from a charming French lady but just missed the fishmonger whose stall, by then, comprised just trays of ice and price tickets.

Slightly out of breath, and a bit flushed, we went to the café and sat down next to Smythe, who was talking to an American woman.

'I see your friends have arrived,' she said. 'It was really nice to meet you, Xander and, by the way, I simply adore your accent.'

'I don't have an accent,' Smythe replied in his pompous accent. 'This is the way English is supposed to be spoken. Good day'

The poor woman didn't know whether to laugh or take offence and we didn't know which way to look. Either way, that was the end of the dialogue and she left shortly after.

'One must keep these colonials in their place you know, Brent,' said Smythe, very pleased with himself. 'You're looking a bit stressed, dear boy. Are you OK? In future you really should try and get here a bit earlier. Bring your own car the next time. Oh look, here's Pippa – and it looks like Sam and Daniel's just behind her. Fortunately, there's not enough seating for all of us. By all means wave but please don't encourage them.'

As we gazed across the crowded café to the square, dust carts began to arrive with industrial hoses attached to the back that the workmen used to spray the tiles where the market had been. Loose cabbage leaves, squashed tomatoes and paper were rallied into the corner for collection. The clearing up was completed in minutes and carried out with military precision. Within half an hour of our arrival the café was all but empty. Market day mornings are a social occasion for the French. They meet up with friends and family for a coffee, a Pastis and maybe a *croque monsieur* and then gently amble back home for a long lunch and a snooze. Smythe, not wishing to remain among the great unwashed any longer than was absolutely necessary, drained what was left of his pichet of rosé into his glass and downed it in one. 'Come on,' he said, grabbing the car keys from the top of the table. 'I have work to do, even if you don't.' Without a thought for the rest of us, Smythe swiftly made his way out of the restaurant and headed towards the car park. Back at the villa, Pippa encouraged us to explore the surrounding areas and told us that after the weekendwe would start work properly with Sam and Daniel, who would be showing us the ropes.

On Monday, Daniel took me on a tour of the grounds and gave me a brief explanation of how his day usually worked. Just before we were due to break for lunch, Smythe wandered over towards us. He gave Daniel a list of verbal instructions and, true to form, Daniel nodded, smiled, said nothing and then completely ignored everything he'd been asked to do. This had obviously become a ritual. As I watched Smythe walk back to his office I knew that he knew that he had just completely wasted his breath. Why he still did this after four years of being ignored was anyone's guess, especially now that Sam and Daniel had now resigned.

Daniel turned out to be a very nice person. Realising what little gardening experience I had, he took me under his wing. He showed me how to make perfect ball shapes out of box hedges, taught me how to use a professional strimmer, cut hedges, how and when to feed plants, what and what not to put in a compost heap and all manner of things that I hadn't realised were necessary to make a garden look good. He took me to his favourite garden centre – it wasn't the best quality or the cheapest but it employed 'Séverine with the lovely arse', which was by far the most important factor. Daniel lent me all of his gardening books in the hope that between them and him I could cram in enough knowledge to keep Smythe happy.

On Tuesday morning at eleven o'clock, I was sitting at the bottom of our steps and had just taken my first mouthful of coffee, when Smythe rushed out of the kitchen, which was almost directly opposite and said,

'Right, Brent, we're off to Bricolage, the local DIY store, to see if we can find some marine glue. Ever used it before? Thought not. Pippa, where are the keys to the Peugeot? Don't suppose you've ever driven a left hand drive before either? I'd better drive then,' he said.

As promised previously, we crawled past the girls' college. Smythe smacked his lips, not realising he was repeatedly muttering the word 'lovely' under his breath. I tried to look anywhere but the college forecourt. I can't remember the last time I felt so uncomfortable. Then, suddenly my head hit the headrest as Smythe slammed on the accelerator, forcing the car to wheel spin through the lights and we were heading off down the Mazamet road. We arrived at Bricolage, screeching to a halt in the disabled parking spot. Smythe flung open his door, narrowly missing an elderly couple pushing a trolley, and jumped out.

'Come on, Brent, we've only got fifteen minutes. Everything shuts at midday – you need to remember that.'

As we walked through the door, he picked up a plastic basket and thrust it in my direction without either looking at me or saying a word. I took the basket, quite amazed at how low down the evolutionary scale he clearly thought I was. The man had absolutely no manners whatsoever and it was obvious in his eyes that as long as he was paying our salary he didn't need to have any. Just before twelve o'clock I put the basket back and we left the shop, empty handed.

'Bloody useless. Don't know why I bother,' Xander said angrily. 'Can't even get marine glue.'

'Well, we are in the middle of the countryside,' I reasoned.

'That's not the point. I'll have to bring some from Cayman.'

'What do you need this for, exactly?' I asked.

'I didn't see the word *engineer* anywhere on your CV, Brent,' replied Smythe, smarting at the fact that some of his valuable time had just been wasted. 'There's no point in trying to explain it to you – come on.'

We drove round trading estates where Smythe pointed out shops where I could buy everything from swimming pool supplies and spares for the sprinkler system to dormouse bait. He knew every back-double, short cut and gravel track in Castres and expected me to remember them all.

By the time we got back to the villa an hour later, I was completely disorientated and my head was pounding.

'You're looking a bit green,' said Debbie, handing me a cheese and tomato sandwich. 'Are you OK?'

'Let's just say, I'm glad the bastard is going back tomorrow. I'm not sure how much more I can take of him.'

I'd drawn the short straw and was taking Smythe and Pippa to Carcassonne airport just before lunch. It was a warm day, around eighteen degrees, so when I walked into the kitchen I was a bit surprised to find Smythe dressed in a full-length raincoat which he was stuffing with all manner of things – books, newspapers, boxes of this, bags of that, rolls of something else. He was by no means a thin chap but he now looked enormous. I noticed that on the floor there were two luggage cases and a set of bathroom scales. Seeing I was looking a little perplexed by the situation, Xander explained,

'Don't want to be paying excess luggage you know. I pay quite enough in airfares. Can't take more than twenty-three kilos, otherwise the buggers fleece you. Pippa, try and get this box in my pocket, would you?'

Pippa obliged. Xander took one step forward and that step was followed by the sound of a huge rip. 'Looks like we'll have to leave the liquorice allsorts behind. Rather partial to one of those on the plane. Never mind. Bye-bye doggles,' he said, making his way to the door.

'Oh, Xander, he knows we're leaving,' added Pippa as Herbie stuffed his nose into his toy box, looking for something to play with. 'He wants to give us a present.'

He's probably glad to get rid of you, I thought.

I loaded the car and soon after we were off to Carcassonne airport. For most of the journey Smythe burbled on about how his ninety-year-old mother had become increasingly difficult over the past few months and how he wasn't looking forward to seeing her at all.

'She's become a right pain in the arse and no one wants to work with her.'

Must run in the family, I mused.

Just before we got the airport, I noticed some impressive sculptures, all about fifty feet high, comprising different coloured, rectangular shapes. 'Wow, look at those sculptures – they're really good,' I said, breaking the silence.

Pippa sighed. 'They're swimming pool linings, Brent,' she said, glancing up from her book. Smythe raised his eyebrows, looked at Pippa and then popped his tenth chocolate éclair of the journey into his mouth.

Shortly after, we arrived at Carcassonne airport where, with much relief, I waved goodbye and made my way back to Castres.

Contrary to what Smythe had told us, Sam and Daniel were moving to a very remote place a few miles away, where they would be looking after a few gîtes in exchange for a peppercorn rent. As the days passed we were becoming good friends with our predecessors. Both we and they were much more relaxed without Smythe around and over the course of a few balmy, wine-soaked, candlelit evenings sitting on their balcony, we began to find out more about each other. It soon became apparent that we all had one thing in common – our intense dislike of Smythe.

'I hate that bastard,' Daniel said. 'The man's a fucking bully. I'm really sorry, Brent. He knows you haven't got the experience, he's just a bully. He just wants someone he can boss around. If I knew you like I do now when I first met you, I would have told you to run – run as fast as you can. Get the fuck out of here. I'm so sorry.'

'It's not your fault Daniel, you weren't to know. And besides, we need the job. What puzzles me is how you managed to stick it for four years.'

'The only reason I stuck it for four years is because after four weeks I was leaving – I was just too lazy to do anything about it. The man's a tosser. I hate him – he's an absolute twat. If he didn't have my mortgage, I would've decked him a long time ago.'

'He's got your mortgage?' Debbie said.

'Yeah, when Sam's business went bust we couldn't get a loan so, when Smythe offered us the money, we couldn't refuse. At the time he meant well but then it all got too much. The bastard used to come and knock on our door on a Sunday morning and ask us out to lunch at *The Grillade*. We had to sit through three hours of him just spouting bullshit. That's all that man ever does, talk bullshit. And I'll tell you something I'll never forgive him for – the amount of times that twat, and that little shit of a girlfriend of his, has had Sam in tears but we couldn't do anything about it. The bastard had got us by the balls and there was nothing we could do about it.'

'Not to worry,' said Sam, trying to lighten the mood, 'it's all in the past now. Anyway, you should hear the number of ways Daniel comes up with to try and kill Smythe,' she said. 'He even dreams about it.'

Daniel laughed. 'Last night,' he said, 'I dreamt that the idiot was strapped to the pilot's seat in a glider at thirty thousand feet and everyone else had jumped out. I was on the ground and was just watching the glider disappear over the mountains when the alarm went off. Bugger, it was such a great dream. These lamb shanks are lovely, Debbie. I'm so sorry you two but I couldn't face another summer with that fucker. I hope you'll be OK.'

A few days before they were due to leave, Sam announced, 'We're having an *apéro* this evening. Just a few of our French friends who want to say goodbye. We'll have a few nibbles by the pool. They want to have a quick look round the house, one last time. I'm not sure if he's told you but when Smythe bought the house it was an old flour mill and the locals are really impressed with what he's done – apart from the fact there's no French furniture in it, that is. He doesn't know they've already seen the house – he'd go mad. But as Daniel and I both say, we've had some of the best parties ever in his kitchen.'

'Yeah,' agreed Daniel, 'you can easily get thirty or forty people in there. Sound system's a bit crap but what can you do?'

At seven o'clock the French started to arrive. Sam and Debbie had been working all day in the kitchen and came back and forth with tray after tray of canapés. Daniel and I took it in turns to open the wine and replenish glasses while the French chatted amongst themselves.

'Been here four years and still can't understand a bloody word they say,' said Daniel.

'I used to be able to,' chipped in Sam. 'I'm sure my French is getting worse. I seem to be forgetting it all.'

'Your French is brilliant, Sam.'

'Not tonight it isn't,' she insisted.

'Oh, don't listen to her,' Daniel said. 'Sam's French is great. It's just their accents round here. It can take some getting used to. Top up anyone?'

'That's true,' agreed Sam, who was busy passing round the canapés. 'Instead of *demain*, they say *deming*. Instead of *vin* they say *ving* and instead of *pain* they say *ping*. Or, as we say, *du ving, du ping, du Boursing*.' The French obviously had had the same advert and joined in the joke at the same time as raising a glass.

At about half past nine, Marcel, our nearest neighbour, produced a small packet of cigars from the breast pocket of his shirt. He showed the cigars to Daniel and asked him for a light. Daniel, slightly worse for wear, thought that he was being offered a cigar, took one and waited for several moments for Marcel to produce a lighter. Realising this wasn't going to be forthcoming, Daniel announced he was off upstairs to the apartment to go and find some matches. Ten minutes later, Daniel hadn't reappeared and the sound of a deep, rasping snore could be heard coming from an upstairs window.

'Oh God, I'm so sorry, he's done it again,' apologised Sam. 'Always does this to me, the rotten bastard,' she said, smiling. 'I'll get you some matches, Marcel, won't be a minute.'

The drink flowed until about two-thirty, when the last of our French guests staggered out through the main gate.

Chapter 14

Later that morning while Debbie and Sam began work in the house, I ambled over the road and found Daniel who was busy in the vegetable patch where he grew everything imaginable.

'Dead brilliant is this,' Daniel said. 'Save yourself a small fortune, Brent. See these lettuces? You can get twelve for two euros at the market. Plant them at two week intervals from now on and that'll keep you going all summer. Smythe's guests love it. You can also do a bit of bartering with the lad next door. He keeps chickens. Scrawny little buggers they are but their eggs are very nice. Tell you what though, if I could get my hands on that bloody cockerel, I'd have it, the little sod. It gets light really early here in the summer and it kicks off at about five o'clock and it doesn't shut up. I hate it.'

'Have you said anything to the owner?' I asked.

'Nah. What can you do? He couldn't give a shite. Besides, he doesn't live round here. Comes in from the town every day, feeds the chickens, takes his eggs which he sells at the market and buggers off. On the sick apparently – bad back. Funny that, I saw him the other day in Burlats digging a plot.'

'Burlats?'

'Next village along. They also say that he's the one who kicked Thyme, which is why she now wheezes a lot – lucky I didn't see him do it. Now, let me explain what we've got here. Smythe will want to know and he'll also expect you to know everything that's here and how much it cost.'

Pen and paper at the ready, I listened intently to what Daniel was saying, trying to take in not just what was there but also the feeding regimes and how to deal with any potential pests and diseases. As well as lettuce there were peas, runner beans, potatoes, red peppers, chillies, cabbages, cauliflowers, courgettes and at least six varieties of tomato. Raspberry, blackcurrant, redcurrant and gooseberry bushes formed a border round the outside and there was also a small area dedicated to cutting flowers.

'Get a lot of slugs and snails down here. Need to keep your eye on them. The old bastard wants me to use those little blue pellets but they're quite nasty. Don't want some of those turning up in your Salade Niçoise. Beer is the best. Put some into a plastic cup,' Daniel explained, 'and sink it into the ground. They love it and they die happy too. It's the yeast that attracts them. Now then, haricots verts and black fly. You'll also need to keep your eye on the weeds here, Brent. Pouring down here one minute and then brilliant sunshine the next. If you don't keep on top of them, you'll be overrun. I like to spend a good hour or so down here in the morning straight after watering, and then again at night for about half hour or so. My advice to you is to get all your watering out the way first thing and then get as far away from Smythe as possible. He doesn't get up until about eleven so by the time he gets to the garden you want to be away. Ask him nothing, otherwise you'll get stuck for hours. You'll learn nothing and just get behind. If you need any help, just give me a call. Doesn't matter how stupid you think the question is, just pick up the phone. Better you ask me than that idiot. Right, come on, it's coffee time. I expect Sam's already there.'

Sure enough she was sitting at the bottom of the apartment steps with a tray of drinks. Debbie, who had given up drinking tea and coffee a few years ago, sipped mineral water from a bottle.

'How you been getting on?' I asked.

'Great,' replied Debbie. 'Sam's been really helpful – look at all these notes I've made,' she said, producing a thick wad of paper.

'Wow, that's almost a book.'

'I know. There are a lot of things that Smythe is very particular about.'

'Fussy, more like,' added Sam.

'Listen to this. Every room has a thermometer in it,' began Debbie, 'and each room has to be set at its own temperature.'

'What?' I said.

'Yeah,' Debbie nodded. 'Where Smythe is during the day, which is mainly the kitchen and his office, it has to be 25°C minimum and even hotter in his bedroom.'

'I told you, that man's a fucking lizard,' added Daniel.

'And the rest of the house?' I said.

'You set the radiators to the minimum, just so the pipes don't freeze – no more than that.'

'What about the guest bedrooms?' I asked.

'That is the guest bedrooms,' replied Debbie.

'Won't they get cold?'

'Probably, but he doesn't care. They're getting a free holiday so why should he pay for them to be warm as well? It's not his problem.'

'We have plenty of extra blankets, don't you know,' said Sam, imitating Smythe, 'and they don't cost me a penny.'

'You'll like this one,' said Debbie with a smile, 'his deck shoes.'

'Go on,' I replied.

'There is an exact amount of polish that you have to use to clean them.'

'Eh?'

'This is unbelievable,' Debbie said. 'One squeeze of the tube – exactly enough to cover the head of a toothbrush. Not only that, I have to use only one brand which he imports from America and I need to let him know when I'm down to the last tube.'

'You're kidding me?'

'No. Wish I was. And there's loads more.'

'The man's bonkers,' I said.

'They're all bonkers in this business,' replied Daniel. 'It's just a matter of degrees. I've worked for some right nutters. None of them as mad as Smythe, admittedly, but one way or the other they're all round the bloody twist. Never met so many anal people in all my life. They all try and make out that they're your friends but they're not – never make that mistake. All they're interested in is themselves. None of them can ever sit still either – always got to be on the go. They don't know how to relax and if that's what having money means they can keep

108

it. And I'll tell you something else – everyone I've worked for so far thinks that you sit on your arse all day doing absolutely nothing. They don't appreciate it. When Smythe arrived the last time, the house was immaculate and the garden looked beautiful, and you know the first thing he said was, "There appears to be a bit of a smear on the kitchen sink. Are you using the product that I told you to Samantha?" That was even before he said hello and that was it for me. We worked really hard for that man and he appreciated none of it and that's why we're off. Sorry to sound so negative, Brent, seeing as you're just starting the job. I really wish I could have said but….'

'Daniel,' I interrupted, 'we needed the money. Still do and then some. Not your fault.'

'Look,' said Daniel, 'we're only twenty minutes down the road from you and I've still got to come back for the bees. A couple of those hives belong to us and we don't want to be leaving them here. You must come and stay for a night or two before the summer. These places can close in on you if you're not careful. Besides, when Smythe's here with his stupid guests you'll get to go nowhere. It's like a bloody prison.'

The two weeks that we had left with Sam and Daniel went very quickly. Before we knew it, a truck arrived to collect their furniture and we were left with Herbie, Thyme and page upon page of notes that we hoped were legible enough to either refer to or type up. We watched as our new friends' antique sofa was winched through the living room window. Box after box appeared from the apartment, as well as from the garage, until eventually we were waving Sam and Daniel goodbye.

'Wow, we're on our own,' I said, as we watched Daniel's van pulling out of the drive.

'Excited?' asked Debbie.

'Not sure if I'm excited or a bit worried really,' I replied. 'It's all a bit daunting.'

'OK, while you make your mind up, we've got some of our own moving to do. Let's start getting our stuff across here. I don't want to be in that man's house any longer than I have to. Come on.'

Having only brought to France what we could fit into our car, we moved in very quickly. Not only did we move in very quickly, we moved into a spotlessly clean and newly decorated apartment. Sam and Daniel weren't messy people after all – they just resented having to do at home what they'd been doing all day for other people.

As I carried the last suitcase down the backstairs joining the Hillside apartment to Smythe's kitchen I said to Debbie, 'There's one thing I really must do that I haven't done since we've been in France.'

'What's that?'

'Weigh myself.'

'Weigh yourself? Is that it? Good grief. Is there no end to the excitement in your life?'

'Clearly not,' I replied. 'There's some scales in Smythe's bathroom, aren't there?'

'There are but you'd better take your shoes off first – look at the state of them.'

'I can do better than that,' I said, taking all my clothes off. I could hear Debbie hoot with laughter as I made my way up the stairs, fully naked, to the bathroom. I'm not sure whether I found the whole experience very liberating or maybe completely disrespectful – either way, I found it very amusing.

With only a week left before Smythe and Pippa were due to return, we wanted to do everything we could to impress our new employers for when they arrived. Debbie cleaned and polished everything until it sparkled. She emptied all the cupboards, washed all the cutlery and crockery and put it all back meticulously. She'd beckon me as I passed the kitchen window,

'Come and look at this, Brent,' Debbie would say with a beaming smile, 'they're going to be so impressed. I've made it all so easy. How Pippa could find anything before I'll never know.' Mirrors and windows gleamed in the spring sunshine, floors were mopped and scrubbed, toilets and sinks were bleached, batteries and bulbs were all gathered together.

110

The pantry was repacked with military precision and bag upon bag of out-of-date products were thrown out.

My time was mainly spent time in the garden, weeding, strimming and mowing the lawn; until, one day, Daniel arrived with a load of plants that Smythe had asked him to buy, and that I was to plant. Opposite Smythe and Pippa's bedroom was a wall with over three hundred built-in terracotta pots. In each one of those pots a fiddly little flower needed to be planted and watered manually. Although there was an automatic watering system for the lawn and the large flower beds, the first two hours of every day were spent walking around the garden with a hose or watering can – there were pots and window baskets everywhere.

The weekend before Smythe was due to arrive, Sam and Daniel invited us to stay for the night at their new home in Montredon-Labessonnié. The car journey to the top of their driveway took only twenty minutes but it was a further twenty to get down into the valley below. It wasn't so much that the drive was long but pothole followed pothole after pothole. We were in a 4x4 but even that struggled. I wondered how many sets of tyres and suspensions had met their end attempting to reach the gîtes below. We wound our way to the bottom and parked outside one of the three newly built houses. As we looked up we could see hills to all sides but no other buildings – this was really remote and felt like being inside a large bowl.

'Great to see you both,' said Sam, who was standing at the kitchen door. 'Daniel's cooking,' she said, leading us inside.

'Hello, you two,' said Daniel, putting his tea towel by the side of the stove. He smiled. 'Must be time for a beer,' he continued. 'Sit yourselves down. What you having, Debbie? Oh, and while I remember and before we all get too pissed,' he said reaching up to a kitchen shelf and into a jar, 'I've found one of the daft bastard's clickers. I always used to keep a spare one for when they arrived.'

'We used to fight about that,' said Sam. 'You know that BMW of theirs? You can hear that engine a mile off. They usually drive down from Calais in the summer and when

Daniel heard the gates opening he'd give it a few seconds, get the clicker out and shut them again, leaving Xander and Pippa on the other side. Not just the once, mind you. He'd do this several times. Must've wound Smythe up something rotten.'

Daniel smiled. 'The man's a bastard. He deserved it.'

'It's his house, Daniel,' said Sam.

'I don't care. He's a fucking idiot,' replied Daniel.

'I wouldn't mind,' Sam continued, 'but the next morning I'd have to call the gate people out to come and fix it. They'd find nothing wrong and charge Smythe over a hundred euros for the privilege.'

'Serves him right for being a twat,' said Daniel. 'Anyway, there you go. Cheers everybody.'

'Busy summer ahead, Debbie? Do you know who's coming?' asked Sam.

'Smythe's Mother…' started Debbie.

'She's a cantankerous old bag as well,' piped up Daniel.

'No she's not,' replied Sam. 'She just doesn't like you.'

'She's like him – she doesn't like anybody.'

'At least you won't have his son coming down this year,' said Sam. 'Smythe really pissed him and his wife off last year.'

'How did he manage that?' I asked.

They've got two little'uns, aged two and three. Michael, Smythe's son, asked him and Pippa to babysit one evening while he and his wife went out for dinner. You'll never believe what he did!'

'Go on,' said Debbie, intrigued.

'Well, when Herbie was young, they had a bit of a problem house training him. So they bought a big metal cage which they stuck him in whenever they went out for something to eat – stopped him making a mess all over the floor. Anyway, when Michael and Alice got back from *The Grillade*….'

'No!' said Debbie, beginning to scarcely believe her own ears.

'Yeah,' said Sam. 'Smythe had stuck the babies in it. They didn't even bother staying the night. They packed their things there and then and left. Not spoken to Smythe or Pippa since.'

'Speaking of restaurants, Daniel,' I said, 'how's yours coming along?'

'What restaurant's that then?' he replied.

'The restaurant that Smythe told us you were starting. He said that's the reason you were leaving.'

'Then he's a lying bastard but we know that already,' Daniel said. 'We told him that we were going to help out our friends, Jack and Jill, with their house, just to get a bit of money in. I tell you, that man's a liability – makes it all up as he goes along. More wine, Brent?'

'Thanks, Daniel' I replied, as our generous host replenished my glass.

'Can I have a crème de menthe please, Daniel,' asked Sam.

'A what?' I said.

'A crème de menthe,' replied Daniel. 'It's what this place does to you, drives you bloody mad. She's had no wine for weeks. It'll be religion next, you'll see. The next time you see her, she'll be Saint Samantha Winters, Our Lady of the Laundry.' He laughed.

'You liking it here then Sam?' asked Debbie.

'Yeah, except it's really eerie. There are no other houses for miles. Never known a place like it. At night you can't see your hand in front of your face. It's pitch black and the only sound you can hear is a dog fox. Quite spooky really. I mean, look at me. Have you ever seen me all dressed in white, and in a dress for that matter? Only wear it so I won't get lost.'

'Or so I can find you if you fall down a ditch pissed, my love,' said Daniel.

'Anyway, look, we've got some news of our own. Is it OK to tell them?' asked Sam.

'Of course it is,' replied Daniel as he brought over a large tray of paella that he placed on the kitchen table. As he lit some candles Sam explained,

'We've got a new job at a château near Bordeaux. It's on a huge estate and we get a beautiful two-bedroomed cottage, so you must come and stay. And you'll like this, it's just down the road from the Pilat Dunes.'

'The pillar what?' I asked.

'The Pilat Dunes,' replied Sam.

'You'll love it, Brent – it's dead brilliant,' said Daniel, who was scooping up some rice with a piece of baguette. 'Been there before. It's the tallest sand dune in Europe, it's good fun. As you climb up, your legs sink into the sand, you can really feel your calves. But when you get to the top you're overlooking the Atlantic. It's brilliant, properly brilliant.'

'And,' said Sam, turning towards Debbie, 'there's Arcachon, a beautiful seaside town full of boutiquey shops. It's so quaint, Daniel's right, you'll love it.'

'Bet you can't wait,' I said. 'This is delicious, by the way, Daniel.'

'Thanks, Brent. No, can't wait,' agreed Daniel. 'This place is doing my head in. It's really scary. For the past few weeks we've been at each other's throats. We're never like that. I thought Smythe's was bad but it never did that to us. I....'

Just then there was a loud beep and Daniel started to ferret around in his trouser pocket.

'Daniel, pass me the bread please,' asked Sam.

'I'm sorry my love,' replied Daniel, who was only half listening and looking at a text message that he'd just received.

'Oh, never mind,' said Sam, reaching across the table for the small basket. As she drew back her hand and sat down, the sleeve of her white, cotton dress caught the rim of her glass containing the crème de menthe and deposited its full contents, including ice, into her lap. For a moment she sat there motionless and open-mouthed. Daniel put his phone down. Sam then stood up and looked down in horror at what had just happened and said, 'Oh my God, what am I going to do? What am I going to tell Jill? It's her best dress! Shit, shit, shit!'

'Tell her you've got the world's first radioactive fanny, my love,' added Daniel helpfully.

'Oh, fuck off, Daniel,' Sam snapped back, running towards the kitchen, closely followed by Debbie. 'Don't worry' and 'I don't believe it' were the last words I heard from either of the girls for a while. I watched through the kitchen window as every cleaning product known to man was produced from under the kitchen sink. Daniel spent a while replying to his text message and went to bed, while I sat up with a cold beer and feet outstretched, listening to the sounds of the night.

When we came down the next morning Daniel had made a full English breakfast for everyone and in the middle of the table was an enormous pot of tea.

'You sleep all right, Brent?'

'Like a log thanks, Daniel.'

'Oh, good. Sit yourselves down. Can't let you go back to that place without a decent meal inside you.'

It was to be a year or so before we went to see Sam, Daniel and the Pilat Dunes but when we did, it was just like old times.

Chapter 15

'Ouch, bollocks!' I shouted, at two in the morning.

'You OK?' asked Debbie.

'No I'm not bloody OK. That sodding thing's just fallen off the wall and smacked me on the head!' I said, throwing the hideous, canary-yellow, metal curtain rail that moments before was just above our bed, to the other end of the room. 'Shit, that hurt!'

'Let's have a look,' said Debbie, reaching for the light. 'You're all right, but I did say to you to take it down,' she went on, brushing away some plaster from her pillow. 'Suggest we bin it and that bloody horrible tapestry that was hanging from it.'

That morning, I woke up with a lump the size of a golf ball just above my right eye and the curtain rail, complete with ghastly tapestry, was consigned to the skip.

'There's a big park just down the road, why don't we take the dogs for a walk?' I suggested.

'Dogs? As in Thyme too?'

'Why not?'

'Because Pippa says she can't walk far. That's why not.'

'And that's probably because she never gets any exercise – that and Pippa can't be bothered with her. Come on, let's give it a go, bet she'd love it.' So we bundled Herbie and Thyme into the back of the car and headed off.

'Look, Brent, she's shaking. What do you reckon that's all about?'

'I don't know but my guess is that that the only time she gets to go in the car is when she's being taken to the vets.'

'Think you might be right,' replied Debbie, who turned round and began to stroke Thyme.

After a few journeys like this, the shaking was replaced by a wagging tail and, despite her blindness, Thyme would scoot round the park at great speed. She was in her element.

In a very short period of time, Thyme's once-matted coat developed into a big ball of well-groomed fluff – she was a different dog from the one that we had first met. Debbie would brush her daily and instead of spending the day in her basket she would wander round the garden and soon found the confidence to make her way up the stone steps to our apartment, where we'd play games. I used to scatter peanuts on the living room floor, which Thyme would hoover up – this was great fun. Sometimes we didn't bother taking her back over the road in the evening and she'd spend the night on the bed with us, which, in hindsight, may have been a bit of a mistake. It's quite surprising how much room a small dog can take up. Not only that, but due to the problem with her ribs, she could snore for France; but she was happy. Her only crime was that she had made the mistake of getting old and therefore, in Pippa's eyes, dispensable.

On the day that Smythe and Pippa were due to arrive back, Debbie tied some pretty pink ribbons into Thyme's hair – she looked fabulous. We had taken Herbie to the local poodle parlour and he also looked good until a few minutes after he got back, when he decided it a good idea to roll around in the mud. Debbie prepared some canapés and before we knew it the BMW appeared at the gates. For a short while there were smiles all round.

'These are rather delicious, Debbie,' said Smythe while eyeing up the plate. 'Appears to be only two left. Brent – do you mind if I have the prawn and you have the salmon?'

'Sounds like a deal,' I replied, offering my hand.

'Oh, I don't think we need to shake on it, do we?' he responded very coolly, putting me firmly in my place. 'So tell me, what's been going on?'

As Debbie and I began to explain the events of the past few weeks, Pippa started to unpack the suitcases which were on the kitchen console. Various tins, pastes and jars of food made their way to the pantry. Debbie looked to see the reaction on Pippa's face as she opened the cupboards, now beautifully set out, but Pippa said nothing, not a word – surely she must have noticed. Suddenly Pippa's face lit up and, having gained all of our attention, asked,

'Have you seen Xander's big cock?'

Debbie and I looked at each other awkwardly. Grinning proudly, Pippa turned round and pointed to a huge, poorly decorated, china cockerel that she had put on the work surface by the door. Smythe smiled in appreciation.

'I think my big cock is going to be the talk of the summer,' he said, rubbing his hands together gleefully.

'Well, I suppose there's a first time for everything Xander,' I chipped in. Smiles quickly turned to scowls and we were back in our apartment shortly after.

'I don't suppose that you've noticed we have a mole problem? Thought not,' Smythe said. 'If you look closely in the rose bed, which you clearly haven't done, you'll notice where they've been. I very much doubt you've ever caught a mole – doubt you've ever seen one have you? Anyway, Pippa and I are going out for dinner later. You need to be out here tonight with a torch. See you about seven. I'll explain all then.'

Just after seven o'clock, I was sitting on a garden chair in the middle of the lawn, shining a torch back and forth along the rose bed. Smythe and Pippa stomped up and down the lawn in some mad attempt to get the moles to surface.

'Have you caught many moles this way?' I asked.

'None whatsoever,' Xander replied, 'but I read an article in Cayman a few weeks ago that said this was a terribly effective method.'

The next morning it was apparent the moles had not succumbed to Smythe's cunning plan and six or seven fresh mounds of earth had appeared on the lawn. At midday he returned from the local DIY store armed with smoke bombs, mole traps and several electronic gadgets. One of the smoke bombs went off shortly after Smythe lit it, causing him to cough, splutter and rub his eyes. On his way to the kitchen, having temporarily lost his vision, he fell into the rose bed, tearing his new polo shirt in several places. Hearing the commotion, Pippa came running to his rescue and off they went, arm in arm, back to the kitchen. The next day a pest control expert arrived.

At eleven o'clock I sat at the bottom of our steps with a cup of coffee, waiting for Debbie to arrive. At ten past she came out of the kitchen door of the main house and walked towards me.

'Bit late on parade, sergeant,' I quipped.

'Oh, don't, Brent, I've just been giving a bollocking.'

'What for?'

'Putting bleach down Smythe's toilets, would you believe?'

'What's wrong with that then? What are you supposed to put down them?'

'Nothing,' replied Debbie. 'He said that bleach discolours the lids when you put them down. He's spent a fortune on toilet seats and doesn't want to have to replace them.'

'They're plastic.'

'I know.'

'He's bloody mad,' I said.

'I know that too. Anyway, on the bright side, after lunch Pippa's taking me into town. At least it gets me away from him, and besides it might be fun.'

'Did she say anything about the house, her cupboards, the silver, anything?'

'No, not a word. Only that there's a few cobwebs in the gym and that if Smythe sees them he'll go mad. You'd better sort it out, Brent – I'm telling you, the man's got a screw loose.'

'Just the one?' I said as I made my way towards the gym.

Good grief, I thought – they've only been here for a day and they're not due to leave until September. This was going to be a long summer.

'Ever used an angle grinder, Brent?' Smythe didn't bother waiting for a response. Instead, he sighed and handed me a small box. 'You'll need safety glasses and, of course, the steel rods which are in the back of the car. Tell me when you've got them in the garage. See you later,' and away he went, leaving me standing in the middle of the courtyard.

119

An hour later he returned. 'I've calculated all of the sizes precisely, so you shouldn't have anything left over,' he said, passing me a list of measurements. 'If you need any help, come and see me but I am rather busy at the moment and I'm sure even you can manage this. Bye-bye.'

I spent the next two days in the garage cutting up steel rods and, when I'd finished, Smythe brought over several tins of rust protector. I still had no idea what this was all about but as one of the ends on each rod had to be pointed I wondered whether Xander was about to go about harpooning moles. Taking Daniel's advice to ask nothing, I waited for Smythe to explain.

'The *arrosagiste* is coming tomorrow morning, Brent,' Xander began.

'The who?' I replied.

'The expert who installed the watering system,' he said with a sigh. 'You're to go round the garden with him and attach the plastic sprinkler heads to the bars with cable ties. I'll see you then.'

Smythe told me that with the heavy winds and rain over the winter, some of the heads had become skewed and now the water wasn't hitting its targets. He used to spend hours in the evenings watching each section, fiddling with nozzles, turning heads a few degrees this way or that, until he was either completely satisfied or soaked through.

'Pork chops and peppers?' Debbie announced as she came through our front door clutching a couple of carrier bags later that day. 'There's more in the car if you wouldn't mind, a bit heavy. And then I've got something to tell you – this'll make you laugh.'

'Be right back,' I said as I went down the steps to get the rest of the shopping, returning shortly after.

As Debbie began to put things away she explained.

'Well, you know we went to the butchers – is our front door shut by the way? Good. Pippa spotted a really nice fillet of beef and asked the butcher to wrap it for her. While he was doing that, his phone rang. We were left standing there for about ten minutes, waiting for him to finish his call. When he'd done, Pippa, who had gone bright-red by this time and was tapping her feet, got her purse out to pay. You're not going to believe what happened next.'

'Go on.'

'The butcher said he'd just sold it.'

'No,' I said, with a huge grin.

'Yeah. "Who to?" Pippa asked. "The person on the phone", he replied. "Perhaps you can come back tomorrow." "Perhaps you can shove it up your arse," she said and stormed out.'

The following morning the young *arrosagiste* arrived. All was going smoothly until eleven o'clock when Smythe, who had just got up, came and found us. In his hand he had a spirit level which he started placing up against each of the heads. More often than not he'd shake his head and let out a heavy sigh, until eventually he lost his temper and shouted,

'I don't know why I bother!' and went back to his office. The *arrosagiste* and I looked at each other and then burst out laughing.

'Do you have a spirit level?' I asked.

'No, it's not necessary. The man is mad. I think he is not well.'

'So why do you bother working for him?'

'The trouble is he owes me three thousand euros from last year that he hasn't paid because he says there is not enough pressure to one of the systems, which is not my fault. If I don't do this today, I think he won't pay me at all for the installation.'

At five o'clock, when the job was completed, Monsieur Roustan, the *arrosagiste*, went in search of Smythe and a cheque – in both cases he was disappointed.

'We've got some visitors arriving later, Brent,' said Smythe. 'Not sure if I've told you but I've sent Debbie the list. Anyway, I notice that the car park over the road needs strimming. Don't want people getting out of their cars into long grass – that just won't do at all. You can park your car on the main road.

121

Should be OK but I'd put the wing mirrors in if I were you – they're not the best drivers round here.'

As I strimmed the grass near the greenhouse, I started to think about the things that Debbie and I could do after the summer and daydreamed of all of the places we could go, as hopefully by that time we'd have a bit of money in our pockets. My daydreaming, however, was soon interrupted by a fizz as something whistled past my ear. The fizz was quickly followed by a bang and the sound of tinkling glass. Instead of a smoked pane of glass there was now a gaping great hole and an offending stone staring at me menacingly from the inside. I'd hit the greenhouse. Fortunately, I'd shot a hole through a pane at the back and as long as I could keep what had happened away from Smythe and Pippa, I had chance to make amends before they knew what had gone on. All I had to do was to measure up, get down to the DIY store and replace the glass.

Needing Debbie's help to take dimensions, I went back to the main house. When I found her, she was with Pippa on one of the upstairs balconies, dead-heading some geraniums. Pippa threw the clippings onto the paving below and having seen me, thought it very amusing to shout, 'Don't worry, the gardener will pick it up! Carry on my good man.'
'Psst,' I shouted up to Debbie. 'Need your help at the greenhouse. Quick as you can. And don't let Pippa see you.'
'What's happened?' asked Debbie, who was looking quite concerned.
'Shhh, she might hear you.'

After lunch I hurried off to the D.I.Y store, returning with a new pane of glass that Debbie and I fitted while our bosses were out having dinner that evening.
'Just got away with it,' I said as I heard the BMW approaching the gates. 'They weren't long.' When I opened the window that looked out onto the courtyard, Pippa was waving and shouting,
'Forgot his wallet! See you later.'

'Where's Brent?' asked Smythe just after eleven the next morning.

'I imagine having his coffee,' replied Debbie.

'Well, go and get him, will you – I need to talk to him.'

'Brent, Brent?' I heard Debbie call from our lounge.

'Here!' I shouted from inside the bathroom.

'Xander wants to see you!' Debbie called back, not immediately noticing he was now standing over her shoulder and listening intently.

'Well, you can tell Xander that I'm in the toilet and I can only deal with one shit at a time.' Neither Debbie nor Smythe spoke to me for the rest of the day.

The following morning, I was summoned across the road.

'There seems to be rather a lot of condensation in the greenhouse this morning, Brent, do you know anything about it?' asked Smythe. Having learned a valuable lesson from Daniel, I shook my head and remained quiet. 'Let's go and have a look,' he said.

He tapped every piece of glass, looking for a gap. Eventually he found it. Unfortunately, Debbie and I couldn't get the pane I'd replaced to snap in properly and we didn't want to risk breaking it.

'No wonder it cost so much to heat last year,' Smythe went on. 'Can't trust Daniel to do anything. I paid him and his mate rather a lot of money to put this up last year and what do I get? I'll tell you what I get...' but before he could say another word, the glass shattered as he tapped the metal retaining clip too hard with his mallet, which he then threw to the ground. Without saying another word, he turned tail and headed back over the road.

As I was making my way back to the villa later that day, I bumped into Xander who had just come out of his office. 'I'm off to pick up some very important guests from Carcassonne in the morning,' he said, 'Please ensure that there is enough oil and water and the tyre pressures are correct. I take it you know how to check tyre pressures? You do? Jolly good. Only I've noticed that yours seem a little low. Tutty bye.'

Over the coming days the house began to fill up with visitors, including Smythe's mother, with whom he had a very strained relationship. Pippa became more and more stressed with the amount of pressure that she said the arrival of new guests was putting on her, which Debbie found to be a bit strange as she did absolutely nothing, apart from lie by the pool. She was rarely seen in the kitchen and unless one of the guests volunteered to cook, the choice was either pizza delivery or a restaurant.

Even so, both Smythe and Pippa vowed, yet again, that the following year they were inviting no one except their best friends, Catherine and Toby, a very sporty couple in their thirties. They'd been coming to the villa every summer for many a year and were scarcely seen during the day. Catherine would be swimming lengths of the pool by eight o'clock and then she and Toby would go for a bike ride at about eleven, sometimes not returning until supper, which suited their hosts perfectly.

'This is Doctor Robert,' said Pippa, proudly introducing me to a morbidly obese, smartly dressed man in his forties.

'Pleased to meet you. What are you a doctor of, Robert?' I asked.

'I'm not a doctor at all, I'm a vet.'

'Oh, are you still practicing?'

'No, I gave it up years ago. There's only so many dogs' anal glands that you can squeeze. Smythe, where's the vodka?'

And with that he walked off. It turned out that Doctor Robert was one of the richest vets in the world. He'd invented an animal product that made him over fifty million pounds, a sizeable chunk of which the tax man was after. That, as it turned out, had some rather unfortunate repercussions on our new employer when one morning a few years earlier, Daniel came down from the apartment to start watering, only to be greeted by twenty or so armed police at the front gate. Thinking that Smythe was one of Doctor Robert's lackeys, they confiscated all of Smythe's computers, who was surprisingly very cool and calm about the whole affair. A week or so later everything was returned along with a letter of apology. They had found nothing.

During his stay, despite Doctor Robert's enormous wealth, he never spent any money, except on himself. He bought no gifts and would sit in a restaurant at the end of a meal with a calculator. So when I was tasked with taking him back to the airport some weeks later I wasn't expecting a tip – which was just as well.

When Debbie wasn't around for our mid-morning break, which was quite often when there were a lot of guests, I'd go and sit with Mrs Smythe Senior who, from about ten o'clock, would sit in a comfortable chair by the pool. In the shade of the trumpet vine, she'd tell me stories, all of which her son had heard before and had become extremely bored.

'I don't really like him you know,' she said one day.

'Who's that then?' I asked.

'Xander.'

'Really?' I replied, a broad grin running across my face. 'So, why do you come here?'

'Well, it's a bit of a break and besides, at my age you never know when you're going to need a kidney.'

My coffee went everywhere. 'Mrs Smythe…' I began.

'Smiff, the name's Smiff.'

'But your son's Smythe.'

'No, he's not – not really. He's plain old Alex Smiff but he changed it, see. Didn't like where he came from, so he changed it. Don't tell him I told you so, he'd kill me. Anyway lovely, you'd best get off otherwise he'll have us both. Thanks for the tea. Bring some biscuits next time,' she winked, before getting back to her book.

Chapter 16

About half past ten one morning, I was watering the plants on the back terrace when I heard a very menacing sound. Snake, I thought, and not a very happy snake at that. Wanting a second opinion, and not feeling brave enough to tackle a French snake on my own, I went to fetch Debbie. As we got back I noticed the sound had got louder.

'What do you reckon?' I asked.

'Don't know but I'm not sure it's a snake. Sounds more like gas to me,' said Debbie.

'Bloody hell, I hope not,' I replied. 'Do you think we should call the Fire Brigade?'

At that very moment, Smythe appeared out of nowhere.

'Can you hear that, Xander?'

'Hear what?' he asked, shaking his head. Within seconds, the hissing sound was replaced with an almighty crack and a huge flume of water burst through the flower bed opposite, completely drenching Smythe. I ran down to the control room and turned off the watering system. Minutes later I returned to the back terrace. On closer inspection, it seemed that Daniel, while digging the earth with a fork, had gone through one of the main pipes, which he'd repaired with gaffer tape and that tape had now succumbed to the water pressure.

Everything seemed to be getting a bit much for Pippa, who was returning from her morning sunbathe.

'Oh, I've got to go and lie down,' she complained. 'I don't how I manage with all of these people coming and going. It's far too much for me. And now I've got backache too. I'm off to bed. Have you seen Debbie?'

I hadn't but I was later to find out that she was having to deal with her own set of problems. There was a separated couple, Hugo and Harriet, staying in the Rose Suite. They absolutely hated each other but in their minds a free holiday was a free holiday and so agreed to put up with each other for a week or two. Apart from the occasional row the arrangement seemed to work quite well. On this occasion, Debbie went up to the suite with her mop, bucket and cleaning materials at the ready. She gently knocked on the door. As there was no answer, she walked into the bathroom and was greeted by one of the loudest farts she'd ever heard. Looking briefly at the bathroom mirror, Debbie saw Hugo sitting on the toilet, smoke billowing from the huge Cuban cigar he was holding.

'Sorry about that, Debbie. Forgot to lock the door. Hang on a minute, here comes another one, ha, ha, ha.' Debbie made a swift exit.

I was walking across the courtyard when I noticed a large van at the gates.

Smythe, who was signing a delivery note, said in his pompous voice, 'At last my barbecue appears to have arrived. Supposed to have been here weeks ago. You'd better make a start unpacking it, Brent. I'll be putting it together myself. I don't really think your D.I.Y. skills are up to it, do you?'

Xander had been very much looking forward to receiving his new barbecue. He'd spent hour upon hour of research, trying to find the right one. It had cost about fifteen hundred euros and, according to Smythe, was the 'must have' party accessory of the summer. As instructed, I laid out all of the pieces neatly on the garage floor and left Xander to it. Every now and then I'd poke my head around the corner where I would see Xander rub his forehead, look quizzically at the bits that he'd laid out on the floor and call Pippa for more coffee. One morning, in sheer exasperation, he asked for my help. As the only set of instructions were in German, my contribution was always going to be very close to zero.

'Xander, I think I can see the problem,' I said. 'It's that piece of crap on the end of your screwdriver.'

Smythe studied hard.

'I can't see a piece of crap on the end of my screwdriver.'

'Wrong end!' I shouted. Not finding my comment at all funny, he threw the implement on the floor and disappeared back to his office.

Pippa suddenly lost her ability to speak, to me at least. Instead, she just glared each time our paths crossed. After five days, the completion of the barbecue heralded a truce and Smythe came to inspect his new toy. He muttered something about that he could have engineered it so much better and off he went into town in search of a gas bottle. He'd researched everything apart from the gas which, he was told by every retailer, wasn't available anywhere in France. And so I started the process of dismantling and repacking the whole thing again. I was instructed to count the number of screws and check them off against the firm's packing list. Everything had to be returned to its right box and inside that box there had to be the corresponding plastic bag.

'They'll find any excuse not to give me a refund,' said Smythe, who was not at all happy. 'There's one piece missing,' he said, glaring at me. 'It's not exactly small – about the size of a fag packet.'

We searched high and low until a few days later a van came to collect the barbecue, minus the small metal plate. Shortly after the barbecue had been collected, another parcel arrived containing two metal, flat-pack garden benches.

'Shouldn't be too difficult, even for you, Brent,' Smythe said. 'It's only about six bolts but as I would like them assembled before the end of the summer, I'd better give you a hand.' We took the benches into the garage under the watchful eye of Pippa. Smythe got out his socket set and triumphantly joined the first two pieces together.

'Oh, Xander,' gushed Pippa, 'you're such a clever engineer – must be in your father's sperm.'

Ewwww, I'm going to be sick, I thought.

The benches turned out to be a further disaster as some of the screw holes hadn't been drilled out. Rather than sending the items back, Smythe took it upon himself to drill them himself.

'You are amazing,' beamed Pippa until her husband, realising that he'd drilled the holes too big, walked off. Pippa, who usually had quite a pale complexion, turned purple and glared at me as if somehow it had been my fault.

'I don't bloody believe it!' she shouted accusingly. 'Isn't that your job?' And she disappeared on the trail of Smythe, who was not to be seen for the rest of the afternoon.

The next day, at half past eight, I went downstairs to open up the pool but Catherine had beaten me to it and had just come to the end of her swim. As she climbed the steps she said,

'You wouldn't do me a favour, would you? It's not much.'

'Sure, how can I help?' I replied.

'Just keep guard, that's all. I need to go out early and don't want to wake Toby up.'

I followed Catherine into the gym, locked the back door and stood by the windows at the front, gazing at the pool. In the background I could hear her peeling off her costume. I tried to focus my mind elsewhere but as much as I thought about weeding the rose bed on the other side of the pool or dead-heading the trumpet vine, it really wasn't working.

'Pass me the towel please, Brent,' she asked in a very soft voice. As I turned round Catherine was naked. She said nothing but smiled warmly as she gently took the towel from my grasp. For a few moments she softly dried her hair, keeping her eyes closed. 'Thank you, Brent,' she whispered, and was soon dressed. Picking up her wet towel and bathing costume she kissed me on the cheek and headed back up to the house.

A week later the final guests were due to leave, much to the relief of Smythe and Pippa, who decided that for their guests' last night it would be a great idea to have a barbecue. He also invited the mayor as well as several other local influential people. Pippa spent all day in the kitchen making marinades, which she took over to Smythe's office for his approval. Moments later she'd reappear with either her thumbs up or declaring, 'Needs more salt' or 'doesn't like it – have to start again.' At about five o'clock I was watering the pots in the courtyard when a very stressed Pippa came flying out of the kitchen door. 'I don't bloody believe it!' she screamed at the top of her voice, 'the busiest day of the year and the bloody dishwasher's just broken down!'

'Anything I can do?' I asked.

'No, it's OK,' Pippa replied, 'Xander said he'll pick her up. Have you seen the keys to the Beamer?'

Unable to use the barbecue that he had ordered, Xander decided to use the brick one underneath our flat. Unfortunately for us he'd neglected to tell us of his plans. As we were sitting down for our evening meal, smoke began to fill our lounge. It was only then that it became clear why Sam and Daniel had put a beer mat over the vent underneath our fireplace.

After the barbecue, the guests began to get into party mood. At half ten they'd all had, in their host's opinion, far too much to drink and started singing. Smythe, who was due to spend another really important day in the office working on his appeal, went to bed, closely followed by Pippa. As the evening progressed the singing got louder until about two o'clock when the whole thing died down. At seven o'clock the following morning Pippa came down to find that someone had rooted through the kitchen drawers and found the key to the wine cellar. Half-empty bottles of very expensive red wine were lined up next to the sink; spent party poppers and party hats littered the floor; and Smythe's fifty-year-old bottle of single malt whisky, which he had been saving for his birthday, lay on its side next to a game of Twister. Whether the guests remembered any of the devastation that they had caused wasn't clear but, by the time they came down for brunch, Debbie and a very stony-faced Pippa had got the kitchen back to normal. The atmosphere, however, could have been cut with a knife and both hosts and guests were pleased to be parting company.

The following day, just before lunch, I went to the kitchen to collect Doctor Robert, who was flying out of Carcassonne. As I walked through the door, all the guests were gathered together, yet there was absolute silence and as I looked at

Debbie, who was standing over the stove, I could see that she'd been crying.

'Who's upset Debbie?' I asked.

'Me,' replied Pippa.

'Why?'

'She put too much butter in the pan to cook the pancakes. Could have caused a fire.' Smythe stood there motionless. Resisting the temptation to say something that no doubt would have got us fired on the spot, I went with Debbie back to our apartment.

'I can't believe it,' said Debbie, fighting back the tears. 'I complimented her the other day on the lousy bloody cakes that she made and now she thinks she's a Michelin-starred chef. She ripped me to pieces in front of all the guests. I didn't deserve that, Brent – I really didn't.'

'We're out of here. I'm not putting up with that kind of rubbish. We don't get paid enough. Look, I'm off to take that fat lump back to Carcassonne and I tell you what, just one word out of turn and I'll be leaving him and that stupid bitch of a girlfriend of his in the middle of the forest. I don't care how rich he is. Who the hell do they think they are? Pieces of shit. When I get back, we need to start looking for a way to get out of here.'

Chapter 17

With the summer drawing to a close, and the villa having to be occupied at all times for security reasons, it was our turn to take some holiday, leaving Smythe and Pippa to look after the property. With great enthusiasm we packed our bags and, on the recommendation of Sam and Daniel, were soon driving down the A9 towards Rosas in Spain.

'A whole week away from those two idiots,' I screamed with delight as we drove through the gates. 'I can't believe we managed a whole summer with those two. What a pair of bastards.'

'To hell with them, we're on our holidays. Woo hoo!'

Our hotel in Rosas was exactly as promised – right on the sea front, with miles and miles of sandy beach and no building work in sight. What wasn't exactly as promised was the manager of the hotel.

'Seven people for two nights,' he nodded.

'No, two people for seven nights.'

'Not what it says here. Did you print out your booking?'

'No, we haven't got a printer,' I replied.

'You might still have to pay. Let me see.'

Some time later, having convinced our most indignant host that we weren't seven people, we checked into our hotel room. Being out of season, the hotel was packed full of senior citizens who were taking advantage of the last of the sunshine as well as the low prices.

As we walked along the front it was like taking a step back in time. All of the restaurants that lined the promenade had photographs on their A-boards to accompany their menus. Both the style of food and the photos dated from the 1970s but it really didn't matter. This was a seaside town and what was on offer was designed to get customers in and out of the restaurants as fast as possible.

The beach, however, was amazing. Every few yards there was an impressive sand sculpture – artists came from all over. Magnificent castles stood tall alongside dragons and sailing ships. There was a larger-than-life bust of the Queen and a few yards along from her was a very convincing sculpture of the Simpsons, sitting on their trademark sofa. For a good while we stood mesmerised by these amazing creations.

Just as spectacular in their own right were the African street traders, elegantly dressed in colourful, flowing robes. At their feet were hundreds of faux designer handbags of all shapes and sizes. As we walked past they would nod politely and smile. We'd stroll along the beach at least once a day, occasionally stopping for a coffee or a glass of wine and watch the world go by. We'd recognise some of our fellow hotel guests as well as some of the slightly eccentric locals, one of which was an elderly gentleman who, with arms outstretched, used to shout at the sea daily at eleven o'clock precisely. Even more peculiar was an extraordinarily odd woman in her early twenties. She would suddenly appear from the tower block behind us dressed from head to toe in designer gym wear. Colour-coordinated from her bandana to her trainers she would go for a march at thirty-minute intervals, striding her way from one end of the promenade and then back again. She would then disappear back to her apartment, returning soon after in a completely different ensemble, equally as matched as the first, and go through exactly the same routine as before. In total, we counted five outfits during our stay, which we felt certain wasn't even a fraction of her wardrobe.

One of the attractions for staying in Rosas, apart from the sea, was that just down the road, in Figueres, was the Dali museum. Debbie was really keen to see one of the paintings that included the melting pocket watch.

'I'm so excited, can't wait,' she said as we drove into a parking space only a few yards away. Unfortunately, can't wait turned into had to wait, for about an hour and a half. Just before us, four or five coachloads of unruly school kids had arrived. Teachers with flailing arms, red faces and hoarse voices tried to herd their pupils through the turnstiles. The poor museum staff, who had clearly seen all of this before, did their best to cope. An argument then broke out between a tour guide, who had just arrived with a coach full of old-aged pensioners, and a frustrated teacher who had lost control of his class. In his boisterousness, one of the larger boys had sent one of the pensioners flying. Farce soon descended into chaos as both tour guide and teacher wrestled each other to the ground. With only egos bruised and following a stern telling off from the local police who had arrived on the scene, normal service was resumed.

Once inside, the museum layout wasn't quite what we were expecting.

'I reckon this was designed by the same bloke who designed Ikea,' I said, as we were forced down one corridor and then the next.

'I know what you mean. If you miss something you've had it,' Debbie replied disappointedly, looking over her shoulder at the vast crowd behind pushing us along. After an hour or so we'd fought our way round, relieved to see the exit sign.

'Sorry about the melting watch,' I said.

'Not your fault. You weren't to know it wasn't there. Anyway, I'm starving. Fancy some lunch?'

'Absolutely, let's get out of here.'

An hour later we'd meandered our way through some winding mountain roads to the picturesque town of Cadaqués, where we sat at a table outside a small restaurant overlooking the bay. Sailing boats bobbed up and down in the brilliant sunshine and we thought we'd arrived in heaven – the setting could not have been more idyllic. As the waitress placed our menus on the immaculate white tablecloth, Debbie and I sat and gazed in awe at the beauty of our surroundings.

'Cheers,' was the first word we said, raising our very large glasses of ice cold rosé to each other.

'Could get used to this,' I said, feeling nicely relaxed for the first time in a very long while.

'Tell you what,' said Debbie. 'If we're still at Smythe's this time next year, we'll definitely come back here. This is just perfect. Now, what are you going to have?'

A plate of *moules frites*, a fish dish and a bottle of rosé (that the waitress had forgotten to put on the bill) later, we strolled, arm in arm, slowly back to the car.

'You can see why this was a favourite of Picasso and Dali,' Debbie said.

'Did they get free bottles of rosé as well then?' I replied.

'You know what I mean.'

'That I do,' I said, wishing our stay could have been longer.

As with most holidays, time flew past all too quickly and before we knew it we were spending our last night in Rosas. We found a fabulous small seafood restaurant underneath a hotel in one of the town's side streets. The fish had been caught that day and was truly delicious. As we picked up the bill, we noticed on the restaurant's business card a cartoon drawing of the chef hugging a fish that was slightly bigger than he was. It made us smile. Completely relaxed, we walked back to the hotel where we were looking forward to a quiet drink by the bar and a good night's sleep before setting off back to Castres the following morning.

Unfortunately, the hotel had other ideas. As we walked towards the entrance we could hear the thump, thump, thump of a bass drum and the chorus to *Rock around the Clock*, sung in a Spanish accent, which was delighting the residents so much that they were all joining in. Those that weren't singing were dancing and those that weren't dancing were cheering and offering words of encouragement to the young female singer, who we could just make out through the crowd. Sitting at her keyboard, she was really getting into the swing of things, as were her knees. They were parting and coming back together in time to the music, which was OK except that she was wearing a mini skirt and there was nothing to screen her legs from the audience. No one seemed to mind and nobody bothered to tell her. Everyone was enjoying themselves to the full and that was all that mattered, so we decided to join in. How or when we got to bed that night, I have no idea.

Gingerly, the next morning, at about nine o'clock, we went down to reception to check out. I put on my sunglasses, took a couple of anti-bangers and hoped that we didn't have to go round too many windy roads before we got to the motorway. Debbie volunteered to drive, at least the first part of the way, while I reclined my seat, closed my eyes and tried to keep whatever I had inside me, which was mainly alcohol, down.

Chapter 18

Far too soon, though feeling much better, we were back in Castres. As we approached the villa gates we could see Smythe and Pippa, dressed in old clothes, standing in the courtyard. Smythe nodded his head and forced a smile.

'Don't mind if I bring the car in for a minute just to unload, Xander?' I said. He shook his head as he bent down to pick up some weeds that he threw into the trailer.

'Been like this all week. Since you went in fact,' said Pippa, not bothering to say hello.

'Like what?' I asked.

'Wind, bloody wind. Seven rotten days we've had of this,' she said, scornfully looking at our tans. 'This and the cicada. They haven't shut up since you've been gone. No wonder people do themselves in – you can't get away from it. And we've had to do gardening, all week. My back is giving me hell and Xander's isn't much better. He's in a really foul mood. I'd keep out of his way if I were you.'

As we walked up the steps to our apartment there was a little yelp of excitement as Thyme came bounding out of the kitchen door of the main house – at least someone was happy to see us. There she was, a big bundle of fluff, running in our direction as fast as her little legs would carry her. She'd just got to the bottom of our steps when Pippa bellowed,

'Thyme Smythe, you don't live there!' With that, Pippa marched over, scooped the little dog up under her arm, turned sharply on her heels and strutted back to the kitchen, slamming the door on her way in.

'Did you have a good time? How was your holiday? Welcome back. That's nice,' I said to Debbie. 'Are these people for real? I didn't expect the red carpet treatment exactly but bloody hell.'

'You know what this is about, don't you?' she replied.

'Yeah. It's about time we were out of here. That's what's it's about.'

'It's about them. It's all about them. They couldn't give a damn about us, our holiday, our anything. They've had to do some work and they hate it. It's as if we planned for the sodding mistral to come when we were away. They couldn't give a toss about us. It's all me, me, me, me, me. Anyway, look, Tuesday's a bank holiday. Let's get out of here then and see what's going on. At least it's a short week.'

And what was going on was absolutely nothing. In the morning we drove around Castres in search of anything just to get away from Smythe and Pippa but everywhere was closed. All the bars, cafés and restaurants had their shutters down and except for a few youngsters sitting on the fountain wall, the town was deserted. The mistral continued to bite and the only other noise to be heard was the sound of shop awnings flapping in the wind.

'Want to go back?' I asked.

'No, not really. I came back from holiday all refreshed and ready to go. We've only been back two days and look at us. It's like we haven't been away at all. It's just horrible.'

'Come on, they're off to a wine tasting at about one – let's stay out until then.'

We drove around for a while and the only building showing any signs of life was the local swimming pool.

'What do you reckon?' I said.

'Must be able to get at least a coffee and a croissant,' replied Debbie. As we reached the top of the escalator we were very pleasantly surprised. In front of us were two restaurants, both very busy.

'*Deux personnes*?' asked a smartly dressed and friendly waitress. She led us to the slightly less busy but more formal of the two restaurants, explaining that although the menus were the same, we would be free of screaming children and would therefore have a much more relaxing time. We had a full view of the pool, and while waiting for our lunch, we watched the French locals thrashing about in the water, having a thoroughly good time.

'Blimey, Debbie, this is amazing.'

'What is?'

'This steak. Best steak I've had since we've been in France and look at the size of it – it's bloody enormous!' We sat, we ate, we drank and reminisced about our holiday, raising a glass to just about everybody we had met during our brief stay away. Having paid hardly any money at all and fully fed and watered, we made our way back to the villa.

'A local swimming pool, who would have thought it? A fantastic restaurant at a pool. If you think about it,' I went on, 'in the UK, you're lucky to get a bag of stale crisps and a Coke – and that's only if the vending machine is working. *Vive La France*! What time is it, Debbie?'

'Just gone two.'

'Great, they'll be gone.'

As we drove up to the gates, our hearts sank – the BMW was still there. A lot sooner than we thought we arrived back at the pool.

'Bastards,' I grumbled, sipping a glass of rosé, 'they should have been long gone by now.'

'You know what they're like, Smythe's always late. Give it an hour they'll be gone.'

We gave it an hour and they weren't. We gave it several hours and still they hadn't gone. We went back to the pool two or three times and I lost the toss in the driving stakes. It was soft drinks for me from then on.

We decided that if we were to avoid our employers for the rest of the day, it would be best to leave it until it got dark. This proved to be a bit of a mistake as I hadn't realised how much wine I'd plied my wife with. Debbie, being slightly more aware of this than I was, had made the decision, once we arrived back, to swap her high heels for the espadrilles that she had bought on holiday. Not wanting to attract any unnecessary attention from our employers, Debbie changed her footwear in complete darkness. It was then about eight o'clock and as we made the short journey from over the road to the front gates, the fresh air really hit her. From being slightly tiddly, my wife could now scarcely stand and was trying desperately to hold on to me. What made things worse, the less she could walk, the funnier she found it.

'Shhh, they'll hear you.'

'Sorry,' said Debbie, putting her hand over her mouth, trying to suppress a snort. We made it out of the darkness and approached the gate as quietly as we could, hoping that we could sneak through unnoticed. In full glare of the courtyard lights I put Debbie in the best position in which I could support her, which was all going well until I looked down at her feet.

'You've got your espadrilles on the wrong feet, you fool. No wonder you can't walk.' With that, Debbie looked down, let out the biggest hoot of laughter I'd ever heard in my life and we both landed up in the flower bed, taking out several plants as we fell. Miraculously, no one noticed as we struggled across the courtyard and up our stairs to the tranquillity of our apartment.

'You haven't ever trained wisteria before, have you, Brent? No, of course you haven't. Can't see you ever having done that, you're only supposed to be a gardener,' said Smythe. 'Pass me the drill.'

'You know what, Xander, you don't have to be unpleasant to me all of the time.'

'I don't have to be pleasant all of the time either.'

'No, just some of the time would be nice,' I replied, angrily. 'You are a very, very rude man.' Without answering, Smythe disappeared up the ladder with his drill. Pippa came out from the kitchen to observe proceedings.

'Oh, do be careful, Xander, we don't want you in hospital again. Shouldn't Brent be doing this? Would you like a cup of tea, dear?'

For an hour or so I stood at the bottom of the ladder, passing up tools, ducking the ones he'd occasionally drop. Pippa shouted words of encouragement, telling him how he was so clever and that it really shouldn't be up to him to do this, making sure that I could hear every word. Just then, the gates opened and I could see Debbie struggling with two heavy bags of shopping. As Pippa was standing next to me and there was seemingly nothing for me to do, I went to help. Angrily Smythe turned round on the ladder and snarled,

'Where's Brent gone?'

Pushing her jaw forward, revealing her bottom teeth, Pippa snapped, 'He's gone to help his wife!'

By the time I'd helped Debbie up the stairs and got back down again they'd gone back into the kitchen.

'We're having some lunch now,' said Pippa. 'We'll see you later. Shut the door behind you.'

That afternoon Smythe couldn't have been more pleasant. He smiled, thanked me as I passed up tools, cracked jokes and tried to make the afternoon a pleasant one.

'Maybe he does back down after all,' I said. 'Perhaps Daniel should have stood up to him a bit more.'

'We'll see,' said Debbie, who was chopping some garlic. 'But that reminds me, I meant to tell you what Pippa told me when we first arrived.' 'When they were first doing this place up, Smythe employed a load of French workmen – plasterers, electricians, plumbers and the like. You know what Smythe's like, he's got to have his nose stuck into everything. He kept going round saying, "We wouldn't do it like that in England, we wouldn't do it like this in England," and so on. This went on for weeks until one day he said it once too often to the foreman, who turned round and said, "Well, you're not in England, you're in France, now fuck off!" And to be fair to Smythe,' Debbie said, 'that's exactly what he did, he fucked off. So, perhaps his bark's worse than his bite after all.'

All seemed to be going quite well until one Saturday morning, just as Debbie and I were getting ready to go to the market, there was the sound of something crashing to the ground followed by the roar of the BMW's engine. As I looked out of the window leading on to the courtyard, Smythe had unwound the garden hose next to the mill and thrown it to the floor.

'What's that all about?' asked Debbie.

'Must be something he doesn't think I've watered enough.'

'But you've been out there for two hours this morning.'

'I'm out there for two hours every bloody morning. That bastard can put the hose back himself. I'm not doing it – ignorant git.'

'Come on, it's not worth it. They'll be gone soon and we can start looking for another job. And Pete and Jen will be here soon – and my mum. Let's just try and ride it out.' Although I was very much looking forward to seeing our dearest friends from the UK, without whom we would never had made it to France, I wasn't quite so sure about seeing the diminutive, feisty woman that we used to affectionately call 'The Bat'.

Soon enough, Smythe's and Pippa's last days were approaching and I did my best to keep out of their way.

'We need to go through the winter list,' said Smythe. 'Suggest you bring pen and paper. Tomorrow morning eleven o'clock. Tutty bye.'

'Here we go,' said Debbie as we tucked into our evening meal. 'Bet that list is enormous.'

'True, but at least we'll have the winter to ourselves. Won't be seeing them for a while.' 'Thank God for that.'

Just before eleven the following morning I walked back from the kitchen garden and met Debbie in the courtyard. Under her left arm she had two box files and in her right hand she was clutching a handful of pens.

'Got it all here,' she said. 'Leaving nothing to chance, I'm not going to give them any excuse to complain. We've done everything he's asked and more.'

We sat at the kitchen table, hardly saying a word to each other. The only sounds were the ticking clock and Thyme's relentless snore. I shook my head, shrugged my shoulders and doodled on the blank piece of paper in front of me. I studied the mural, paced up and down the kitchen and ate several of Xander's chocolate biscuits. At ten past eleven, the swing doors opened and through came Pippa with a tray complete with teapot and biscuits.

'Sorry we're a bit late,' she apologised, 'but Xander didn't have a very good night's sleep – he worries so much you know. This court case is driving him mad. Coffee anyone?'

We waited and we waited and we waited. Pippa shuffled around, occasionally disappearing into the house, presumably to try and nudge Smythe along. Just before midday he appeared.

'Sorry about the delay,' he said. 'Been doing a lot of thinking.'

'Thought I could smell burning,' I muttered.

'Well, the thing is,' he began nervously, 'Pippa and I have racked our brains and I'm sorry but we just can't find a way to keep you. Your gardening, Brent, really isn't good enough. The thing is, we really need someone with more experience.'

Debbie and I looked at each other momentarily in disbelief and then tears began to roll down her face. Pushing up her glasses with her index finger, Debbie tried to stem the flow. It had come as a big shock.

'I think the best thing is…' Smythe began.

'That's so unfair, Xander,' Debbie interrupted. 'You knew when we started that Brent had very little gardening experience. You promised to teach him.'

Pippa, anticipating that there was more than a fair chance that the situation was about to get quite nasty, went over to the sink and began to wash up the breakfast dishes.

'I just haven't had the time,' said Smythe. 'I've been stuck in my office all summer with the appeal. I just haven't had the time.'

'That's not Brent's fault,' argued Debbie, her tears turning to anger.

'No, I don't suppose that it is, which is why we're giving you a rather long notice period – six months in fact. You can go before if you like or you could take the winter off and, I don't know, Brent, maybe write a book,' he suggested. 'There's not much to do here but you'll still get paid. Anyway, have a think about it, must get on. I've got a Skype call with my very expensive barrister shortly and I'm nowhere near prepared.'

And off he went to his office. Debbie and I followed him out of the kitchen door and headed up to our apartment.

'Can't believe the bastard's just sacked us,' I said.

'I can,' replied Debbie, who was looking through her notes. 'Thought they were being too nice to us. I wouldn't mind but I spent ages putting this lot together. We've done loads for that man and you've learned so much. Daniel taught you loads. There's nothing wrong with the garden. You know what did it, don't you?'

'Not really, no.'

'You snapping at Smythe. Daniel was wrong, he doesn't always back down. Not with you, anyway.'

'The man's a bully.'

'I know, just saying. Right, what shall we have for lunch?' asked Debbie, gazing into the kitchen cupboards. 'Looks like either sardines on toast or burgers with rubbish cheese.'

'Burgers. Look,' I said, beginning to feel relieved that we were going to be getting away from Smythe, 'at least we've got six months to find something else. Six months ago we didn't have a job.'

'We still haven't got a job!' Debbie replied jokingly, the colour beginning to come back to her cheeks.

'True, but at least we've got a bit of money in the bank and we'll have quite a bit more by the time we leave. Time for a celebration, I would've thought. Can we afford Champagne?'

'Bloody French,' sneered Smythe. 'Have you seen the news, Brent? No, of course you haven't, why would you? The tanker drivers have gone on strike and everyone's queuing up for petrol. We go back to the UK tomorrow and there's no sign of any let up,' he said while checking some calculations he'd made on his notepad. 'It's taken me a few hours, which I can ill afford quite frankly, but I've worked out exactly how much fuel we need to get to Calais. Get down to Bricolage and buy five twenty-litre Jerry cans and fill them. I suggest you get a move on – the shop shuts for lunch in twenty minutes. Here's some cash.'

The queues were enormous. Drivers were limited to twenty litres per vehicle and when they saw me filling plastic containers instead of my petrol tank, they weren't at all pleased. I watched as angry faces glared at me through car windows. I watched them shake their heads and mouth profanities in my direction but what could I do? Smythe couldn't care less about the French drivers or how they got to work. He needed to get to Calais the following day at whatever cost and that was that. Xander phoned me more times that afternoon than in all the time that we had been in Castres. I went to petrol station after petrol station and eventually returned, mission accomplished, at about seven o'clock.

'Jolly good,' he said. 'Jolly good.'

'You should've seen the looks I was getting from some of the locals,' I said but Smythe couldn't have been less interested. He was in his office trying to decide what he could take with him. There were cables everywhere. While continually changing his mind about what he did and didn't need, mains leads and cables that joined pieces of equipment together had all become intertwined. It reminded me of our annual fight with the Christmas tree lights.

Eventually, at around midnight, we saw a very tired looking Pippa and Xander leave his office and head back to the main house.

As usual, Smythe was not seen until eleven o'clock the following day.

'Now, how are we going to get all of these into the car as well as the dogs? Pippa, come and help.'

'Isn't it illegal to take this amount of petrol darling?' she replied, looking very concerned and clearly worried about her own safety.

'I don't care if it's illegal or not,' snapped Xander. 'I've got a meeting with a very expensive barrister on Monday and if I miss it he'll still charge me. Now come on.'

Due to be leaving midday at the latest, Smythe, at one o'clock, as stressed as I'd ever seen him, lowered himself into the driving seat of the BMW.

'No time for goodbyes,' he said, pointing his clicker at the gates. Seconds later, he roared through them.

'Yippee!' I screamed at the top of my voice and walked up to the villa.

'Where are you off to?' asked Debbie.

'Weigh myself!' I shouted, already starting to take my clothes off.

Debbie laughed. 'Blimey, that didn't take long. Better leave the rest until you get inside – you don't want to frighten the neighbours!' she said as I watched her walk back to our apartment. Leaving all of my clothes on the kitchen floor, I ran naked up the stairs to Xander's bathroom. As I stood at on the scales I heard a sound that had become very familiar over the summer and that sound was coming from Smythe's BMW, which was getting closer and closer. What the hell was he doing back? More importantly, how was I going to explain this one?

'Oh fuck, fuck, fuck!' I shouted as I ran down the stairs, getting to the swing doors just in time to see Debbie walking out of the house with my clothes under her arm. I heard the gates close and Smythe's voice booming through the air. What do I do now? What had they forgotten? Where could I hide? I knew they hardly ever used the *salon* at the far end of the house so I ran as fast as I could and hid behind one of the sofas, my heart going ten to the dozen. The problem was that the *salon* was more like a conservatory – it was surrounded by glass. If Smythe or Pippa walked down to the end of the house, I'd be caught. But there was no reason for them to do that, surely? Just as I was beginning to calm down I heard a scratching noise. As I turned round, Herbie, who had jumped out of the car, was pawing at the window – he'd seen me. I tried to shoo him away but the more I waved my arms about the more he wagged his tail and scratched at the glass door, trying to get in.

'Herbie what are you up to?' demanded Pippa, the clip clop of her shoes getting louder and closer. What the hell do I do now? I thought. I bolted through the side door, climbed the small wall containing the miniature flowers and hid behind a tree in the woods, hoping that no ramblers would be passing through. An agonising ten minutes later I heard the BMW's engine start and roar down the road.

'What the hell were they doing back?' I asked.

'Forgot the dogs' passports. Left them on the kitchen table.'

'Bastards, bastards, bastards,' I said, as I began to get dressed. 'Bloody hell, that was close.'

Debbie laughed. 'That'll teach you!'. You might as well go and weigh yourself again. You've probably lost another half a stone in the last ten minutes.'

'Funny.'

We spent the rest of the afternoon soaked in rosé, celebrating our employers' long awaited departure. Pippa emailed a couple of days later to say that we'd be pleased to know that they'd arrived back safely and that Smythe's concerns about the petrol had been unwarranted and that he was absolutely seething as every motorway service station between Castres and Calais was open and that there was no problem at all with filling up.

Chapter 19

'Six months isn't long at all really is it?' Debbie said.

'No, and I can't see us getting anything before Christmas,' I replied. 'We've just got to sit tight, save every penny we can and keep looking.'

We sent our CV to every agency that we could think of, trawled websites and patiently waited. Although we had a little bit of money put aside we'd agreed not to buy each other Christmas presents and that we'd have a fabulous lunch instead. One thing that the French love at Christmas, and do so well, is seafood. Our local supermarket had the most spectacular display of everything that the sea had to offer. A bed of ice covered an enormous counter full of crab, langoustines, sea bass, turbot, monkfish, bream, gurnard and tuna. There was every variety of shellfish that anyone could possibly think of and lobsters swam around in a tank just in front of us. Debbie was in foodie heaven. The queues were enormous but the rewards were worth the wait. Box upon box of oysters were being scooped up as fast the shop's staff could get them from the storeroom. It was a wonderful experience and we decided, come what may, we were going to have a fabulous feast. We were also looking forward to the Castres Christmas market, at the time voted the fifth best in France. It was due to take place over two weeks and was even open on Christmas Day. Anticipating something quite special, we were a bit disappointed to find a series of tiny Swiss chalet-style booths, selling hot chocolate, sweets and ceramics and being the only people there it didn't take us long to get round. But it really didn't matter – we were going to be spending Christmas on our own and, soon after, our closest friends from the UK would be arriving.

Jen, stylishly and immaculately dressed, breezed through Arrivals at Toulouse airport. Greeting me with a big hug and a warm smile she said,

'Hello, Brent, it's really good to see you. You're looking well. How's Debs? Pete won't be a minute. Stopped again at Customs. Don't worry, he's used it by now. Happens every time he goes abroad. Not sure if it's his Irish passport or the way he looks at the officials. Probably both.'

'You look great. Haven't changed a bit,' I replied, taking her arm and picking up her case. 'How was your flight?'

'All right, a bit bumpy but all right. Here he is now,' Jen said, looking towards Arrivals. Sure enough, there Pete was, smartly dressed, rolling a cigarette and looking slightly grumpy.

'Hello, Brent, nice to see you old chap. Bloody French. Only been here five minutes and someone's already rifled through my bags. Don't know what they expect to find in there, didn't bring much. Come on, let's go,' and off he marched towards the exit, leaving me and Jen trying to keep up.

'Much warmer than back home,' said Pete as we drove along the Mazamet road. 'What's the temperature, Brent?'

'About twelve, Pete.'

'Minus two when we left this morning,' Pete said. 'T-shirt weather here. You've got a pool, should've brought my trunks.'

It occurred to me then, that since coming to France I must have been spoilt by the weather as it didn't feel at all warm to me.

'You find it easy enough driving on this side of the road, Brent?' he asked.

'Took a bit of getting used to. One or two scary moments to start with but I think we're OK now.'

'That's a bit of a relief,' said Jen. 'Glad we left it for a bit before we came to see you! We've got a cat to get back to you know.'

Debbie and I had been gone for the best part of a year by then and although our lives had changed quite dramatically, it was great to see that our friends hadn't changed at all. The same gentle ribbing that we were used to at home, as well as their genuine warmth and affection, was still there. As we drove down the long avenues lined with plane trees Pete asked,

'What are all those black cardboard cut-outs along the road, Brent? And why the yellow crosses? Looks like a bloody rifle range!'

'They're all dead, Pete.'

'Of course they're all dead, they're made of cardboard,' he quipped. Jen laughed.

'Accident black spots, where people have been killed.'

'Killed? This road's as straight as an arrow so it's true what they say then, they still can't drive. Mad bastards.'

'Here comes one now,' said Jen, nervously looking out of the back window. We were going along at about sixty when a white Peugeot came within inches of our bumper before pulling out and overtaking. A few moments later a motorbike did exactly the same thing.

'Can't stand motorcyclists,' said Pete. 'They're all barmy as well.'

'There are no motorcyclists over here,' I replied.

'Oh, really? What was that then?'

'An organ donor on two wheels.' Pete laughed.

When we arrived back at the villa, Debbie and Jen greeted each other with open arms and big smiles that briefly turned to tears. Jen had brought a huge bunch of flowers and Pete thrust a bottle of Hennessey XO into my hands and whispered,

'We'll make a start on that later.'

Debbie showed Jen around the villa while Pete, with his builder's hat on, took me round the outside and pointed out all of the 'crap rendering', as he put it, and the shoddy workmanship of the building in general. That evening, over a home-cooked supper and a bottle or two of wine we caught up with each other's news.

Slightly worse for wear and with varying degrees of hangover, the next morning we bundled ourselves into the car and headed off towards Albi, the birthplace of Toulouse Lautrec. From a distance we could see the magnificent red-bricked, thirteenth-century Gothic Cathedral. We strolled through the pretty streets, had a quick peek in the *salons de thé*, bistros and tourist shops and eventually arrived at the entrance to the huge cathedral. As the right hand door seemed to be stuck, I gave it a shove. From the other side of the now partially-opened door there was a yelp. So popular was the service going on inside that there was standing room only at the back and in my eagerness to get in I'd managed to clip the heels of a poor French madame. Profusely apologising to her and agreeing with the others that we weren't going to be able to see very much, we left. As we walked down the steps we were passed by a big, burly chap who did exactly the same thing as I had done, except with far more force, which resulted in madame flying past us, shouting some very unreligious words as she went.

'*Merde, con, putain!*' she screamed as she hobbled down the road, clutching the back of her ankle. Ten metres further on her final humiliation of the morning arrived as the heel of her right stiletto snapped and over she went. The crowd which came to help her was not appreciated by the injured party as *madame*'s patience had long since run out. The offending shoe was soon making its way, at speed, through the Albi air at head height, causing many to duck. The first shoe was closely followed by the second and the poor woman, now in stockinged feet and still very upset, disappeared down a side street.

'That'll teach her to swear in church,' said Pete. 'He doesn't like it you know. Very disrespectful. There'll be a thunderbolt any minute – you watch.'

We sat outside a *salon de thé*. Pete and Jen ordered coffees, Debbie had mineral water and I asked for some breakfast tea. My tea arrived in a huge pot, inside of which were two small tea bags complete with string.

'This'll take forever to brew,' I said, lifting the bags and squeezing them with my spoon on the inside of my cup. All of a sudden, the waitress came flying out from behind the counter, through the queue of waiting customers and started wagging her finger in my direction.

'Non, non, non. This is not how we do it here,' she said, taking my tea bags and lowering them back in the teapot. 'This is English tea. You should know better. Thank you.' And off she disappeared.

'Welcome to France,' I said to Jen, who was giggling uncontrollably behind her hand.

'I told you they were bloody mad, Brent,' said Pete, rolling a cigarette, at the same time smiling nervously at the waitress who was keeping a beady eye on us through the *salon*'s window. 'Lunatics, the lot of them. Remind me why it was France you decided to come to.'

On the way back to the villa we stopped at a couple of clothes shops along the Mazamet road. Debbie tried on a pair of ankle boots that she liked but put them back as she decided we couldn't really afford them. I tried to change her mind but she was quite adamant.

'Come on, fifty euros was all we had in the world when we got to Castres. I'll never forget that. I just can't do it, I'm sorry. Anyway, we're not here to look at clothes. We're supposed to be going to the toy shop over the road. Come on, let's go.'

'How about a pop gun?' asked Pete, turning to Jen who had picked up a jigsaw puzzle.

'Sounds good to me.'

'How old is Diddy now?' asked Debbie, referring to Pete and Jen's grandson.

'Twenty-seven,' I chipped in before Jen had the chance to answer.

'No he's not!' she gently scolded. 'He's five. Mind you, you're right, Brent, he's very advanced for his age. He's a very intelligent young man. Knows all his films. You ask him. Any western, he'll tell you,' she said proudly, at the same time filling her basket with other bits and pieces.

The long weekend that Pete and Jen were due to stay was passing very quickly and it wasn't long before their final night at the villa had arrived. Debbie, Jen and I were sitting round the kitchen table, waiting for Pete to join us. 'Pete, you nearly ready?' Jen shouted up the stairs.

'Won't be a minute,' he replied, 'and they'd better not be serving any of that French jollop.

'It's not French, Pete, it's Italian,' Jen replied.

'Not having any of their jollop either.'

'Do they do steaks there, Debbie? He likes his food plain,' Jen explained. 'He likes to know what he's eating. Good honest food.'

'Of course they do. Everything there is really fresh,' Debbie replied, getting into the car.

'This is nice, Brent,' said Jen as we sat down at a table near the window.

'It's one of the nicest restaurants we've found,' I said. 'It's nothing posh but the staff are friendly and it's pretty good for what it is.'

Shortly after we ordered, our food arrived.

'What do you expect me to do with that?' Pete asked the somewhat bewildered waitress, who was busy handing round our starters.

'I expect you eat to it, monsieur,' came back the answer with lightning speed.

'You can expect again then,' said Pete, looking suspiciously at his asparagus soup. 'What's that dollop in the middle?'

'What is that what?'

'That dollop,' he replied, pointing accusingly at a grey torpedo-shaped object that was floating in the middle of his soup.

'You don't want the *truffes*?'

'Of course I want the truth – do I look like an idiot?'

'Pete, she means truffle,' I helpfully added.

'Truffle? Oh, I see, not only do they think I'm an idiot, they also think I'm a pig.' With that, the waitress whipped away Pete's bowl of soup.

'I'll get you another one without the *truffes*,' and off she marched towards the kitchen.

'Sorry, Pete, that's my fault,' I said looking at the menu. It says here, *Asparagus soup with a quenelle of truffles*. I didn't see that bit, sorry.'

'A whatty of truffles?' Pete asked.

'A quenelle,' I replied.

'And what exactly is the difference between a quenelle and a dollop, Brent?'

'About seven-pound-fifty.' Pete laughed.

By the end of the evening and after much merriment, Pete and the waitress had become best friends. Pete presented her with a plastic carnation that he'd taken out of the vase on the table. She presented him with the bill and an enormous complimentary glass of brandy, and at the end of what turned out to be a thoroughly enjoyable evening we made our way into the Castres night air.

The following morning, and much too soon for all of us, the car was being loaded and Debbie came to say a very teary goodbye to our dearest friends.

'Thanks for everything, Debbie,' said Jen, hugging her tightly.

'I can't believe you're going. You've only just got here.'

'It'll all be fine, you'll see,' reassured Jen with big smile.

'Thanks a lot, old boy,' said Pete. 'And give my love to that waitress next time you're there.'

'If we're allowed back in, you bollocks!' I replied.

'Oh by the way, we've got you a little something,' said Jen, handing Debbie a carrier bag. Debbie put her hand inside and pulled out the pair of boots that she'd been looking at. Unable to speak and with floods of tears starting to stream down her face she turned away and walked quickly back to the apartment, closing the door gently behind her.

As I started the engine, Debbie's face appeared at the lounge window. Trying desperately to hold herself together, she waved us goodbye. I was fine until we got to Toulouse airport. Without uttering a single word, because I quite simply couldn't, I hugged our friends one last time and drove back to Castres.

Chapter 20

It wasn't long before I was making the journey back to the airport but this time to pick up a completely different proposition. I stood next to the car park machine with my ticket at the as I had no doubt that Marlene would want to make a quick getaway. With bags under each arm and looking extremely confused, the diminutive, though not to be underestimated, Marlene marched through the arrival gates. Dressed from head to toe in black, and looking slightly menacing, she could have easily been mistaken for a mafia matriarch instead of a bewildered British tourist. I stood only a few yards away from her, waving my arms furiously but such was her anxiety, she saw nothing. With her eyes focused on the doors marked *Exit*, she bundled her way straight through the crowd of people waiting for their own friends and relatives to arrive.

'Sorry dear, sorry dear,' was all I could hear as I hurriedly paid for my parking.

'You only just got here?' she said scornfully as I approached her, slightly out of breath. 'The plane was a bit delayed so I thought you might have been here before now. Never mind. Look, Brent, I haven't had my morning coffee yet. We're not in any great hurry are we?' she said, fumbling around in her handbag for her purse. 'Oh look, there we go. Come on, I'll treat you.'

Marlene sighed. 'I thought you might've sorted that out before we left,' she said as I searched for some loose change to pay the excess parking fees that I'd accrued over coffee. 'Debbie told me we're having lunch at one o'clock. How long did you say it takes to get there?' she asked, staring impatiently at her watch.

'About forty minutes.'

'Well, it's half past twelve now. You'd best put your foot down. You should have said. I could have waited. What did you say the name of the place was where you live?'

'Castres,' I replied, already beginning to try and recollect the exact moment that we took leave of our senses and decided to ask Debbie's mother to come and visit.

'Are you sure?' she asked, looking confused and rifling through her handbag.

'I think I know where I live.'

'Debbie told me it was Carcassonne. I'm sure it's here somewhere.'

'What is?'

'The email from Debbie. I'm sure she wrote Carcassonne. Oh, never mind,' she replied, dropping her handbag on the floor.

'That's where we were told.'

'So did he move?'

'Did who move?'

'Your boss.'

'No.'

'So why did he tell you Carcassonne?'

During the journey back Marlene delivered an endless monologue ranging from her grandchildren to the road works in Henley town centre to her one-woman campaign to persuade Café Rouge to re-instate the *Daily Telegraph* in the morning instead of the *Daily Express* so that she could do the crossword.

'You've missed it.'

'I've missed what?'

'The turn off to Carcassonne. I suppose that'll be another delay.'

'We don't live in Carcassonne.'

'Oh, so you don't. What's it like?'

'What's what like?'

'Carcassonne.'

'Don't know. Never been there.'

'Never been there! With all that history, it's the first thing I would have done. Oh well,' she said. 'Do you two ever go anywhere?'

'Hello, dear,' said Marlene, relieved to be out of the car. 'I'm so sorry we're late but I was waiting a good ten minutes for Brent at the airport. Something smells delicious. I've really missed your cooking. What have we got?'

'Hello, Mum. How was your flight?'

'Oh, don't worry about that. Now, where's my room? Brent, be a love and bring my bags, would you? Now, Debbie I've got something for you. Oh, where is it?'

As I walked up the hill with Marlene's suitcases I watched her ferreting through her handbag at the same time as passing Debbie handful upon handful of sweet wrappers. Far from being embarrassed she found the whole episode very amusing. Chuckling quite hard she said to Debbie,

'Can't do without my sweeties. No, it's not in here. Maybe I packed it. Never mind, I'm sure it'll turn up.'

'What will? Can I help?'

'No, dear, I got you a little surprise, nothing much – just something I doubt you can get over here. Anyway, let's sit down and you can tell me all about Carcassonne.'

'Castres.'

'Whatever.'

After lunch and thoroughly exhausted by my mother-in-law, we left her to it and went to our apartment.

'She's incredible,' said Debbie, exasperated and collapsing onto the sofa. 'She's like a human whirlwind. She's only been here a couple of hours and I've already got a headache. Remind me when she's going. And another thing – I'm sure they're lovely but if I hear one more word about my sister's kids…. What now?' she said as the intercom buzzed.

'Don't look at me – it wasn't me that invited her,' I replied as Debbie picked up the handset.

'She's too cold to sleep apparently. Needs another blanket. It's twenty-four degrees outside for God's sake. What's wrong with her?'

'She's not human.'

'Surprised it's taken you this long to work that out. If I'm not back in ten minutes, call the murder squad.'

Over the course of dinner, Marlene produced a list of places that she wanted to see during her short stay and on top of that list was Carcassonne. Dutifully, the following morning, we set off. Debbie and I thought that the walled city was absolutely beautiful but Marlene was looking a little less than impressed.

'If I knew it was going to be full of tourist shops and restaurants, I wouldn't have bothered. We've got twin girls. What use is a plastic sword and chainmail to me? If you two had come here before I could have saved myself a lot of time. I haven't got long you know. What about this Albi place that you went to with your friends?'

'It's very nice,' I replied as we sat at a table outside a charming café in the square. 'It's where Toulouse Lautrec was born.'

'Are you sure, dear?'

'Of course I'm sure. We've been there.'

'I thought that Toulouse Lautrec was born in Lautrec, or was it Toulouse? Debbie?'

'Yes Mum?' replied Debbie, who was busy people-watching and had switched off from the conversation a long time ago.

'Where was Toulouse Lautrec born?'

'Albi.'

'So why is Albi not called Lautrec?'

'I'm sorry?' replied Debbie, completely confused.

'Haven't you been listening to anything Brent and I have been talking about?'

'No, not really.'

'Now that you're back with us, dear, what's so good about Albi?'

'Well, lots of things, but I suppose it's best known for having one of the most magnificent cathedrals in the world.'

'I didn't come to France to visit a cathedral. We've got plenty of our own thanks very much,' replied an ever more

158

anxious Marlene. 'Did I tell you I went to Yorkminster with the girls a few weeks ago? Beautiful it was and they've got a Betty's tea rooms there. I bet there isn't one in Albi.'

We didn't make it back to Albi but we did go to Lautrec, famous for its pink garlic. We had lunch at a small bistro in one of the cobbled streets. Marlene bought a few souvenirs and by the time she was due to leave the following day she was much more relaxed, until she got to the airport. As I watched her go through the departure gate, barging past people, catching some with her handbag, I saw one of Marlene's gloves fall to the ground.

'*Madame, madame, vous avez…*' but she was having none of it. Off she marched, leaving a bemused gentleman waving a single black leather glove in the air.

Chapter 21

'Thank God that's over,' said Debbie as I walked into our apartment.

'I meant to ask you, what was the mysterious surprise that she was looking for?'

'No idea,' replied Debbie, who was engrossed in her computer. 'She didn't mention it again but I did find an empty box of Milk Tray in her bin when I went up there,' she added.

'What you up to anyway?' I asked.

'Looking for jobs.'

'Anything?'

'There's a couple. One's just outside Nice and the other, Cannes.'

'Through agencies?'

'Unfortunately not, free ads.'

'Oh, good,' I said, sarcastically.

'They might be all right.'

'Bloody well won't, I bet you. Flaky as hell, all of them – cheapskates. They don't want to pay the fees, they don't want to declare you and then they treat you like crap.'

'They can't all be the same as Smythe,' Debbie replied, while updating our CV.

'According to Sam and Daniel they are, and they should know.'

'We'll see. I'll send our details anyway. Nothing to lose.'

Over the next few weeks Debbie had arranged two interviews for us back in the south of France. Finding accommodation, however, was proving to be both difficult and expensive. They were all due to take place during the first week of the Nice carnival. After a long time searching, I'd found a relatively cheap hotel where we would stay for three nights, accompanied by Herbie and Thyme.

Excited to be going back to familiar territory, we packed the car and began the six-hour journey to Nice.

'Love it. Great to see palm trees again,' I said as we drove along the coast road. 'Look at the sea and that sky, not a cloud in it. Woo hoo. I am so pleased to be back.'

And we were pleased to be back, very pleased, until we got to the small backstreet where our hotel was. The road was being dug up, there was scaffolding everywhere and there was no sign of a car park. We drove around the block two or three times, still unable to park, and the time of our first interview at a bistro a kilometre or so away was getting uncomfortably close.

'I can't see us making it, unless we drive straight there,' I said.

'I need to change and I've got an awful feeling that I left my makeup bag at home,' Debbie replied.

'One sec,' I said, pulling over and double parking outside our hotel. Two minutes later I was back. 'You've got to be kidding! Family room? They're having a laugh. Not a bloody family room at all. Six single beds all in one room and littered with ashtrays. It's a builder's room. It's for six blokes.'

'Thought it was a bit cheap.'

'Come on, let's get out of here.' Instead of a sixty-euro room, all we could find was one for a hundred and seventy-five euros.

'We've got no choice,' said Debbie. 'There goes the budget.'

As I went up to our room, complete with bags and two very weary dogs, Debbie went in search of makeup. I had just enough time to walk Herbie and Thyme on the beach, feed them and get them back upstairs before meeting Debbie in the hotel foyer.

'How did you get on?' I asked.

'Not exactly what I wanted but it'll do. I'm just going to pop in to the Ladies to put it on. Be right back.' Several moments later, heavily stressed from the day's events, we ran down the street towards the bistro. With less than a minute to go, we made it.

As we walked through the front door, we could see that the dimly lit room was packed. The carnival was clearly underway and we could hardly hear ourselves speak over the very loud jazz music that was coming through the bistro's speakers. As our eyes scanned the candlelit tables we were able to make out a man in his early forties wearing a long-sleeved casual shirt with unbuttoned cuffs, who was waving a piece of paper in our direction.

'Hello, I'm James, you look exactly as you do on your CV, which is a bit of a relief,' he said, turning to his much younger girlfriend and laughing. 'This is Annabelle,' he said, sidling up to her. 'Sit down, what can I get you?' Putting one arm over the back of an empty chair and squeezing the other one down the back of his partner's jeans, he said to Debbie, 'So what made you decide to become an actress?'

'I'm sorry, what?' replied Debbie in disbelief.

'What made you decide to become an actress?' he repeated.

'I am not an actress,' was the stern response.

Seeing the look on Debbie's face, James awkwardly began to shuffle through the papers in front of him. Had we come all of this way and gone through everything that we had been through for some buffoon not even to bother to read our CV properly?

'Oh sorry, I seem to have got you confused with someone else. Never mind.'

Whichever CV he had found the most interesting, it clearly wasn't ours. We talked for about an hour, often having to raise our voices above the music, while our interviewer continued to grope his girlfriend.

'What's the place like where you're working now? he asked.

'I can show you,' I replied, handing him my Blackberry. As I went to take it back, James pulled the phone back towards him.

'Just looking to see if you've got anything interesting on here,' he said, continuing to scroll through my photos. 'Nah, doesn't look like it,' passing it back across the table.

After an hour or so of struggling to hear each other, we agreed to visit James' property the following day.

Debbie and I retrieved the dogs and found a small beach side restaurant.

'What a tosser,' I said, tucking into my *moules frites*.

'You'd think he would have bothered to check, wouldn't you?' she replied. 'We've come all this way and he didn't even bother to find out who we were or have the correct CV. How bloody rude. How dare people. Who do they think they are? Drives me mad. There's just no respect. I could have killed him.'

The next morning at ten o'clock we drove up to the hills behind Nice and arrived at a large, gated property. As we got out of the car there was no sign of his girlfriend but we spotted James a few yards away, who was talking to his gardener. He glanced over his shoulder towards us and continued his conversation for a good ten minutes. We let Herbie and Thyme stretch their legs and just as Debbie said, 'Come on, this is ridiculous, let's get out of here,' James shouted,

'You'd better keep the dogs in the car, my gardener's putting weed killer down. Come on, I'll show you the guardians' apartment. I take it Annabelle told you it won't be ready for another three or four months, maybe longer than that knowing the French,' he said.

'No, Annabelle didn't,' Debbie replied, scornfully.

James showed us around a small apartment which was in the very early stages of being renovated. Everything had been stripped back to the bare minimum and we were told that the main house was in a similar state and obviously that would take priority. At the end of a five-minute tour, James wrapped up our brief visit by saying,

'Well that's about it then. See ya. Sylvain will let you out. Be in touch if we're interested. Right, I've got some calls to make.'

'Come on, look on the bright side,' said Debbie as we drove out. 'We've got another one tomorrow. Can't be anything as bad as that idiot.'

'You wanna bet?' I said. 'Mind you, it is in a vineyard so there are some benefits.'

'You just better make sure you don't drink all the profits.'

'I was coming to that.'

The following morning, we drove to a small village just outside Vidauban, less than an hour from Nice and although not far in distance there was a complete change of landscape. Spotlessly clean meandering roads, palm trees and a clear blue sea were replaced by swathes of scrubland, umbrella pines and narrow tracks that caused Debbie to cower at the sight of any oncoming vehicle. How could an area so close to the playground of the rich and famous seem so barren and desolate? We passed huge fields populated with row upon row of vines that reminded me of gnarled, old hags' hands sticking out of the ground. A cold chill ran down my spine as I imagined breaking down here in the middle of the night but I was soon brought back to reality by my wife saying,

'I think we've just missed it. There was a sign back there.'

'Not according to TomTom.'

'I'd trust the sign if I were you, my love.'

'Yep, wouldn't be the first time,' I replied, turning the car round in a layby. On many occasions since arriving in France the GPS had sent us down pot-holed single lanes and almost unnavigable tracks, only to land up on the same road that we had originally turned off twenty minutes previously. Not only was it not quicker, our tyres and suspension, as well as our patience, had taken a good battering.

'You have reached your destination,' a very proud posh woman's voice announced from the little box stuck to the windscreen as we drove a further mile or so down a rickety old track, flanked by vines as far as the eye could see.

As we approached the entrance to the château, two huge black Schnauzers bounded up to the car, jumping up at the windows.

'Boys here, come here!' shouted an exasperated woman in her forties. Pushing back her hair through her fingers, the poor woman, dressed in country attire, obviously had no control over her dogs. She motioned to us to park next to an old Land Rover.

'Hello, I'm Felicity, or Flick as my friends call me,' she said nervously. 'I'm so sorry about the boys, they just don't listen to me. Lucky you haven't got an expensive car, what,' she continued, ignoring the small scratches the dogs had made on the paintwork. 'They're after your dogs you know – can be vicious little buggers. I'd lock them up but every time I try, they go to bite me. Right, lunch should be ready. Lavinia!' she called in a shrill, piercing voice, 'our guests are here,' at the same time ringing a hand bell which was in the middle of the pine kitchen table. 'I know it's a bit *Upstairs Downstairs* but it works well.'

As we sat down for lunch Felicity began, 'Now then, tell me all about yourselves, or would you prefer me to tell you all about here? Of course you would,' she went on, while awkwardly attempting to peel a prawn with her knife and fork. 'That's why you're here.'

Felicity talked for the next hour, barely stopping to take a breath. By the time she had finished telling us about the vineyard, the delicious wine that her and her husband exported all over the world, her mad dogs and her precious horses, Debbie and I were exhausted. 'There's not much housekeeping to do,' she explained, which was evident by the sticky kitchen floor, the mud spattered windows and grubby wall tiles. 'Debbie, it is Debbie isn't it? Yes, I thought so. I'm sorry, I have a terrible memory for names and we tend to go through rather a lot of housekeepers here. The previous one only lasted a couple of weeks. She arrived one morning, was extremely rude, right to my face I'll have you know, and walked straight back out again. I ask you. Now, where was I? Oh, yes. Debbie, you'll be spending a lot of time in the garden with Barney.'

'Brent.' Debbie corrected.

'Brent? We don't have anyone working here called Brent. Who's Brent?'

'My husband.'

'Are you sure?' replied Felicity, nervously flicking through our CV. 'Of course you're sure. How silly of me. It was you that married him after all. The thing is, Debbie, the garden is huge and then there's the vineyard. I doubt you'll even see the inside of the house come harvest time and then there are just so many other jobs to be done. I hope you enjoy gardening, Debbie. Doesn't appear to say much about it on your CV. Now, I appear to have done all of the talking, it must be your turn,' she said, having tired herself out by her marathon monologue.

She was right – she had done all of the talking and somehow, since arriving at twelve o'clock, the time had slipped round to two-thirty and not only had we not seen the grounds, we had hardly said a word. It was then our turn to try and convince Felicity that we were the right people for the job. A further two hours and several bouts of verbal incontinence later, delivered to us by our very genial but eccentric host, we made it back out into the fresh air and were given the grand tour.

The garden was a mass of well-kept box hedges and topiary as well as a not so well-kept swimming pool full of sludge. Around its exterior were discarded wellies, children's toys that had been there since the summer and a rusty trampoline with a sagging floor.

'This is my husband, Jack,' said Flick as we followed her into a large building that housed several aluminium wine vats. 'Ask any questions you like. Jack loves to talk about wine making. He has a real talent for it. That and keeping away from me. Ha, ha.' Dragging up as many wine-related questions as we could think of, we asked away only for Jack not to be given the chance to answer a single one of them – Felicity was far too quick.

An eternity later and armed with a bottle of red we said goodbye to Jack and were given a brief tour of the wine shop, which comprised a makeshift counter and six or seven pallets, stacked with boxes of wine bearing the château's name. Just after six o'clock, thoroughly brow beaten and barely able to speak, we made our way down the drive, hotly pursued by two mad dogs who helpfully removed some more paintwork from our car. In the rear-view mirror I watched Felicity, who found this all very funny, disappear into the distance.

'Sweetie, I don't think I can do this all in one hit. Five hours is just too much. Shall we stop half way?' Debbie asked.

'Good idea. I'll have a look on the map. How do you think it went?'

'If we don't get the job after all that.... Mind you I'm not sure I want it, she's nuts.'

'Blisteringly bloody mad, I'd say. Can you imagine that all day, every day? No wonder her husband spends all of his time in his wine shed. You're right, she's bloody bonkers.'

'Look, let's discuss it over a glass or two,' replied Debbie, closing her eyes and reclining her seat.

'Need to get rid of this headache first – my head's spinning. There's some anti-bangers in the glove compartment. Pass me the water, would you? And the map at the same time.'

'Your last slave died of what exactly?' replied Debbie, wearily reaching for the glove compartment.

'Asked one question too many.'

For a few minutes we pulled over at the side of the road while I pored over our now well-worn map of France.

'Nimes looks about half way, we'll stop there.'

'What's in Nimes?' yawned Debbie.

'Not got a clue but it's big and might be all right – that's where denim comes from.'

'Thought denim came from the States.'

'Nope, de Nimes, from Nimes.'

'Ooh, smarty pants.'

'They're all the same you know,' I said.

'What are?' asked Debbie as we drove into a car park, just off the *autoroute*.

'Buffalo Grills.' I replied, easing my way into a comfy, red-seated booth. 'Except the pinball machines.'

'Sorry?' replied Debbie, whose mind was elsewhere.

'Pinball machines. They're all....'

167

'Shall we order?' interrupted Debbie, who was understandably far more interested in the menu than my burbling on about pinball machines.

'Thought anymore about today?' I asked.

'Only that, that woman's barking and right now, I'm too tired to think about it. Can we leave it until tomorrow?' Debbie said, toying with the obligatory salad starter that the chef had drowned in mayonnaise.

A rack of barbecue ribs and a huge burger with peppercorn sauce later, we strolled back to our cheap hotel room, where we decided to open the bottle of red that Felicity had given us.

'She reckons it's really good this year,' I said, while battling with the rubber cork from hell.

'What's it like?' Debbie asked, when I finished struggling.

'Ready steady…shit, that's awful. Disgusting,' I said, with my face screwed up like a prune. Tastes like someone's drunk it once already. I've had some bad wine in my time but that's unbelievably bad.'

'Just as well we brought some rosé,' said Debbie, who appeared from the bathroom in her dressing gown.

'I'll tell you what,' I said as I turned round, having opened a new bottle – but it was too late. Worn out from the day's events, Debbie was fast asleep on the bed.

Chapter 22

Around lunchtime the next day we were back in Castres and approaching 'The Gates of Hell', as we had come to call them. Menacingly and slowly they beckoned us in. As we drove through, the phone rang.

'Hello, is that Brent?' asked a very bubbly young lady.

'It is.'

'Great. Rachel from Staff First here. I've got some good news for you. I sent off your CV last week and I've got you two interviews.'

'Brilliant. Where are they?' I said, raising my thumbs and smiling at Debbie, who was trying to listen in.

'One's in a place called Ramatuelle, not far from Saint Tropez apparently, and the other one's just down the road from there in Grasse, which is only about half an hour away. Now, how flexible are you?'

'Pretty much. The owners aren't here at the moment, so we can meet up at any time'

'Good, because the couple in Ramatuelle are only there for a few days and they want to see you tomorrow morning. It's the only time they can do it. And, I've persuaded the chap in Grasse to see you the day after. He's very busy you know. Shall I confirm?'

'We've only just got back from round there. It's five hours away. Literally just driven through the gates!'

'Sorry about that but they're both fantastic jobs, Brent. I think you and Debbie could be ideal. You might not get this kind of opportunity for a long time. If not, there's plenty....'

'OK, Rachel, I get the message,' I interrupted. 'I need to speak to Debbie, can I call you back?'

'OK, but I said I'd get back to them within the hour. Let me know. Byeeeeee!' she screeched as she ended the call.

'Bloody hell. Why is it none of the people from employment agencies come with a volume control? They always shout at you. I'm not deaf. At least I wasn't,' I said, rubbing my ear. 'You realise that if we do go, we're going to have to leave here in a couple of hours. Either that or stupid o'clock tomorrow morning.'

'I know. Let's do it.'

'Are you sure?'

'What choice do we have? It's a job,' said Debbie, as we walked up the stairs, closely followed by Herbie and Thyme, who headed straight for the kitchen.

'OK. Look, I'll just check emails and then I'll call her.'

'Fancy a sandwich? Cheese and…' began Debbie.

'I don't believe it!' I shouted, shortly after logging in.

'What's wrong?' replied Debbie, who came running into the office.

'Just got an email from that Felicity.'

'That was quick. What does she want?'

'Remember her saying that she had two couples to interview?'

'Yep. Not sure I believed her, though.'

'Well, believe this. Apparently she can't split us so she wants us to write, you'll like this, in no more than a thousand words, why we are the most suitable candidates for the job.'

'Well she can fuck off. We spent six hours at that place and she still can't make her mind up. What's wrong with her?'

'It gets better. Listen to this,' I said. 'She wants to know exactly what my strengths are – cheeky bitch. Who does she think she is?'

'Look,' reasoned Debbie, who was making her way back to the kitchen, 'we weren't going to take it anyway, the woman's nuts.'

'True. Actually, come to think of it, what would you say my strengths were?'

'Oh, I don't know,' replied Debbie, who was peering into a jar of Branston Pickle. 'Squishing down the bin when it's full, leaving the freezer door open, dragging your muddy boots through the house, leaving the lid up. How many do you want?'

'Thanks for that,' I said. 'Look, I'll write back before we go and tell her to poke it – daft mare.'

'Anything other mails?'

'Yeah, the job descriptions have just come through. Usual stuff – housekeeper, cook, gardener, handyman. One's a Swiss couple and the other's a Scottish film producer.'

'Wow. Never know, might to get to meet someone famous,' said Debbie, who was already beginning to repack our suitcase. 'I think we should just try and find somewhere to stay when we get there, otherwise you'll be sitting on that thing, looking for somewhere all afternoon. Come on, sweetie. Print out what we need and let's get out of here.'

Five hours later we were back in familiar territory and spent the night in a charming hotel just outside the village. At ten o'clock the next morning we arrived at a very grand château at the top of Ramatuelle. As there was no intercom or doorbell we went back down the drive, which was flanked by vines, and stopped at the wine shop.
'Hello. You must be Brent and Debbie,' said an elegantly dressed French lady. 'I'm sorry, I saw you but I was on the phone. Mr and Mrs Durrenberger are on their way back from Monaco. They apologise but they will be about ten minutes late. Come, I show you outside,' she said, wrapping her scarf several times around her neck. 'You drive to the gate. I meet you there.'

As we drove through there was a charming little cottage on the left hand side surrounded by fruit trees.

'Wow, that must be ours,' I said to Debbie enthusiastically.

'Looks fabulous,' she replied, her eyes lighting up. 'I think we could be very happy here, provided this lot aren't nuts as well.'

We continued along the drive and parked just outside the kitchen door of the main house and waited for Madame to catch us up.

'What's that?' asked Debbie, referring to a strange whooshing sound that became louder as we walked just beyond the house.

'No idea, let's have a look.'

It wasn't long before our curiosity was satisfied as within a few short paces we were overlooking the sea.

The huge château was perched on top of a cliff and what we could hear was a swirling wind. There wasn't a cloud in the sky and the view was quite breath-taking. A handful of sailing boats were being tossed about by the waves and on the beach below we could see some determined sunbathers who were struggling to keep their windbreakers from blowing away.

'*Magnifique n'est-ce pas?*' said Madame who, after a few minutes, had caught up with us.

'*Très jolie,*' I nodded in agreement.

'I leave you to look around the gardens. They won't be long. Nice to meet you. Bye-bye.'

'This all looks rather impressive,' said Debbie once the lady had gone.

'That's what worries me.'

'How so?'

'It's all so immaculate. Look at this topiary – there's not a leaf out of place. And the lawns, perfectly straight lines. You could eat your dinner off the terraces, not a mark on them. I bet this is where they keep the tools,' I said, reaching for the metal handle on the shed door and giving it a tug.

Nothing could have prepared me for what happened next. Suddenly, a huge pair of paws and the head of a very angry Beauceron appeared at a small grill just in front of my face. The dog barked, I yelled and Debbie laughed.

'Fucking hell, I thought I was going to die,' I said, as I sat down on the bench opposite. 'Little bastard.'

'You're shaking, are you OK?'

'Yeah, just give me a minute.' As I was beginning to catch my breath, the familiar sound of tyres on gravel was getting louder.

'Hello, I'm Peter and this is Ingrid,' said a tall, silver-haired man in his seventies. Casually dressed in a pink polo shirt, red trousers and deck shoes, he went on, 'I see you've already met Bella. She's very nice really,' he added, 'once you get to know her, that is. Hello Bella my beauty,' he said in a soft, reassuring voice. With that, the dog let out a sigh, whimpered and slunk to the ground. We'd only just met the man but he was already beginning to remind me of a Bond villain.

'Let's go and sit on the terrace and I can tell you a bit about the garden. Ingrid, would you get some drinks please?' he said to his petite, immaculately dressed wife. 'You see, one of the issues that we have here, Brent, is the topiary,' Mr Durrenberger explained, pointing to an enormous ball on the opposite side of the swimming pool. 'You see the problem? It is supposed to be a ball. My guardian has made it look like a bloody mushroom! Who wants bloody mushrooms growing in their garden? Not me, I can tell you. And look at this shit,' he went on, pointing to the gravel just in front of the bench we were sitting on. 'No attention to detail whatsoever, that man.' As I glanced down, I could just make out under the surface some thick, black plastic piping that I recognised to be part of the mains water supply. 'Should have buried it properly. Now every time I sit here, what do I have to look at? Black plastic pipe. I didn't buy this house to look at black plastic pipe and mushrooms. The man's an idiot. Thank you Ingrid,' he said to his wife, who was nervously trying to place a tray with a large jug of water and glasses on to the white, wrought iron table in front of us. 'Now, the swimming pool. I take it you know about swimming pools, Brent?'

'Yes.'

'Good, you see there are a lot of missing mosaics which should have been replaced last year, but weren't. I think the guardian and his wife spent most of their time in the pool when we weren't here, which is not allowed. We don't let our guardians in the pool. Are you allowed in your current employers' pool?' asked Mr Durrenberger.

'Yes, not when they are in residence of course, but at all other times. I think it's quite normal,' replied Debbie.

'Then, perhaps we are not normal,' he said firmly. 'Right, let's show you the villa and your accommodation.'

The marble-floored entrance hall was large enough to house two decent-sized apartments on its own. Life-sized Roman and Greek statues were carefully arranged alongside period tables, chairs and writing desks. At the far end, a

173

classically decorated lounge with sliding glass doors, which must have stretched at least fifty feet, overlooked the Mediterranean. To the right, a tapestry draped from the ceiling to the top of the imposing fireplace. The now, very familiar sofas that looked impossible to sit on for any length of time were flanked by ornate side tables and enormous gilded lamps.

'Excuse me,' said Mr Durrenberger, 'I have a few phone calls to make so, if you wouldn't mind, I'll let Ingrid take care of this part but I'll see you before you go.'

We followed Mrs Durrenberger up the marble staircase to the first landing, where she stopped to show Debbie a brass light switch.

'Now, Debbie,' she began with a very intense look, 'I'm very particular about how things should be cleaned. I've spent a long time testing all sorts of products and it is very important that the right one is used for the right job. This switch for example,' she said and began to lecture Debbie for a further twenty minutes about how the switch should be cleaned. Feeling that this really had nothing whatsoever to do with me, I sidled away to have a look at some of the huge paintings on the walls. Were they originals? I had no idea. As I was trying to decide, something caught my eye. The walls appeared to have velvety flowers coming out of them. Never having ever seen anything like that before, I reached forward to touch one of them when the distinctive voice of Mrs Durrenberger, who was now standing right next to me, said,

'This wallpaper is flocked, Brent.'

'Looks perfectly OK to me,' I replied.

Ingrid didn't know quite where to look or what to say, unlike Debbie, who was glaring at me and looking decidedly annoyed. Any attempt I made from that moment on to either smile or attract my wife's attention was completely ignored. How was I to know she was standing right behind me? Rude to creep up on me like that, I thought.

'There's a real art to housekeeping, Debbie,' I heard Mrs Durrenberger say as we traipsed from one bedroom or bathroom to the next. 'You'll need to keep your hair up when you're in the main house. Hairs, hairs. There's nothing more annoying than hairs – that and sticky fingerprints. I'd come into our bathroom sometimes after our previous housekeeper and there were so many fingerprints it looked like a crime scene from one of those cheap television detective series.'

An hour or so later we were sitting in Peter's study.

'Well, if everybody's happy,' he said hesitantly. 'I assume everybody's happy?' he continued, looking at the three of us for agreement. 'We should talk about when you can start and of course the nitty-gritty.'

He talked at length about our salary while poring over page after page of figures. He talked about this charge and that, referred to his calculator on many occasions, grumbled, got his rubber out, wrote something down and then rubbed that out and eventually declared, 'Right I've got it!' Expressions of relief could clearly be seen on the three faces sitting opposite him until he gazed into the air saying, 'Just a second,' and appeared to start the whole process again. Ingrid, aware that the situation was becoming uncomfortable, for at least three of us, offered helpfully,

'Why don't I show Debbie and Brent their accommodation?'

'No, no,' replied Peter, raising his right hand in Papal fashion. 'I won't be a minute.'

He was right about that. At least a further twenty minutes we spent glued to our cane seats. When he had eventually finished, Peter showed us a page full of numbers that only he understood and then asked Ingrid to show us where we would be living.

As I got up, I could feel that my trousers were damp round the thighs. Not only that, they had become attached to the chair that I, slightly embarrassingly, started to take with me. At least we'll be outside in a minute, I thought, and the fresh breeze would soon dry me out again. It came as a bit of a surprise when Ingrid led Debbie and I down some stairs just inside the kitchen door. I imagined this was a secret passage leading to the cottage – how exciting.

At the bottom of the stairs was a poorly lit corridor that smelled quite damp.

'One moment,' said Ingrid, who was fumbling for a light switch. 'I'm sure it's here somewhere. There you go,' she continued. Slowly, the round, plastic-covered ceiling lights began to reveal our surroundings. Overhead, running along both sides of the corridor, were large lagged pipes encased in aluminium wrapping. There was a small trailer used to carry a dinghy, nautical ropes, a pair of flippers and a snorkel. I could see four or five doors on either side of the corridor that led into empty rooms. Mrs Durrenberger, who obviously hadn't been down here for a long time, opened the first door. 'Nothing in here,' she said, 'nor here, or here, or here.' Surely she knew where the door to the garden was? 'You see the thing is they've moved out, otherwise they could have shown you.'

'Who've moved out?' I asked.

'Your predecessors.'

'Moved out of where?'

'Here of course. This is your apartment – where did you think we were?'

As Mrs Durrenberger disappeared into another room, Debbie whispered to me, 'This is ridiculous.'

'I know. Hang on, I'll be back in a minute.' Up until that moment I hadn't really taken any notice of where we were so I went to go and have a good look at the rooms that Ingrid had been darting in and out of. When I eventually caught up with Debbie and Mrs Durrenberger they were in the kitchen, which housed a twenty-year-old cooker, a rusty fridge-freezer and a pair of muddy wellington boots. Several wires dangled from the ceiling, and the kitchen units that were at least as old as the cooker were covered in grease. Looking up, there was a tiny window where I could just make out a flowerbed. We were shown another room that had previously been a lounge as well as a shower room and it was simply disgusting.

'It's really up to you how you use the space,' Ingrid said. 'You can make it however you wish. Obviously, it'll need some redecoration before you get here but that won't be a problem. Shall we go back up?'

Soon after, and hiding our disappointment, we said our goodbyes.

'Just one question before we go if you don't mind,' I said as I opened the car door.

'Sure, go ahead,' replied Peter.

'The cottage in the grounds, who lives there?'

'It's not really lived in at all,' he said. 'My daughter occasionally comes down for a week in the summer with her family but not always. I'm sorry, did you want to see that too? It's really beautiful inside. I can get Ingrid to show you if you like.'

'No, that's OK,' I replied, noticing the dejected look on Debbie's face. 'We can always have a look when we come back. Thanks again.'

'Nice to meet you,' Peter said, as he opened the kitchen door. 'We'll be in touch with all the details. Look forward to seeing you again soon. I'll open the gates. Bye.'

'Bloody hellfire!' I shouted, shaking my head in disbelief. 'What the hell was that all about? That really is taking the piss. Cheeky bastards.'

'You know what, Brent? It wasn't even an apartment.'

'How do you mean?'

'In an apartment, rooms lead off each other. There was none of that. No, it wasn't an apartment at all. It's a basement storage area – you saw all of the boating equipment, it's storage! Just cupboard after cupboard and no natural light. And, and,' she said, shaking with anger, 'central heating pipes in every room, which I bet clank in the middle of the night. We'd be boiled in the winter and frozen in the summer. What's wrong with these people? What do they think we are – a pair of moles? I'm so angry, I'm so angry, Brent. There is no way I'm living there – not for any money.'

We stopped at a small bistro in the town that boasted a very reasonable menu. As free wi-fi was also available we took the opportunity to write and thank the Durrenbergers for their time, adding that despite our advancing years, we weren't yet ready to be put into storage. They didn't reply.

177

Although our next interview was to be for a position just outside Grasse, for reasons we didn't know at the time we were asked to meet our prospective employer at a hotel in Draguignan, a market town about thirty miles north of Saint Tropez. We decided that it would be best to make the hour or so drive, find the hotel where the interview was to be held and, ideally, stay there for the night. After lunch, we took the dogs for a nice long walk along the beach at Ramatuelle. Once Herbie had had enough of chasing sticks, and Thyme, who had developed a love of the waves, was completely drenched we headed off to Draguignan, arriving at about five-thirty. Unusually for France, most of the hotels, including the one where we were due to be interviewed, wouldn't accept dogs. We went up this street and that but no one would have us. It was around seven o'clock and getting a bit dark when Debbie said,

'I keep seeing a sign for the Hôtel de Ville. That's the town hotel, isn't it?'

'That's what it translates to,' I replied. 'We've been down that road a few times already but I couldn't see it.'

We thought it best to have a walk around and pulled over to the side of the road.

Having spent a good ten minutes searching with no success, Debbie said, 'Let's ask somebody.'

'*Excusez-moi madame, où se trouve l'hôtel de ville?*' I said to a lady who was struggling along the pavement with two heavy bags of shopping. Looking a little perplexed, she raised her eyebrows and motioned to the large building in front of which we were standing. National flags waved proudly from the brickwork above but there didn't seem to be much light from the inside. Seeing that we were more than a little confused by the situation, our helpful bystander put her bags down, looked at her watch and said,

'*Fermé, maintenant, il est fermé. Bonsoir, monsieur, dame.*'
She picked up her bags and continued on her way, looking almost as confused as when we'd stopped her.

'Closed, closed? How can the biggest hotel in the town be closed?' I said.

'This is France my love, they can do what they want. Perhaps they're on holiday.'

'What, are you mad? This time of year? Not even the French are that barmy.'

Once back in the car, I reached for the glove compartment.

'This might explain it,' I said, after checking our pocket French–English dictionary.

'What might?' asked Debbie.

'*A hôtel de ville* apparently isn't a hotel at all.'

'Oh no?'

I smiled. 'No, it's only the bloody Town Hall. No wonder that woman thought we were mad.'

'Good grief, Brent, our French needs to improve. But that is funny though. Back to the drawing board.'

Eventually we found somewhere a couple of kilometres out of town and, although not ideal, Herbie and Thyme were welcome and, more importantly, we had located the hotel where we were due to be the next day. Once installed in our room, we sat at the computer and tried to find out as much as we could about Duncan Forbes, the film producer. It seemed that, having spent much of the seventies and eighties as a character actor, he was now a very successful and wealthy owner of an independent television production company. In his time, he'd been behind quite a few well-known costume dramas as well as some other films specially made for television. And, according to the newspaper reports, he wasn't afraid to speak his mind and could be quite intimidating.

'Be interesting to see how you two get along then,' said Debbie with a wry smile.

At eleven o'clock the next morning we sat and waited in the enclosed garden at the back of the hotel. At twenty past, I began to wonder if we were in the right place at all and started pacing up and down.

'These people are always late. Sit down and stop worrying. He'll be here,' said Debbie, who was reading her book.

I wandered round and spent a few minutes testing my knowledge of the various plants in the flowerbeds, out of which Herbie or Thyme would occasionally poke their heads. At half past eleven the door to the hotel burst open and through it came a man in his mid-sixties, as wide as he was tall. Stretching out his hand and marching at pace in our direction, he introduced himself.

'Hello, I'm Duncan and this is Kristina,' he boomed, pointing to a blonde woman in her late thirties who was dressed in very short hot pants, a flimsy top and bright-red high heels. 'Coffee everyone?' he said in a manner that came across as more of an order than a question. He didn't look at Debbie or I, nor did he wait for a response. He simply clicked his fingers, 'Kristina,' he barked, 'ask at reception for some coffees and make it quick, we haven't got long.'

Obediently, his companion placed several files, which she had just put on her lap, onto the table and hurried towards the door that led into the hotel.

'Now then, the thing is this,' Duncan began, 'the people you'll be taking over from don't know that they're going. There's nothing wrong with them as such,' he explained in a heavy Glaswegian accent, 'but unfortunately I can't keep them. Michael's Australian, his visa runs out in March and I can't afford to be seen employing someone illegally. If I was a little less high profile, I might be able to get away with it but I'm not. That's the price of fame for you. The papers would have a field day. If *The Daily Mail* got hold of it,' he said with a smile, quite bizarrely appearing to relish the thought, 'I'd be front page news. The upshot of this is that I've got to have some very delicate conversations with Michael and his wife, Sarah, over the next few weeks, so please bear with me.'

Duncan brushed lightly over our CV, asking the odd question but nothing in depth. I got the impression that he'd quite possibly made his mind up before our meeting and just wanted to confirm that we were who we said we were. Just as the waitress arrived with the tray of coffees, a broad grin ran across Duncan Forbes's face. He looked at his watch, pointed at Kristina and said,

'Right, we'd better be off darling. Sorry to cut this short,' he apologised, turning to Debbie and I, 'but we're having lunch in the mountains and if we don't leave now...Look, if you've got any other questions, send me a mail,' he said, handing me his card as he got up from the table. He stretched his hand out, said goodbye, tucked his paperwork under his arm and disappeared back through the hotel door as quickly as he had come through it. Kristina followed, struggling to keep up in her six-inch heels. Moments later, the door was flung back open and through it popped Duncan's head. 'Would you mind settling up for the coffee?' He nodded. 'I'll see you right when we next meet. Bye-bye.'

'No wonder he's rich and we're not,' I said.

'How so?' asked Debbie, picking up her bottle of water.

'Sails through life, never having to pay for a cup of coffee. Must add up to quite a bit. You can take the man out of Scotland....'

'It's not a bad thing though is it?' interrupted Debbie.

'What isn't?'

'He said he'll settle up the next time we meet. So, he obviously wants to see us again.'

'Bet he says that to everyone.'

'Oh, behave, it's only a cup of coffee and they seem nice enough. Wonder what their place is like.'

'No idea but I nearly stuck my foot in it.'

'Really?'

'Yeah, I thought that was his daughter.'

'You didn't? Bloody hell, you can be a liability sometimes.'

'What did you expect me to think? She's about half his age. What would happen if the *Daily Mail* got hold of that one?' I replied with an appalling Scottish accent.

'They already did,' said Debbie. 'I read it when I was googling him last night.'

'Front page news?' 'Hardly. Come on, let's round up the dogs.'

When we got back to Castres we phoned the agency to ask if they'd had any news. Mr and Mrs Durrenberger were refusing to return calls but the news from Duncan Forbes was very positive.

'Really?' I said.

'Absolutely,' replied Rachel. 'I'll send you the email.'

I made myself a cup of coffee and was looking forward to receiving Duncan Forbes's comments about us. Patiently, I sat at our office desk with notepaper and pen, ready to respond to any points he had to make. What arrived a few moments later came as a bit of a shock – just three words: *Keep 'em warm*.

'What did you expect my love?' said Debbie, as I scratched my head and gazed suspiciously at the screen. 'Page upon page of how wonderful he thought we were? He's not that sort of person.'

'No but, *keep 'em warm*?'

'Look, who cares as long as we get the job? Besides, he's probably got a million and one things to do in his world. We're hardly likely to be top of his priorities.'

'I suppose.'

And we did get the job. Three weeks later Duncan's accountants sent through the contracts. 1 May 2011 we were going to be starting our new job in the south of France. The only problem was that our successors in Castres were due to start at the beginning of April and Smythe wanted our apartment back. Where to go? Mandelieu was just down the road from Grasse and Paul and Ruth would probably need help but we just didn't want to go back.

'France is vast and full of big, empty houses. We must be able to find somewhere,' I said enthusiastically. 'We can go anywhere, absolutely anywhere.' For the first time in a long while we had a bit of money in our pockets. Not only that, we had a job to go to in our favourite part of the world and we'd got a month's break ahead of us – a month to get Smythe out of our system.

'La Grande Motte. How about La Grande Motte? It's on the way,' said Debbie.

'I thought you said it was a bit *Kiss Me Quick*. Are you sure that's where you want to go?'

'Well, it is a bit tacky, or at least it was. Haven't been there for twenty years. Anyway, it's out of season so we should be able to pick up an apartment really cheap. Let me have the computer.'

Debbie, who had made up her mind, spent days in front of the screen, occasionally popping her head out of the office door and shouting, 'Come and have a look at this one, what do you think?' Each time the quality of the apartment rose so did the price. But Debbie was on a mission. She'd dreamed of going back to La Grande Motte, the place where she had such fond memories as a child. One sunny Tuesday afternoon she appeared on the terrace where I was reading the local newspaper and announced triumphantly, 'Done it! We're going to La Grande Motte. Pack your bags!'

'Really?' I said.

'Really. Come on, I'll show you Look at this,' Debbie said excitedly, once we were back in the office and in front of the computer. 'Four weeks in an apartment overlooking the sea and in one of the best pyramid Buildings. All mod cons, nice kitchen – all for eight hundred euros. I know it's not the five hundred that we wanted to spend but we're there for four weeks so we want something a bit nice. You're going to love it, I promise you. I can't wait to show you around.'

For the next few days Debbie spoke of nothing else. It was as if all of her Christmases had come at once. It was the happiest I'd seen her in a long time. It seemed that our luck was finally beginning to change for the better.

Chapter 24

'Just promise me one thing,' pleaded Debbie. 'Try not to upset them before we go. We've only got one day left and that's it. After that we never have to see them again. Please.'

'OK, I promise.'

The next day, the Gates of Hell opened and in rolled the BMW. Debbie and I waited like obedient children in the courtyard for the car to stop. The interior was jammed to the roof with bags and boxes – there wasn't an inch left of space to be had. Out of the car struggled an even larger Smythe than the one that had left in October.

'Looks like you had a good Christmas,' I said cheerily. Smythe scowled.

'Twenty seconds – less than twenty seconds it's taken you,' said Debbie through gritted teeth. 'He hasn't even got out of the car yet.'

'Sorry, just came out.'

'Go on, go and help him with his bags – and be nice!'

'I see that the light above the garage isn't working,' said Smythe, completely ignoring my offer of a handshake. 'Never mind, you can fix it tomorrow. Once you've put these things away perhaps you and Debbie would like to join us for a glass of wine – tell us what's been going on.'

How they had managed to cram so much into one car was quite amazing. The large boxes we had taken from the car were stacked high on the centre console in the kitchen and many more boxes and bags had gone either to the garage or upstairs. An hour or so later, Debbie and I sat opposite Xander, who was holding a generously filled glass of white wine. Pippa was wandering around, holding her head and groaning at the prospect of deciding where everything she and Xander had brought could be put.

'Where's it all going to go? Where's it all going to go?' she kept repeating, before coming to join us. Daniel's words, 'That woman's fucking demented,' suddenly flashed across my mind.

'Help yourselves, I'm not going to serve you. It's a long time since I've been a waiter.' 'You've never been a waiter, dear.'

'Quite right, they don't get paid nearly enough.' Smythe laughed.

'You seem to tip them rather a lot,' said Pippa, who had suddenly become quite jovial. 'I'm surprised they haven't all got Ferraris,' she continued, finding her joke very funny and taking a large gulp of rosé.

'That way I get larger portions,' Xander replied, clearly very proud of himself. 'Anyway, back to more mundane matters. Rather sadly, we need to talk about your impending departure. George and Carol arrive the day after tomorrow so I thought we could put them up in the Hillside suite while you do the handover. We'll obviously pay you for the next couple of weeks and….'

'Xander,' I interrupted, 'we're leaving tomorrow. We've rented somewhere.'

'You didn't tell me,' he said scornfully, the air of bonhomie having quickly evaporated.

'But you didn't say anything about a handover. We assumed that because George and Mildred are due to start….'

'Carol,' growled Pippa, who got up from the table and began to snort like an angry bull.

'Look, Xander,' said Debbie, 'we thought that as you hadn't told us differently, we'd need to be out by the first.'

Pippa, who had resumed pacing up and down the kitchen and rubbing her forehead, furiously snapped, 'Xander, you haven't got the time and besides, you don't know….'

'I'll have to do it myself then,' said Smythe, raising his voice above Pippa's. 'Not really very convenient. That's another job I'll have to do. OK, see you tomorrow,' Smythe added, turning his back towards us. 'Close the door behind you.'

Leaving our unfinished glasses of wine behind we slowly made our way out. As the latch gently slotted into place I heard Pippa say in a very soft, yet reproaching, voice, 'I told you, you should have written to them.'

'You think he'd be pleased. Save himself two weeks' money,' I said, opening the kitchen drawer and searching for a corkscrew. 'You know what? If we'd told him that we hadn't made plans to be out of here tomorrow, you know what he would have said? I can hear it now,' I continued, imitating Smythe, '"you've had six months to find somewhere. I think that's quite long enough, don't you?" And anyway, if I'm so bad at this job, why's he asking me to do a handover anyway? I could....'

'Look, we're out of here tomorrow,' interrupted Debbie, who was struggling to zip up a bulging suitcase. 'Give me a hand, would you?' she said, trying to force the canvas lid down. 'Forget it. This time tomorrow, we'll be by the sea, eating lobster and drinking Champagne cocktails – he'll be a memory. And what's more, it'll be some other poor sods that are going to have to put up with him. Come on.'

'I know but....'

'Just leave it. Now, what are you wearing tomorrow? Pass me the small case down. I'm doing the bathroom next. Are you going to bother having a shave in the morning?'

Wanting to spend no more time with Smythe than we absolutely had to, we'd packed the car by eleven o'clock the next day and were ready to go. We'd worked out that with a bit of luck and a fair wind we might just make it to La Grande Motte for lunch. All that we had to do, or so we thought, was to wait for Xander to get up and hand us our final pay cheque. Smythe had other ideas. Obviously angered at the fact that he was going to have his time wasted by having to show our successors the ropes, he was about to waste ours. He called us to his office, where he declared that he wanted to go through every expenses receipt since our arrival a year earlier.

'You get these every month!' protested Debbie. 'Why are you leaving it until now?' she said, angrily staring at the pile of manila envelopes stacked up in front of Smythe, who was slowly sipping his coffee.

'You don't really think I've had time to look at them all, do you? I've been far too busy with my court case. Anyway, let's get on.'

Debbie sat next to me and glared at Xander while I gazed out of the office window at the lawn which had developed a few mole hills overnight. Xander painstakingly went through every receipt, occasionally stopping to give the room a large burst of fly spray.

'I see you broke something on your first week, Debbie,' he said, looking at an invoice. 'Not very good is it? Eighteen euros. Perhaps I should deduct it.'

'I broke what?' asked Debbie, reaching for the piece of paper.

'A plastic fridge tray apparently,' Smythe replied. It had become apparent to Debbie that he was much more interested in inconveniencing us than the receipt for eighteen euros. 'Thirty-five degrees in the Cayman,' he announced, passing the piece of paper across the table at the same time as looking at his computer screen.

'What makes you think I broke it? The crack was probably there before we got here,' snapped Debbie, who was trying to remember if she had, indeed, broken the tray or whether the crack was already there when we arrived.

'I doubt that very much. Samantha was an excellent housekeeper. I'm sure she would have told me. Let's carry on. Next....'

'Hang on a minute, that's a bit strong,' I started. 'You know what, Xander?'

Xander sighed. 'If you want any chance of getting the money that you believe you're owed, I suggest you leave Debbie and I to it. Actually, I'm not really sure what you're doing here,' he said with an air of disappointment.

'You invited me.'

'Close the door behind you. Now then, Debbie....'

I went into the main kitchen, made myself a cup of coffee and went at sat at the bottom of our apartment stairs. Moments later, Pippa came past me on her way to the gym.

'Still here then?' she said, peering into the back window of our car. 'Perhaps I should check the silver before you go?' she said. I ignored her and took a sip of my coffee.

'Hopefully won't be too long now,' she continued. 'Xander's not in the best of moods today, I'm afraid.'

'You can tell the difference, can you?'

'Bit of bad news from his barrister. They can't guarantee a court slot, so Xander has had to book him for three days. And at thirteen grand a day, that's quite expensive.'

I spat my coffee out.

'I know, but if he wins he'll get it all back and he's pretty confident this time. I'll see you before you go. Must get on.'

At lunchtime I popped my head round the door of Smythe's office. Debbie forced a smile though it was obvious to me that she was being ground down by Xander's microscopic examination of the expenses.

'You OK?' I whispered. Debbie nodded, puffed out her cheeks and raised her eyebrows.

'Novembarr,' Smythe said, completely ignoring me.

'Won't be too long,' said Debbie hopefully, as I quietly closed the office door on my way out. I thought she was being a bit optimistic – something which was confirmed as I saw Pippa carrying a tray of sandwiches and a pot of coffee over to Smythe's office at about one o'clock.

With little else to do, I watched some television and drifted in and out of sleep until just before five o'clock, when our front door was flung open by a triumphant Debbie, who was waving a cheque in the air.

'Got it, finally got it,' she said, punching the air. 'The bastard tried to wriggle but we've got it – all two thousand four hundred euros of it,' she said, giving the cheque a kiss. 'Tell you what though, my head is pounding. Would you mind driving?'

'No, of course not. So that means we're leaving here with how much exactly?' I asked.

'I calculated it to be about six grand. Not bad eh?'

'Great. That means I can have a couple of hundred euros in the casino. Woo hoo,' I said, rubbing my hands together.

'No you will not. Not after what I've just been through to get it, you won't. You'll be lucky to land up with a scratch card,' Debbie replied. 'Anyway, let's get out of here. Pass me a couple of anti-bangers would you? There's some in my bag.'

As Debbie went to get a bottle of water, I wandered around our apartment one last time. I smiled as I looked at the two holes above our bed where the metal rail had been. I thought about the good times that we had had with Sam and Daniel and I wondered if we'd ever be back. I certainly hoped not.

'You got the keys?' asked Debbie.

'I think....'

'Come on, dithery,' replied Debbie, who was still pumped up from her battle with Xander. She picked up the keys from the mantelpiece, tossed them over to me and grinned. 'La Grande Motte here we come, and don't spare the horses.' With that, Debbie flung the door open again and charged off down the steps. Seeing us head towards the car, Smythe and Pippa, accompanied by Herbie, came out to say goodbye.

'Aren't you going to say goodbye to Thyme?' asked Pippa.

'I don't think I can,' replied Debbie, her face all of a sudden becoming filled with sadness. 'I don't think I can. The thing is...' and then the words just wouldn't come out; Debbie was far too upset.

'Me neither,' I said. 'I'm sorry, Pippa, I just can't do it.'

Debbie and I had become more attached than we realised to Thyme. Now a bundle of fun and fluff and with a personality as bold as any dog, despite her being scarcely able to see, Thyme had really blossomed. Our only true concern about leaving *Rose des Vents* was what was going to happen to her when we left. We wondered whether the people taking over from us would treat her as well. We so wanted to take her with us, but couldn't. We just hoped that she wouldn't give up.

As we got into the car, Pippa handed us an envelope with a card inside. On the outside of the card was a picture of two dogs. On the inside she had written, *Thanks very much for looking after us. Love Herbie and Thyme.* Next to the message, Pippa had drawn a paw print in biro.

With all four of us trading false smiles, Debbie and I drove out of the villa's gates.

A month or so after we left Castres, Sam wrote to us to say that Pippa had written to her and that Thyme had been put to sleep.

Chapter 25

'Wow, look at that,' I said excitedly as we neared La Grande Motte. Out of the window I could see a group of six or seven Camargue horses running through the marshes that were adjacent to the busy main road. Giant bulrushes occasionally obscured them but there was nothing that could have prepared me for the sight of those magnificent animals galloping freely in the early evening sun.

'Told you,' yawned Debbie, who had just woken up from a good hour's sleep.

'I know but....'

'Didn't believe me, did you?' she said, stretching out her arms.

'How's the head?'

'Much better thanks,' replied Debbie, who was rooting around the glove compartment for her hairbrush. 'Tell you what, I am hungry though.'

'Be there soon.'

As we drove through the town centre, Debbie said, 'This is different.'

'How do you mean?'

'Well, I know it's been a long time but it looks so clean. It used to be full of shabby-looking buildings, cracked pavements, boarded-up shops – now look it at. It's amazing!'

Having never been to La Grande Motte before, I had no way of being able to make a comparison but it certainly wasn't the run-down seaside town that we had been expecting. The shop walls were freshly painted, the pavements were lined with manicured bushes and brightly-coloured flowers were planted in large stoneware pots. We soon found our pyramid so we parked and took the lift to the third floor. At the door we pulled a set of keys that were attached to a piece of string through the letterbox. I made several trips to the car and twenty minutes later I put the last carrier bag on the bed. I opened the doors that led to our balcony and instantly smiled. Twenty metres or so in front of our building was the harbour, where boats of all different shapes and sizes were bobbing up and down in the soft sea breeze. Below us, the street lamps that lined the walkways between the pyramids, shaped like giant lollipops, were just starting to come on in the evening gloom. A handful of people were walking their dogs, there were some young couples strolling along with prams, and the occasional skateboarder came scooting past. Shops selling beachwear and accessories started to pull their shutters down while the town's bars and restaurants began to come to life.

As I stood on the terrace, taking in the scenery for a short while, Debbie put our things away.

'We're about to become French promenaders,' I said.

'Do they have promenaders in France?' replied Debbie, who had come to join me.

'Not sure. Come on, let's go and find out.'

Wrapped up in winter clothing we strolled arm in arm along the quayside.

'Look at that,' I said, pointing towards a couple who were each tucking into a dessert topped with a small mountain of squirty cream.

'Nothing the French like more than a sticky,' said Debbie. 'That's what my dad used to say. Quite normal this time of day, an espresso and a good old sticky! Speaking of food, are you ready to eat?'

'Absolutely. What do you fancy?'

'Fish,' Debbie replied, clutching my arm. 'Fish, fish and more fish – must be the smell of the sea. Actually, never mind the smell of the sea, the smell coming from this restaurant is rather nice.' For a few moments we huddled round the menu that was displayed in a glass cabinet just outside. 'Seems OK to me,' said Debbie, beginning to look quite excited. 'It's a bit more expensive than we're used to, what do you think?'

'What do I think? I think we order everything on the menu and refuse to leave for a week. Anyway, we can always offer to do the washing up. Come on.'

We were greeted by a very personable waiter, who ushered us to a table with an immaculately ironed tablecloth, large, gleaming wine glasses and a small basket of freshly baked rolls. Moments later, he handed us each an impressively bound menu with the name of the restaurant, *L'Ombrine*, emblazoned on the cover.

'An aperitif, monsieur?' asked the waiter.

'Sounds good to me. Two Kir Royals,' I nodded in Debbie's direction, who approved immediately.

'I'm so happy, Brent. La Grande Motte, I can't quite believe it. Pinch me,' she said, offering her arm. 'Ouch, not quite that hard – bastard.'

'Sorry.'

For a while we studied the menu, which boasted just about every kind of fish imaginable. There was so much choice that we were finding it impossible to make a decision until Debbie said, 'I know it's a bit extravagant, but look, there's a seafood platter here for thirty-five euros.'

'I saw that and there's another one for thirty-nine.'

'Would you mind?'

'Would I mind what?'

'If I ordered one of them? Can try a lot of different things that way.'

'Of course not. I'll tell you what, why don't you order one and I'll order the other? We can share.'

'Really? Are you sure it's not too expensive?'

'Come on. How often do we do this? We've earned it.'

'*Voila monsieur*,' said our waiter, putting our drinks in front of us. '*Vous avez choisi*?'

'Yes, we've chosen,' I said, looking at Debbie, who was clearly delighted with our choice of restaurant.

'You're looking really happy,' I said, raising my glass.

'Happy? I'm giddy as a whelk!' replied Debbie, who was looking in every direction at the waiters bringing food to the other diners.

'You're what?' I said.

'Giddy as a whelk,' she replied, turning towards me. 'Something my father used to say.'

'Never heard that one before.'

'He probably made it up. As you know, raving mad my family. Don't worry. Plenty more where that came from. Look, here's ours,' Debbie said, clapping her hands.

The waiter cleared the middle of the table and put down two very large silver platters of fish and shellfish. Piece after piece of cod, salmon and red mullet were beautifully presented alongside langoustines, crab claws and oysters. Scallops and squid were plentiful, as were cuttlefish and prawns. Debbie gazed for a few moments, mesmerised by what was in front of us, and then said, 'Ready, steady....' She picked up her cutlery and some other weapons that were beside her and began to work away at a crab claw. There's nothing she likes more than breaking a shell open and prizing out the last, tenacious piece of meat. Crack, bash, crack was all I could hear for a few moments. Debbie, oblivious to everyone and everything around her, was in her element but it wasn't important. She was happy and that was all that mattered, to me at least.

'Look at that,' I said, momentarily managing to distract her attention. At a table to our left a further impressive but completely different assortment of the sea's finest delicacies was just arriving. An enormous glass, three-tiered stand was being placed in front of an eagerly awaiting party of four. All manner of seafood elegantly sat on beds of ice, waiting to be devoured.

'Fruits de mer,' said Debbie. 'Very nice if you don't mind it cold. Mind you, they have got a big bowl of chips. How are you enjoying yours? Sorry, should've asked earlier – too busy eating,' she apologised, looking at the amount of food left, which didn't seem to be going down.

An hour and a half later, and bursting at the seams like a pair of trawlers after a good day's catch, we slowly strolled along the quayside and back to our apartment.
'Come on, sweetie, wakey, wakey,' said Debbie, nudging me in the ribs about ten the next morning.

'Where's the fire?' I said wearily, pulling the duvet over my head.

'Come on, lazy, get out of your pit. The Sunday market's on and there's so much to see. Hurry up,' she said excitedly, already putting her shoes on.

With my eyes scarcely open, about ten minutes later we were walking along the avenues of La Grande Motte. Debbie hadn't forgotten a thing. She'd take this short cut and that, take a small detour here or there and talk enthusiastically about some of her early childhood memories.

'We used to slide down this slope,' she said. 'Boy, did we get into some trouble! Ruined all of our holiday clothes. We used to play hopscotch here and just over there was where we used to ride our bikes.'

All of a sudden Debbie stopped abruptly and squeezed my hand very tightly. 'Look,' she said, pointing at a sign at the top of one of the pyramid buildings. And there it was, emblazoned in huge letters: *Le Club*, the apartment block where Debbie had spent so many happy memories as a child

'I wonder if we can get inside?' said Debbie, leading me over to the steps. We stood there for a few minutes, peering through the locked iron gates. Just as we were about to leave, an elderly lady who was just leaving her apartment opened the door and held it open for us. We walked up some more steps and into the courtyard, in the centre of which was an empty swimming pool. 'We used to spend hours in there,' Debbie said. 'I'll never forget one summer when it turned completely green and no one knew what to do about it. There was nearly a riot. Residents went mad – including my mother, as far as I remember.'

'I don't get that. Why do you need a swimming pool when you've got all of that sea? Not exactly far away is it?' I asked, slightly confused.

'You see all the apartments?' Debbie began.

'Yes.'

'They've all got balconies, so mums and dads can look out at what's going on. They don't have to move. Besides, in the summer the beach is mad, it's like a zoo. All the French come here from Montpellier and it's impossible to move – not a square inch to be had. Look, that's our apartment there,' said Debbie, pointing to a large, first-floor balcony.

'Shall we go and knock?'

'Not sure I can,' she replied, clutching my arm tightly. 'Not just yet anyway. Maybe before we leave. Come on, let's go.'

Moments later we were in the midst of a bustling Sunday market. Markets are something that the French tend to do very well and this was no exception. Fresh fruit and vegetables, as far as the eye could see, were being sold alongside hams, sausages and, of course, cheese. Cooked portions of local delicacies were displayed on large circular trays, butchers' vans were aplenty and all manner of stuffed olives were in abundance. Fishmongers, bakers and a good selection of artisan food producers had come to La Grande Motte – and it wasn't just food. Leather goods, watches, kitchen gadgets, all types of clothing from suits to t-shirts were all on offer. Taking our time to stop at almost every stall, at midday we left the market with two bags of fresh vegetables, a pair of reading glasses and some very smelly cheese. Lunch was followed by an afternoon snooze, a walk along the beach and a few games of backgammon.

The next morning Debbie, who was just about to take a bite out of her toast, asked, 'Where shall we go today?'

'You know the area my love, I was rather hoping you'd tell me,' I replied, sipping my coffee.

'Well,' said Debbie, who was spreading out a map on the table. 'Thought either Aigues-Mortes, Palavas or maybe Le Grau-du-Roi.'

'I know about Aigues-Mortes. Haven't got a clue about the other two.'

'Well, Palavas is a nice seaside town. We used to go there just for the *soupe de poisson* – the region's renowned for it. Also, I'm pretty sure that's where the flamingos are. Le Grau-du-Roi,' Debbie added, still poring over the map, 'has an amazing aquarium and an indoor artisan market which is pretty special. Anyway, you decide, my love. I'm going to put some makeup on.'

'OK, let's try the flamingo soup,' I said, rinsing our plates. 'Take long to get there?'

'About twenty minutes,' replied Debbie, who was putting her jacket on looking round for the car keys.

It wasn't long at all before Debbie's memory was proved to be correct. To the side of the coast road, in amongst the marshes, were groups of beautiful, pale-pink flamingos huddled together. They took no notice whatsoever of the traffic that was belting along at sixty or seventy miles an hour only a hundred yards or so away. What were these magnificent birds, which I'd always associated with Africa or South America, doing roaming free in a seaside town in the south west of France? I didn't think anybody back home would believe me if I told them about the flamingos, so I asked Debbie to pull over so I could take a couple of pictures.

'Told you,' she said as we stood by the side of the road in the howling wind. Debbie jumped up and down and rubbed her hands together to try and keep warm while I took some photos. 'Too bloody cold to be standing here,' said Debbie as we got back into the car. 'How's my hair?'

'Looks like you've come on your bike.'

'That's attractive,' she replied, looking in the rear-view mirror. 'Pass me my brush, would you?'

We cancelled our walk along the beach that we had planned earlier and found a small beachside restaurant, decorated with fishing nets, lobster pots and an old ship's wheel. There, we enjoyed two fabulous bowls of *soupe de poisson*, some char-grilled *gambas*, *frites* and some rather strong but delicious home-made aioli.

Over the next few days we visited Aigues-Mortes, which was also amazing – the ancient walled city didn't disappoint. Of course, there were tourist shops with plenty of postcards and souvenirs of the Camargue, mostly depicting bulls, flamingos and guardians riding the semi-feral horses but, in the main, the city had retained most of its charm. We walked along the ramparts where we looked out onto incredible scenery. We sat in the pretty square and enjoyed a coffee and a chat and visited most of the artisan shops, as well as bagging a few goodies from a rather large emporium dedicated to sweets. Not surprisingly, having seen at first hand the French people's love of all things sweet, this was the busiest place of all.

The day before we left La Grande Motte we went to Le Grau-du-Roi where we bought some Camargue rice, an artist's palette populated with small glass pots, each containing a local tapenade or dip, and a couple of bottles of local wine. Unfortunately, having run out of time to visit the aquarium, we went back to the apartment, promising ourselves that we would go the next time. We did, however, make it to the casino. Fifty euros lighter and an 'I told you so' later, we left to have dinner at the Yacht club, where we enjoyed a delicious meal in elegant surroundings overlooking the sea. The following morning, we packed the car and headed off towards Grasse.

Chapter 26

We pressed the buzzer on the villa wall belonging to our new employer, Duncan Forbes, and waited. After the third or fourth time ringing we heard a voice coming from somewhere inside the gates.

'Is that you Brett?' asked a man with a heavy Australian accent. 'All right mate, I'll just go and get the clicker. Not sure what I've done with it. Chloe, Chloe!' he shouted, 'Have you seen the clicker? Won't be a minute.'

For several minutes more Debbie and I stood patiently, surmising that our arrival wasn't one that had been eagerly anticipated or even wanted for that matter. When the gates finally opened they revealed a tall, lanky man in his late twenties. Dressed in a green and gold hooped rugby shirt, knee-length shorts and flip flops, he offered his hand.

'G'day mate, I'm Michael. Bring your car in, you can park it anywhere you like, except in the garage,' he said, pointing to a three sided, rickety old shack that looked like it could fall down at any moment.

'When we go you can put yours in there.' In there, as he had put it, was an old soft-topped BMW, an American army jeep and a very sad-looking, maroon, twenty-year-old Renault, which I took to belong to Michael and Chloe. 'Right, I'll just show you where you'll be staying until we go.'

As we began to walk towards the house, a young golden retriever came belting past us and disappeared out of the gates as fast as his legs would carry him.

'Jasper, come here you little bastard. Won't be a minute,' Michael said, running into the road after the dog. About ten minutes later, and out of breath, he returned holding Jasper by his collar. 'He's always doing it. You've gotta watch him. Beautiful animal though, we absolutely love him. Wish we could take him with us. He was a rescue dog – me and Chloe got him. Unfortunately, we made the mistake of putting him in Duncan's name – we're so going to miss him.'

As Michael closed the gates we heard a huge screech of tyres coming from the road behind us. That screech was soon followed by a lot of swearing. 'Happens a lot round here,' Michael explained. 'People drive too fast mate – the roads are really narrow. Every now and again you hear a bang. Can be quite funny sometimes. It's like stock car racing, except you don't have to pay to watch it.' Michael laughed.

'Hilarious,' muttered Debbie, who was clearly not amused by the man's comment nor by his welcoming skills. We walked through the courtyard, passing the front entrance to the house on our right, down a few steps, and entered the villa via the conservatory.

'That's Cocoa,' said Michael, pointing to an elderly black Labrador who was just inside the door, lying in his basket fast asleep. 'He doesn't do much these days. He's blind and he's got arthritis. Be careful. Don't get too close, his breath stinks. Strong as an ox though. He made the mistake of coming up to our apartment once. When he couldn't get in, he tried to go back down but missed the steps. It's a good fifteen-feet drop. You know what? Not a scratch. He's a tough old boy, ha, ha, ha. Come on,' continued Michael, who opened a door to our left, 'I'll show you the lounge.'

It soon became apparent that this house was very different to Smythe's. Everything had been designed for comfort and not for show. The cream-coloured sofas were there to be sunk into and all kinds of knick-knacks adorned the small shelves that were recessed into the burnt-orange, rag-rolled walls. An enormous television covered the width of the far wall and bowls of sweets were dotted around the sideboards. On the coffee table there was a goldfish bowl full of wine corks, a handful of magazines and a cigar cutter. Having had a brief look around, Michael took us through another door that led up to a landing, where we were shown our room, which was almost immediately opposite the front door.

'Why don't you guys have a look around yourselves for a bit? Have a trip round the garden. We'll meet up about seven. Chloe's going to make us something to eat. These stairs,' he said, starting to climb them, 'lead up to our apartment.

Just knock on the door. Either that or you can come up from the outside. See ya later mate.'

Until Michael and Chloe's departure we were due to stay in the red room. Red, rag-rolled walls, a red carpet, a red-and-white striped duvet cover and a single red chair made up the bedroom. The bathroom could have come straight out of the shower scene in Psycho.

'Shocker,' I said to Debbie, who was busy unpacking.

'I know,' she replied, shaking her head. 'We're only in here for a couple of weeks. Hopefully, upstairs won't be as bad. Anyway, even if it is, Duncan said we can redecorate it. Come on, let's go and explore.'

Walking back down the inside stairs and through the lounge, we arrived in the library. The few pictures that graced the walls were mainly of Duncan with his friends in party mode or of him pointing directly at the camera as if to say 'I'm watching you.' In one corner, an antique writing desk looked a little out of place and to the side of the cloakroom was a strong door, leading to the wine cellar. At the far end was a glass-paned, wooden door that looked out onto the garden.

'Come on, let's go and have a look,' I said, unlocking the door. In the middle of the lawn was a swimming pool.

'Brrrrrrr,' I shivered as I knelt down and waved my hand in the very cold water.

'I take it it's not heated then?' said Debbie.

'If he's anything like Smythe it won't be until about a week before he gets here. Anyway, what's up there then?' As we looked to our right we could see a series of stairs leading up to different levels of the garden. 'Careful, this banister doesn't look at all safe. Look, it's really wobbly,' I said, offering my hand to help Debbie.

We walked along the first level that comprised a simple strip of lawn, thirty metres long by two metres wide and a small, paved path running alongside. Three-quarters of the way down, on the right, was an office that resembled a cricket commentator's box and at the end was a three-sided shack that, much like the garage, looked as if it could collapse at any moment. Inside the shack were several exercise bikes, cross-trainers, some weights and a television. On closer inspection we could see that, as nothing had been covered, much of the equipment had rusted; battery covers were missing and cobwebs dangled from just about everywhere.

'Doesn't look like this gets used much,' Debbie said. 'Look at the state of it.'

'Wouldn't have thought so, considering the size of him,' I replied.

There was nothing except vegetation on the next two levels but as we got to the top we saw there was a large log cabin. Inside there was a small, glass-fronted fridge and some wicker chairs with removable cushions. For a few moments we stood outside on the wooden decking and began to take in the view. Surrounding us was woodland and very little else. To the rear of the cabin we could just make out a chimney stack belonging to a neighbour, which was almost completely obscured by a line of Cypress trees that had been planted inside our grounds. Privacy was obviously very important to Duncan Forbes.

At seven o'clock we made our way up to the apartment.

'Hello, I'm Chloe,' said a boyish-looking woman in her late twenties. She was dressed in a short-sleeved, floral dress, three-quarter-length black leggings and was walking around in bare feet. Her natural voice was hoarse, which didn't come as a great surprise as, from the moment we arrived, she didn't stop talking. We sat in the lounge for a full hour listening to Chloe, who completely ignored any questions that either Debbie or I had to ask. She stood with her hands on her hips, verbal claptrap flowing from Chloe's mouth at breakneck speed while Michael, who was sprawled out on the L-shaped sofa, stared mindlessly at his computer. Our only distraction was that, as Chloe spoke, her legs got wider and wider to the point whereby she was almost doing the splits. Still talking, every now and then she would disappear into the kitchen, before eventually announcing, 'I'm sorry, but this lasagne's been in the oven for nearly two hours and it's still not done. I'm not really a cook. More of an outdoor type,' she apologised. '

Anyway, I think the oven needs replacing. You'll have to ask Duncan. Nothing to do with me anymore.'

Chloe ignored Debbie's offer to help and, half an hour later, brought through four plates of barely cooked layers of pasta sandwiched between some extremely unappetising filling of raw mince.

Much to our relief, the food succeeded where we hadn't. Its crunchiness kept Chloe quiet for a while, which gave Debbie and I time to study the décor in what was to become our new home. The long lounge wall had been coated several times in thick, blood-red paint and the rest of the room was painted bright-yellow. From where we were sitting we were able to see into the bedroom, which was, at least, all one colour – lime green. There were no bedside tables, lamps or even a dresser. There was a solitary chair in the middle of the room and a small built-in wardrobe. The bed was raised some six inches from the floor and was supported on two of the corners by a couple of empty, wooden wine boxes.

'The bed's a bit basic mate but Chloe and I are used to roughing it so it didn't bother us. If it's a problem for you, perhaps you could ask Duncan.' Above the bed was a single light fitting with three spot lamps and a full-length wavy mirror had been glued to the wall just inside the door.

'That was delicious, thanks, Chloe. Is it OK if I just use your loo?' asked Debbie.

'Through the kitchen on the left,' replied Michael. Soon after Debbie was back and gestured to me to go and have a look.

'Sorry, me too,' I said, getting up from my seat. Having seen the rest of the apartment, what came next shouldn't have come as a shock; nonetheless, it did. The walls in the tiny bathroom had been painted turquoise, with a thick, white wavy line running all the way along the top. This, we were told, was actually a wave and represented Chloe and Michael's love of the sea.

'That apartment isn't even student accommodation,' said Debbie angrily, as we made our way back to the red room.

'They've ruined it. I can't live in that. It's a hovel. I tell you what, if we'd seen the place before we took the job, I would've had second thoughts,' she said, slamming our bedroom door behind her. 'This is bad enough,' she added, scowling at the walls, 'but Jesus....'

'Maybe we'll get a budget to decorate....'

'Decorate? Decorate?' Debbie snapped. 'It'll take six months just to scrape the bloody paint off. Come on, let's get out of here.'

'Where to?'

'I neither know nor care. Just so long as it's away from those two clowns. For God's sake. Turquoise bathroom,' I heard Debbie mutter as she opened the door.

'There are about ten different walks we take Jasper on,' announced Chloe the next morning, as the four of us stood in the kitchen. 'I'll take you on one of them,' she said, looking at Debbie, 'and Michael can show Brent some of the places he's going to need to know around town.'

'Come on, mate, let's take the jeep,' he said, swiping the keys from the work surface. 'You're going to love it. Reminds me of back home, cruising up and down the beach. Chloe, you seen my sunnies? See ya later, girls.'

Michael ran through the courtyard, grabbed his sunglasses off the dashboard and started the engine. As I got into the passenger seat, Jasper jumped in the back. 'Ah, you got to love him, Brett,' said Michael, stroking Jasper on the head. 'Not today mate. You're staying with the girls. You behave yourself. Chloe, Chloe!' he bellowed at the top of his voice.

Minutes later, I was being bounced around at high speed along the backroads of Grasse. Seeing I was looking less than comfortable, Michael said, 'Don't worry mate, when people see this thing heading in their direction they tend to get out of the way. See what I mean,' he went on, narrowly missing a small car that had pulled over and whose wheels were perilously close to the ditch at the side of the road.

Michael took me to every garden centre, DIY store, builder's merchants, supermarket, dry cleaners, *boulangerie* and wine shop that he could think of. He also showed me some of Duncan's favourite restaurants. Keen to show off his knowledge of the area, Michael zipped down one road after another.

'Best way to do it mate is get lost a few times. That's what I did – great fun. Only way to learn. We're used to that in Australia. I used to go missing for weeks, no one ever worried. I reckon my father was quite disappointed when I found my way home.'

'Really?' I said, raising my eyebrows.

'No, not really, mate. Don't look so shocked, only joking. Oh, look, there's the girls.' About a mile or so from the villa we saw Chloe and a very downcast-looking Debbie walking towards us.

'You OK?' I asked. Debbie, hands in pockets, forced a smile and shrugged her shoulders.

'Come on, let's do it,' Michael said, excitedly jumping out of the jeep. With one hand each on Jasper's collar, he and Chloe began whispering in his ear. The whispering became louder and louder until Chloe and Michael eventually screamed, '*Allez, allez, allez*!' They then released Jasper, who went charging off as fast as his legs would take him.

'Right, let's follow him. See you later girls.' With that, Michael and I hurtled down the road in hot pursuit of Duncan's dog, who was already a good way ahead of us. 'Watch this mate,' said Michael as we drove past Jasper. Michael slowed down. Jasper ran past the jeep, disappeared under the front wheels and back out again.   'Isn't he just the best? I'm so going to miss that dog. I wish we could take him with us.'

'You never know, you might be able to, provided you don't kill him first, that is.'

'Ah no mate, it's just a bit of fun. He knows what he's doing. Come on, you little bastard, keep up,' Michael said, as we drove through the villa gates, closely followed by Jasper.

Jumping out of the jeep, Michael said, 'Brett, why don't you go and have a bit of a potter round the garden? I've got a couple of things to do in the tool shed.'

I wandered around the grounds for about half an hour but with no visible sign of any gardening equipment so unable to do much, I went back to see Michael. He was looking intently at an instruction manual for a lawnmower, which was in the middle of the floor and surrounded by bits.

'Are you servicing the mower?' I asked.

'Well, I'm not in here fucking spiders mate,' Michael replied with a big grin. 'Something my father always used to say.'

'He must be a real charmer.'

'Oh no mate, he's just Australian, that's all. Pass me the Philips would ya?'

Leaving Michael to the lawnmower that he never managed to put back together, I went in search of Debbie, who was in the villa kitchen. She'd emptied every cupboard and drawer and was cleaning all of the crockery and cutlery and organising the space so that everything could be easily found.

'This place is filthy,' she said. 'Doesn't look like Chloe spends a lot of time in here. Have you seen her by the way? Something I need to ask her.'

'I saw her about ten minutes ago, dangling from a tree.'

'Dangling from a tree? What's she doing that for?'

'I think she's trying to evolve. Would you like me to go and get her?'

'No, it's OK. It can wait,' replied Debbie, who was scrubbing away at the work surfaces.

The next few days were spent with each of us doing our own thing. Chloe could often be seen wandering round the grounds with a chainsaw and when she wasn't doing that she would either help Michael in the garage or walk Jasper for hours on end. She never came into the house and Michael was rarely seen in the garden.

It all seemed to be going OK until one day at about five in the afternoon Chloe appeared in the kitchen, where Debbie and I were having a chat, and announced,

'We're all taking Jasper out for a walk,' to which Debbie replied,

'I'm sorry, I haven't got time. Too much to do here,' she said, squeezing out her mop.

206

'You've been out for two walks in five days,' snapped Chloe, looking angrily at Debbie.

'I know, I've been busy,' she replied, turning her back on Chloe.

'Listen, Debbie,' said Michael, raising his voice, 'Jasper is the most important thing to Duncan and Kristina and we've only shown you two of the walks.'

'Michael, I don't want to be rude,' replied Debbie, swivelling round and glaring at our predecessors, 'but,' she said quite firmly, 'I'm perfectly capable of walking a dog, thanks very much. I need to get on. Now, unless there's anything else....'

With that, Chloe stormed out of the conservatory door. Seconds later we could hear voices coming from the road. As Debbie and I peered over the wall to the side of the lawn we could see Chloe, her arms pumping along like a couple of pistons and her ponytail swishing from side to side. Jasper was already some way in the distance. We heard Chloe shout to Michael,

'Who the hell does she think she is? Bitch has only been here five minutes. He's no better either.'

A further two days passed before we saw them again. We were sitting in front of the television in the main lounge, eating our dinner. Michael and Chloe appeared at the glass-paned door that led to the upstairs. In contrast to how we had previously left them, they were now all smiles and full of bonhomie – we were beginning to smell a rat. They asked about how we'd been getting on, whether we were settling in and were quite apologetic that they hadn't been around more. As they got up to leave, and thinking that entente cordiale had been fully restored, Chloe, rather unsubtly, winked at Michael, who nodded back.

'Oh,' said Chloe, reaching for the door, 'I forgot to mention that my mother, grandmother and a friend of hers are all coming to stay here for a week. I'm picking them up from the airport in the morning. They've been so worried about us, losing our jobs and everything....'

'Duncan's OK about this, is he?' Debbie asked. 'He hasn't mentioned any of this to us.'

'We haven't told him actually,' Chloe replied abruptly. 'He doesn't have to know, does he? I mean, we're in charge and while we're here we can do what we like. You can do the same when we're gone,' she said, confidently.

'I think you'll find, Chloe, that as it's his house, Duncan's got every right to know, don't you? Are you seriously trying to tell us that you weren't going to tell him?' Debbie asked.

'I didn't want to worry him, he's a busy man,' replied Chloe, whose face was getting redder by the minute. 'He's got a lot on his plate.'

'He'll have a bit more on it now then,' Debbie said, quite firmly. 'Besides, this is our handover period, for which you are being paid very handsomely. How are you going to do that if you've got people coming to stay?'

Chloe flew out of the door, closely followed by Michael. Their apartment door slammed shut and, once again, we could hear raised voices. Duncan phoned the next morning to find out how things were going, so we felt obliged to tell him what had happened.

'Amazing behaviour,' was all he said.

Chloe's mother arrived as planned and didn't say a single word to us the entire time that she was there. A week later she left and three days after that Chloe and Michael followed suit. We stopped taking Jasper round the ever-increasingly dangerous roads and, instead, drove the short journey to Gourdon, where there was mile upon mile of forest and open tracks. He could run freely without fear of being run over. Occasionally he'd pick up some smell or other, disappear in amongst the trees for ten minutes or so and then return to us, covered in all sorts of debris. How dirty he came back really didn't matter – Jasper was safe.

We decided that lying in his basket all day, just popping outside occasionally to go to the toilet, wasn't doing Cocoa any good at all.

'We've been here before,' said Debbie, referring to Thyme. 'What is it with part-time owners?' she said, snatching his collar.

Leaving Jasper behind, we took Cocoa to a nearby field. Cocoa's nose went into overdrive and despite his bandy back legs, that dog could pull. Wagging his tail, he dragged us this way and that until our arms could take no more, so we let him off the lead. He'd zigzag around and bump into the odd tree or two but it didn't seem to bother him one iota. If there was any mud to be had, he'd roll around in it with all four legs in the air. He seemed to find this all very amusing and the only thing he loved more than his walk was the shower when he got back. Trying to push Cocoa out of the large shower room next to the swimming pool took a monumental effort from both Debbie and I. She'd pull, I'd push, while Cocoa dug his heels in. In the end, we discovered that the only way to get Cocoa to move at all was to bribe him with food. It was clear that he was beginning to enjoy the attention and his confidence grew with each passing day. One morning as I wandered into the conservatory looking for Debbie, she grabbed me by the arm and said, 'Cocoa has just frightened the hell out of me, the little sod.'

'Really?' I replied. 'How did he manage that?'

'I thought he was asleep, so I tried to sneak past him quietly. Just as I got past him he let out the loudest bloody bark I've ever heard in my life, the little bastard. He hasn't barked since we've been here. I nearly peed myself! He thought that it was hilarious. He rolled on his back, wagged his tail and stuck all four feet up in the air. I could have killed him,' Debbie said and then laughed.

From that moment on, Cocoa had found his voice again, which he used to great effect. It didn't take him long to realise that if he barked long and often enough, someone would come and give him a hug. He also became more adventurous. Often when we were having dinner, we'd hear a scratch at the door and Cocoa would come barging through and plonk himself on the sofa, which, quite often, was where he refused to leave until the following morning.

Chapter 27

'What if they don't like my cooking? I mean, suppose they hate it? I don't know what they like. We could be out of here,' Debbie said, uncharacteristically crashing pots and pans around.

'Don't be daft, they'll love it. Come on,' I replied, doing my best to reassure her. 'Have a bit of confidence, it'll all be OK. Anyway, I'm off to the airport in a minute – anything I can do before I go?'

'Well, you could light the candles in the living room.'

'Bloody hell fire!' I shouted as I picked up a box of matches. 'How many are there?'

'Fifty or sixty,' replied Debbie from the kitchen.

'Isn't that dangerous?'

'It's what Chloe said. He's got a thing about candles.'

'I think the word you're looking for is obsession. It's like a bloody shrine in here. Right, I'm off to the airport,' I said when I'd finished. 'I'll give you a buzz when I've got them. Eighteen, by the way.'

'Eighteen? What's eighteen?'

'The number of the fire brigade,' I replied.

'Very funny.'

I kissed Debbie goodbye and waved through the kitchen window at a very worried-looking face that was doing its best to smile back at me.

When collecting people from the airport I have a habit of getting there way too early and, consequently, end up paying a fortune for parking. Whether it's because I think I'm going to get stuck in the traffic jam from hell on the way there or that the flight will be early I'm not sure but this time was no exception. By the time Duncan burst through the Arrivals door I'd finished my third espresso and was feeling quite wired.

Wearing a brown fedora, yellow jacket, blue shirt and pink trousers, he was not easy to miss. Tucked under his arm was an English newspaper, which he dropped. A kind old lady bent down to pick it up and tapped him on the shoulder. He turned round, smiled at her and said firmly, 'I'm sorry, no time for autographs, we're in a hurry.' The bemused woman muttered something in German and threw the paper in a bin.

'Keys, Brent,' Duncan said, stretching out his hand. 'Parked in the Kiss and Fly?'

'Yes.'

'You wait for Kristina. I think she's brought half of London with her,' he said before marching towards the exit.

'Nice to see you again. I take it you've got Duncan?' asked Kristina, who was pushing a trolley full of luggage. 'That's good – he's always dying to get out of these places.'

By the time we got to the car, Duncan had put the roof down and was sitting in the driver's seat and revving the engine impatiently.

'I'll sit in the back,' offered Kristina.

'No, no,' I insisted, pushing the front seat forward. As Kristina closed the car door, Duncan put his foot down and went screeching along through the car park towards the barrier.

'Ticket,' bellowed Duncan, reaching over his left shoulder and clicking his fingers. Hurriedly, I took the ticket out of my wallet and passed it to him. Once out of the airport, Duncan put on the radio, which he turned up to full volume.

As we arrived at the villa, Jasper came to greet the car. True to form, and catching us all off guard, he seized his opportunity and belted out of the gates as fast as legs his legs would carry him.

'Don't just stand there, Brent, you'd better go and get him,' ordered Duncan. 'You can get the bags out of the car when you get back. And hurry, it'll be dark soon. Come on, Kristina,' he said, walking quickly down the path towards the kitchen.

'Wow, this is delicious, Debbie,' I heard Duncan say as I dragged Jasper by the collar into the conservatory. 'Crab and sweetcorn soup is one of my all-time favourites,' he added. Similar amounts of praise came for the spicy pork in lettuce wraps and the red Thai curry.

'That's the most wonderful meal I've eaten in a long time. I'm really looking forward to this summer,' said Kristina, who had already changed into some shorts and a skimpy top.

'You'll lock up later won't you, Brent?' asked Duncan, getting up and making his way to the lounge.

'Of course,' I replied as I watched him pick up the box of Cuban cigars that were on the coffee table.

'I think that went rather well,' said Debbie, who was washing up.

'Didn't it just? Told you, you didn't need to worry,' I replied, giving her a hug. 'Well done you.'

An hour or so and a few glasses of rosé later, Debbie, very pleased that her cooking had been so well received, was fast asleep next to me on the couch upstairs.

My night, however, was far from over. At about half past eleven, I came down our spiral staircase on the outside of the apartment. I walked past the kitchen and gazed through the conservatory into the lounge, where I could see Duncan puffing on an enormous cigar. The television was blaring – Kristina was nowhere in sight. So, I went back upstairs and came back down at half-hour intervals until around two o'clock when I saw that the lounge was empty. Through the window I could see that none of the candles had been extinguished, no lights had been turned off and the doors that led to the swimming pool were still wide open. I was just about to go into the conservatory when the door leading from the lounge to the upstairs opened. In walked Kristina, looking slightly sleepy and dressed in a silver, silk night shirt that barely covered her dignity. Shuffling along slowly into the kitchen, she ambled over to the large American fridge. She opened the door and bent over.

'Holy moley,' I heard myself say, hoping that I hadn't said it too loudly.

In Kristina's eagerness to reach something at the back of the fridge she hadn't noticed that her shirt had ridden up past the small of her back, leaving nothing to the imagination. The fridge light had illuminated everything. Putting my hand over my mouth for fear of blurting something out I retreated into the shadows, which turned out to be quite a wise move. Kristina, suddenly aware of her predicament, stood bolt upright and pulled the hem of the shirt down as far as it would go, at the same time shimmying from side to side. She then came over to the conservatory door, against which she firmly pressed her nose. With clam-like eyes she looked from side to side, trying to peer into the darkness. For what felt like an age, I stood motionless, holding my breath. Eventually, Kristina made her way up the inner stairs, pausing once, briefly, to look back at the conservatory door. She put her hand to her mouth, hoping that she may have just got away with her mistake but allowed herself a little smile as she went back to bed. As the conservatory door, when opened, made a huge clunk that could be heard all over the house, I left it a further half an hour before I came back down from our apartment, so as not to arouse any suspicion.

'Did you sleep OK?' asked a very chirpy Debbie the next morning.

'Not really. Took ages to get to sleep.'

'Why so?'

'They didn't go up until gone two and by then I was past being tired. Buggers left all the lights on, doors open and not a candle blown out. Sorry, didn't get a chance to tidy up. Place looks like a bomb's hit it.'

'I better go then.'

By the time Debbie got downstairs at a quarter past eight, Duncan was already sitting at his writing desk. Dressed in a polo shirt, sarong and flip-flops and listening to some classical music, he was oblivious to Debbie. An hour or so later, a barely awake Kristina came down and sat at the long wooden conservatory table, where she ate some cereal and gazed at her laptop. Not long after that she disappeared upstairs with Duncan, coming back down soon after in some very short shorts and running shoes. He was dressed in a pale-blue tracksuit and a floppy hat and was carrying a walking staff. Clearly, he thought he looked like Gandalf. I thought he looked like a squashed Smurf.

'Got the water? asked Duncan. Kristina nodded. 'We don't want a repeat of last year. Hospitalised for two days you know. Right, come on,' and off they went through the gates, preceded by an exuberant Jasper.

During the course of their long speech on our first night at the villa, Michael and Chloe had told us how that with Kristina being Danish, she had persuaded Duncan, while out for a walk, to take a drink from the stream that ran along the side of the road. Having been used to natural spring water where she lived, Kristina hadn't considered the perils that lay in wait for them in what was essentially a filthy French ditch. An ambulance in the middle of the night and forty-eight hours later, Duncan and Kristina were discharged somewhat sheepishly from Grasse General Hospital. Since that time Duncan would only drink bottled water, including in his coffee – he wasn't taking any further chances.

'Come on, Brent. We're going to be late!' shouted Duncan one lunchtime.

'Late for what? I asked.

'Oh, didn't I tell you we're off to the *Colombe D'or*?' he said, clapping his hands.

'Er, no, you didn't, sorry.'

'We're supposed to be there at one. What time is it now?' he asked, putting his jacket on.

'Five to.'

'You'd better hurry up and get changed then. Kristina!' he bellowed. 'Kristina, come on!'

I passed Kristina on the way to our apartment. She was struggling to do the straps up on her sandals and her hair was still wet from a shower. It seemed that I wasn't the only person that Duncan had forgotten to tell about his plans.

This behaviour, I was to discover, was quite normal for Duncan. He would only ever leave the villa to go to a restaurant at the time he was supposed to be there. He thought nothing of keeping people waiting. He and Smythe were perhaps not so different after all.

Forty minutes later and with Kristina and I green at the gills from Duncan's fast and erratic driving, we arrived at the famous restaurant in Saint-Paul de Vence. The town, with its many art galleries and artisan shops, is a huge tourist attraction and a table at the *Colombe D'or* usually needs to be booked months in advance. Thinking that this was likely to be a long lunch, I made the forty-minute trip back to the villa. As I drove through the gates, I saw that our reliable old Honda CRV had been replaced by a Ferrari.

'Debbie, Debbie,' I said as I opened the conservatory door, 'I see our company car's arrived.'

'Ah, the Ferrari,' replied Debbie. 'Thought you might like it. Belongs to Duncan's friend, Giles. He dropped it off when you were out. Coming back in a couple of weeks so until then, it's all Duncan's.'

'Lucky boy. Where's the keys?'

'Never you mind. We've got some chopping to do,' Debbie said, handing me a bunch of parsley. 'They're in tonight.'

'Anyway, what party?' I asked.

'Sorry, didn't I tell you? Duncan has a party every year on the fifteenth of August.'

'His birthday?'

'Not quite – Napoleon's.' Debbie smiled, who was taking some salad out of the fridge.

'That's very patriotic of him.'

'No, not really,' replied Debbie. 'At the end of the meal, there's a toast to Wellington.'

'That'd be right. Now, how do you want these onions sliced?'

At three-thirty I got the call to hurry back to the *Colombe D'Or* as they were, apparently, almost ready to leave. Just before six o'clock Duncan and Kristina came outside with their friends, who were waiting for their chauffeur to arrive. Within seconds, an impressive red Bentley, complete with a man in a uniform and cap, drove towards us through the crowded streets. Most people stared admiringly – most people apart from Duncan Forbes, that is, who shouted at the top of his lungs, 'Oh a Bentley, a bloody Bentley. How fucking vulgar!' His attempt at humour succeeded in stunning the whole square into silence. Nobody knew where to look. Kristina, looking very embarrassed, dived into the back of the car. Thankfully, we were soon heading back to the villa. Duncan and Kristina went straight to their room and were not seen again until dinner.

The next morning, I was on my way to the garage when I heard a voice behind me shout, 'Come on, Brent, get in!'

As I turned round, Duncan was dangling a set of keys and pointing towards the Ferrari. With his baseball cap turned round and wearing shorts and a t-shirt, Duncan Forbes had decided that we were off to do a bit of cruising along the Côte d'Azur. Under normal circumstances this might seem quite a cool thing to do – unfortunately Duncan was obviously anything but normal. I'd never driven a car with flappy paddles on the steering wheel before and it soon became clear that neither had Duncan. Having spent an age kangarooing through the backstreets of Grasse, I suggested that Duncan press the button marked 'A' for automatic – a suggestion which he completely ignored. Instead, much to the amusement of the onlooking public, we bounced along the coast road to Cannes in our seventy-thousand-pound Ferrari. I found the whole episode very amusing and at one point I had tears of laughter streaming down my face. Duncan mistook this for me having a thoroughly good time and promised, once we'd got back to the villa, a repeat performance in the near future. Fortunately, that promise never came to fruition.

As the summer got into full swing, the villa began to fill up with guests who had all been invited to Duncan's big summer party. Ferrari-owner Giles arrived with his airhead girlfriend, who was considerably younger than him. Her sole contribution to proceedings was to wander around the poolside in a skimpy bikini and say to anyone passing, 'Hi, Honey, you all right, Honey?' and, 'What time's lunch, Honey?'

'Oh my God!' shouted Duncan one morning at about eleven. 'Brent, Brent, where's Brent?'

'What's up, Duncan?' I said, running from the garden into the conservatory.

'What's up? I'll tell you what's up. Alistair and Rosemary are arriving at lunchtime and they've just told me they're bringing their fourteen-year-old son with them.'

'And that's a problem because...?'

'It's a problem because there's only a double bed in their room. You'd better go out with Debbie and buy a single – they'll be here in a couple of hours. Shit!'

'OK, but Debbie's doing your lunch.'

'To hell with lunch!' he said angrily. 'You'd better get going.'

Debbie and I got in a car and went to scour Grasse for a bed. We'd only been gone half an hour when Duncan phoned.

'Well? Well?' he said.

'We're nearly there now,' I replied.

Every ten minutes from that moment on, Duncan phoned for an update. Each call was more panicked than the previous. Within an hour we'd got a bed and had loaded it into the car. We were about fifteen minutes away from the villa when the phone rang yet again.

'You'd better hurry up!' screamed Duncan, 'they could be here any minute.'

'What's he going to do?' I asked, having had enough of his manic behaviour. 'Go to bed as soon as he gets here?'

The phone went dead.

As the gates of the villa opened, Duncan and Giles were standing in the middle of the courtyard with their arms folded. Neither of them said a word. Instead they glared as they watched Debbie and I struggle to unload the bed, which we had wedged into the back of the car.

As well as the great and the good from the world of television, a few of Duncan's family had made the trip, including his eleven-year-old godson. One afternoon, he came running out of the house, screaming at the top of his voice. Thinking that a scream so loud would have at least warranted a murder, I went rushing over.

'Are you OK?' I asked the distressed young chap.

'No, no I'm not,' he whimpered, his face all screwed up. 'No, I'm not OK.'

'What's happened?'

'It's Uncle Duncan,' the boy snivelled.

'Uncle Duncan? What's wrong with Uncle Duncan?'

'Nothing's wrong with Uncle Duncan, but, but….'

'But?'

'But his skirt's just fallen off and he's not wearing any pants. Ewwww, I think I'm going to be sick,' and off he ran. Unfortunately, Uncle Duncan's skirt fell off quite a few times over the summer, including once in Debbie's presence, who was fortunate enough to be behind and not facing him.

'What shall I do with this?' Debbie asked one evening, as she was looking at the dregs of some red wine that barely covered the bottom of a glass decanter.

'He's obviously brought it out to the kitchen for a reason,' I replied. 'It's been in the lounge for a while. Maybe he expected you to get rid of it earlier. I'd wash it up if I were you. There's sod all left. See ya later,' I said, as I went out through the conservatory door.

An hour later, I was back. Debbie was looking very red and visibly upset.

'What's up?' I asked.

'I've just been bollocked for throwing away his wine. He said it cost five hundred euros a bottle. That's what's up,' Debbie replied angrily.

'Then he's a lying bastard. He buys all of his wine from the auctions down the road. Look,' I said, picking up a thick brochure with dozens of wine bottles on the front cover, 'this is where he buys his wine from. Comes from hotels that have gone bust. He pays bugger all. Be lucky if that wine cost more than about twenty quid. I bet he's actually pissed off because I didn't decant it properly last night.'

'Really?'

'Did you see all of that sediment stuck to the side of the glass? It's my fault, not yours.'

'It doesn't matter whose fault it was – you should have seen the look on his face. He was so angry. I thought he was going to explode. He really frightened me.'

'I'll tell him it was my fault – I'm not scared of him,' I said, putting my arm round Debbie.

'Just leave it. Please leave it, Brent, we've only just got here. It just came as a bit of a shock, that's all.'

I left Debbie preparing dinner for the guests and went to the bins at the bottom of the garden, where I found the bottle in question. I then went back upstairs and straight onto a few wine websites.

'Forty-five quid. Forty-five quid! That's all that bottle cost retail and he won't have paid that. The man's a bloody liar. I told you.'

'It doesn't matter,' replied Debbie. 'It doesn't matter, Brent. It's not worth getting involved. There'll only be one outcome.'

'I know. Just saying, that's all.'

'Help me set the table, would you?' asked Debbie, whose wind had clearly left her sails.

Chapter 28

The next evening at about seven, dressed in a white tuxedo, open-necked shirt and black trousers, Duncan came flying down the living room stairs, followed by Kristina, who was dressed just on the right side of naked, and announced,

'Right, we're ready. Let's go. Brent, have you got the car out yet?'

As usual, we were going to be late. The destination this time was a wedding reception that was being held at a castle in La Napoule, a few minutes along the coast from Cannes. Thinking it not the right thing to do to comment on Kristina's attire, interesting though it was, I turned my attention to Duncan.

'You look great Duncan,' I said with a smile, 'though, thought you might have worn a kilt.' With that his face contorted and he barked, 'Who the hell do you think I am? Some fucking thick Jock, looking for a small part in Braveheart?' He was furious and the subsequent car journey was, pretty much, silent.

'Be here for about eleven,' demanded Duncan, jumping out of the car and running towards the bride and her father, who were moments from the castle doors. 'If we're going to be any later, I'll call you!' he shouted back over his shoulder. 'Oh, and bring your car when you come back, we might have to drop some people off. The Merc's not big enough' he added, rushing into the castle. My final vision as I drove away was one of the bride and her father going to Kristina's aid as, in attempt to keep up with Duncan, her high heels had given way and she, very unfortunately, had landed up in an oleander bush.

I made the short journey back to the villa and was back at the castle by ten to eleven. Eleven turned into twelve, twelve became one and, eventually, at two-thirty the following morning, Duncan, Kristina and some of their friends, all worse for wear, came spilling out of the castle.

'Sorry about that, Brent,' apologised Duncan, who was in a much better mood than when I'd left him. 'We thought it was just the reception but it turned out it was the complete wedding. Come on, you lot, get in!' he shouted, puffing on his cigar and turning up the radio. With the music blaring and with no consideration whatsoever for the residents of La Napoule, we deposited Duncan's guests at various hotels before heading back to Grasse, arriving at the villa at about three-thirty.

With only ten days to go before the big party, Debbie was busily organising menus. She was to cook for forty people, and in a very small kitchen, so there was a lot of planning and preparation required. Quite often she'd lie awake into the early hours, switching the light on every now and again to write something or other down. She'd hired tables and chairs, crockery and cutlery, wine glasses and decanters. Huge, white, stately tablecloths were soon to arrive as well as bunting, depicting both the French and British flags.

It was eleven o'clock one morning when Duncan came into the kitchen and announced, 'We'll be eating out this evening, Debbie. If we could just have something light and tasty for lunch, that would be fine. I think there are only twelve of us. Thank you,' he said and headed back to his office.
'He always does this to me,' complained Debbie, picking up her purse and looking at the clock. 'He never gives me any warning. Look at the time! I'd better get to the supermarket.'
'I know, the man's clueless but look, you can have a rest this evening. They're going out and I've got to take someone to the airport, so you'll have the place all to yourself. You'll be fine.'
'I suppose. See you later,' said Debbie, taking the car keys from the hook on the wall.
At six o'clock I left to go to the airport. Debbie was having a well-earned afternoon snooze and I was looking forward to sharing a bottle of rosé with her, free from Duncan and his guests, when I got back. At eight o'clock I drove through the

villa gates, parked the car in the garage and began to walk towards our apartment. As I made my way across the courtyard I heard a small voice whispering from somewhere in the shadows.

'Brent, Brent, help!'

As a cold shiver ran down my spine I could just make out the silhouette of Debbie, who was sitting on the steps leading to the upper levels of the garden. 'Brent,' she whispered again, her voice quivering.

'What's happened?' I asked, noticing that Debbie's arms were grazed. 'Christ, what's happened?'

'I went over on my ankle. I fell down the stairs and it's so sore. I'm sorry.' I looked a little closer and could see that her left leg was extremely swollen from the knee down. 'It really hurts, Brent, it really hurts,' she said, rubbing her eyes and trying to hold back the tears.

'How long have you been sitting here?' I said, shaking my head.

'I don't know. A while I think. I thought the pain would have gone by now but it hasn't. Oh, God, what have I done? Ow, ow, ow, it hurts, Brent. It really hurts.'

'Put your arm around my shoulder. Let's get you inside.' With that that I picked Debbie up and carried her through the conservatory door and into the kitchen. 'Come on, let's have a look at you,' I said, beginning to see the full extent of her wounds. It didn't seem to me to be a minor fall.

'You think I'll be OK?' asked Debbie, who was clearly in a lot of pain but doing her best to hide it.

'I'm sure you'll be fine,' I tried to reassure her, 'but I think we need to get some ice on that leg as soon as possible and if it's no better by the morning, we're off to the hospital.'

'Oh, I hope not. I can't afford the time. I just can't.'

'So what happened? What were you doing outside in the first place?' I asked, taking a bag of peas out of the freezer.

'About seven Kristina knocked on the door, woke me up. She said that Duncan had changed his mind about going out and could I bring some drinks up to the chalet. I wasn't really awake, Brent, and I couldn't find the torch. I just slipped.'

'For fuck's sake!' I shouted. 'Can't these bastards do anything for themselves?'

'Shhh, Brent, they'll hear you,' said Debbie, who then had tears rolling down her face.

'I don't care. Selfish load of wankers. I've a good mind....'

'Leave it, please leave it. For me, please? Don't say anything.'

Just then the conservatory door opened.

'Oh, oh...' began a male guest, who walked into the kitchen, carrying a tray of empty glasses. 'Is she OK?' he said, looking quite alarmed as he stared at Debbie's leg. 'Only, the thing is, we could do with some more drinks. Duncan's asked. No hurry, just when you can,' he said, smiling awkwardly and placing the tray next to the sink.

'I'll be there in a minute,' I replied calmly, until he closed the conservatory door behind him. 'Moron.'

A quarter of an hour later I walked up to the chalet with a tray of drinks.

'I hear Debbie's hurt her leg,' said Kristina, feigning concern.

'Unfortunately, she has,' I replied, resisting the urge to say something inflammatory.

'I'm sorry to hear that. Look, tell her not to worry about the washing up,' she said helpfully. 'It can wait until tomorrow. I'm sure Duncan won't mind. Can we have some straws for the Mojitos? Thanks, Brent.'

That night Debbie sat on the bottom of our steps and pulled herself up one by one to our apartment. Eventually, she made it to the bedroom but she didn't sleep.

By the following morning there was no visible improvement in Debbie's leg and so, despite her initial protest, we drove to Grasse hospital where, after only a short wait, Debbie was put in a wheelchair and taken to radiography. Minutes later we were back in the emergency department and waiting for the results. Doctors bustled around, darting in and out of the office, clutching pieces of paper and holding X-rays up to the light until, after about an hour, a woman doctor with a warm smile approached us. Before she could say anything, Debbie pleaded, 'Please tell me it's not broken. Please tell me it's not broken.'

The doctor looked at the X-ray. 'No, it's not broken. What you have....'

'Thank God for that,' interrupted Debbie, tears of relief running down her cheeks. 'I was so worried I'd have to wear a cast.'

'Madame Tyler,' the doctor said, calmly.

'Yes.'

'Madame Tyler, you have torn ligaments.'

'Which means?'

'Which means you have to wear a cast for six weeks.'

'No, no, no. I can't do that,' Debbie sobbed. 'I haven't got time. The thing is....'

'Wait there. I send a nurse,' replied the doctor, who wasn't in any mood to be argued with.

An hour later, myself and a very disgruntled Debbie, who was hobbling along on crutches, left to go back to the villa. When we walked into the conservatory Kristina looked quite shocked. Duncan, who was staring at his laptop, just raised his eyebrows.

'Oh, Debbie, I'm sorry, you must take it easy,' Kristina said, gazing into any empty mug. 'Although, there are quite a few of us for lunch today. Would you like some help?'

'No, no, it's OK,' replied Debbie. 'Would you like another coffee?'

'Yes, please. Could one of you bring it up to the pavilion? I've got a Skype call. Byeeeeee!'

Determined not to let her temporary disability get in the way, Debbie continued to plough ahead with her plans for the party. With very little help from me, she also somehow managed to change the beds and do the washing and ironing.

Duncan, desperate to be seen as a benevolent employer, used to make a point of praising us in the presence of his guests. 'This is far too good for you lot,' was a common phrase that he used as I would collect the empty dinner plates.

One evening a few days later, as I was walking back to the kitchen, he said, 'Brent, go and choose me a nice red from the cellar, would you?'

Not knowing one bottle of wine from another I chose the dustiest-looking one from the hundreds that were on display.

'Excellent,' said Duncan as I showed him the label. I returned to the kitchen where Debbie was starting the washing up and uncorked the bottle. Feeling rather pleased with myself for having made a good choice and not wanting to make the same mistake that I had made before, I slowly began to decant the bottle of wine through a coffee filter. Moments later, Duncan burst through the door and then turned to make sure it was shut properly.

'Why's it taking so fucking long?' he snarled, clenching his teeth.

'I'm trying to make sure you don't get any sediment, Duncan.'

'What? What?' he snapped. 'That's the best bit – gives it all the flavour. Just pour the bloody stuff, will you? We haven't got all night.'

For a few seconds I stood there hardly able to believe my own ears. I looked at Debbie, who knew exactly what I was thinking.

'Don't,' she said. 'Just don't.'

Within the space of a few seconds, we could hear Duncan's exaggerated laugh ringing through the house. Who exactly was this Jekyll and Hyde character?

Chapter 29

The day of the party finally arrived and the setting could have hardly been more perfect. It was thirty-two degrees outside, there was a gentle breeze blowing and just in front of the swimming pool, Debbie had carefully chosen and decorated a long table, set for forty guests. For the first time in Duncan's house, everything matched. Sparkling wine glasses and bright, blue water goblets were placed with precision on the immaculately ironed, white tablecloth. Alongside were gleaming, white plates and shiny cutlery. Suddenly a voice boomed over the balcony above that led to Duncan's bedroom.

'Bugger me, looks like the treaty of Marseilles,' bellowed our mercurial host. 'Brent, Brent! Get some more mosquito spray up here, fast. Can't go to the party looking like the Elephant Man, can I?'

As the guests started to arrive, Debbie began to bring out plate after plate of freshly made food. Terrines, Mediterranean salads, Coronation chicken, as well as plates of thinly carved beef fillet, were carefully arranged on the serving tables. Two large silver platters, each displaying a beautifully presented salmon en croûte, were brought out, as well as many other summer dishes. With Duncan sitting at one end of the table and Kristina at the other, lunch was served. Everybody looked very happy and compliments were coming back to the kitchen as fast as I could relay them; all seemed to be going very well. One of the guests had brought a Yorkshire terrier with him that he kept by his side. As it was Sunday, which was when Jasper and Cocoa used to get a treat, and not wishing any dog to be left out, I approached the gentleman.

'Would your dog like a pig's ear?' I asked.

'Don't be ridiculous, he's Jewish!' snapped the man and scooped the terrier off the floor.

Towards the end of the meal there was a buzz at the gate and a band of merry musicians arrived that had been booked by one of Duncan's guests. They serenaded Kristina and all of the other female guests with every cheesy song that anyone could possibly think of. They devoured several plates of food, drank copious amounts of wine and disappeared after about half an hour. Later on, and with Duncan declaring the party the best one ever, his guests started to slowly trickle away, many of whom popped their heads round the kitchen door to say thank you to Debbie.

Everything seemed to be running quite smoothly in our new job until we handed in the month's expenses. Duncan summoned us to his office, where he was sitting at his desk looking very angry.

'This must be some kind of fucking record!' he shouted, looking at the spreadsheet that he maniacally began to wave in the air. 'Five grand, five fucking grand! You've spent five fucking grand in August. What are you trying to do to me?' Duncan asked, his face contorted with fury.

'Two thousand of that was on the party, Duncan,' said Debbie, who was beginning to shake with fear.

'Spent less than half that last year, less than half!' Duncan replied. 'You'd better start clearing things with me properly from now on. Off you go.'

'Five grand, five grand,' we heard him say as we left him, scratching his head in a manner reminiscent of Fagin.

'He said that it was the best party ever. He never mentioned anything about a budget. I can't believe what he's just done,' Debbie said angrily, as we walked back up to our apartment.

'You know the problem with Duncan?' I replied. 'You never know where you are with him.'

'You're right,' said Debbie. 'You've always got to be on your toes with that man.'

'Worse than that my love – it makes him bloody dangerous. Put the kettle on, we need to have a think.'

When I went down to the swimming pool the next morning Duncan was sitting having coffee with the five or six remaining house guests, which included Giles and 'Hi Honey'.

'Brent,' he said, 'you see these cushions here?' pointing to one of the very old, threadbare, stained seats that was opposite him. 'They're very expensive to replace. If you leave them out at night, they get soaked by the watering system and rot. I think we've already spent enough money this month, don't you? And another thing....'

While Duncan's guests fidgeted uncomfortably in their chairs, our mercurial boss continued to dress me down. He'd changed overnight from a man who hadn't a care in the world to someone who noticed absolutely everything, right down to the last detail. Suddenly, everything was under scrutiny. I stood there, trying to switch off from the tirade of abuse that was coming my way, while at the same time playing over in my head Debbie's words, 'Don't, Brent, just don't.'

'Thank you, Brent,' said Duncan as I put a cup of black coffee on his desk on the Tuesday morning. 'I'm flying to London tonight. I'll take myself to the airport. Kristina will be leaving at the same time. I'll be back late tomorrow. I'm going to Birmingham.'

'Oh, really?' I replied, feigning interest.

'Yes,' replied Duncan, 'I've got a lecture on crisis management.'

'Oh, that sounds interesting,' I replied with equal enthusiasm. 'Who's giving it?'

'I am of course,' he snapped. 'Who the bloody hell do you think is giving it?'

'Oh, I see.'

'And there's a programme on later about my production company. I've asked Giles to record it for me, don't let him forget,' he said, menacingly wagging his finger.

Later that evening, as I walked into the lounge I saw Giles on his mobile at the same time as fiddling with the remote control to the TV.

'I can't get this thing to work. Hang on a minute, have a word with Brent,' he said, very quickly passing me his phone as if it had got some kind of contagious disease. At the other end was a very testy Duncan.

'This is my fucking job. Television, it's what I do. I need to see that programme. You'd better find a way of recording it,' and then the phone went dead.

Unfortunately, we didn't find a way of recording his programme at all. Duncan Forbes's Sky Box had packed up, and no doubt, he was going to find someone to blame. I went in search of the instructions and guarantee, which I found. Despite Duncan's assurance that the box was almost brand new, it turned out to be almost five years' old.

'Giles and Hi Honey have asked us to join them for a Chinese takeaway tomorrow night,' I said to Debbie in our apartment, later that day.

'They're friends of Duncan's,' she replied. 'I'm not really sure that that's appropriate. I mean, what if he comes back when we're eating? I don't think he'd like it. You'd better try and put them off. Pass me the stapler, would you? I'm just printing out our new CV.

'He said he won't be back until late, so we should be all right,' I reasoned.

'Yeah, but you know what he's like – he could turn up at any minute. Wouldn't put it past him. Anyway, I think it would be a good idea to give Duncan a wide berth until he's calmed down.'

'I'll speak to Giles.'

'Thanks.'

I caught up with Giles and Hi Honey who were sitting by the pool, tapping away on their tablets.

'Look, we'll only be half an hour,' said Giles. 'He won't know we've even been here.'

'Besides,' argued Hi Honey, 'Debbie could do with a night off cooking. Come on. Give her a break. It would be nice to get to know you both. You go and get the menu, Brent and I'll phone them in the morning.'

'You speak French, then?' I asked.

'No,' she replied. 'Don't need to. They're Chinese.'

'You speak Chinese?' I said. 'That's impressive.'

'No, silly. They're Chinese so they speak English. At least, they all do back home. Don't see why it would be any different here. Right I'm off for a...' but before she could finish her sentence, there was a loud splash and Hi Honey disappeared under the water in the pool.

The only way we could have really got out of it was by offending them and we didn't want to do that.

As we chatted over our Chinese, we found out that Hi Honey had spent the past four years getting wasted with her chums on Australian beaches and that Giles had spent a similar amount of time blowing his inheritance on fast cars and having a thoroughly good time. Having met only six months previously they decided that now would be a good time for them both to settle down and were due to get married just before Christmas.

At eight o'clock and just as I was about to take my first mouthful of crispy duck, our worst fears were realised. In the distance we heard the metal gates close. Duncan was back. He marched along the side of the conservatory, gave us all a stern look and disappeared into his office.

'I think it would be better if we weren't here,' I said, picking up my plate.

'I'll go and see him,' replied Giles, a little nervously.

In the distance, I could hear the sound of flip-flops slapping along the terrace at high speed and I just caught the words, 'Wait for me honey,' as the conservatory door slammed shut. Debbie and I quickly extinguished the candles and retreated to the relative comfort and safety of our apartment. Such was Duncan's ill temper the following morning, I was glad to be tasked with taking the defective Sky Box to the local television repair shop. Despite telling us at our interview that as he lived in an old house, Duncan fully understood and, indeed, expected for things to go wrong, he didn't really accept it at all.

Although Giles and Hi Honey were going to be staying at the villa for a further ten days, I was due to take Duncan and Kristina to the airport at the weekend and we were very unlikely to see them again until Christmas. Debbie and I were looking forward to a, hopefully, stress-free couple of months.

'I'm going to take Jasper up to Gourdon,' I said to Debbie the next afternoon. 'Be good to get rid of a few cobwebs. You be all right with Giles and whatsername?'

'Yeah, of course. See you later. Have fun.'

'Bye,' I said, grabbing the car keys and the dog's lead from the kitchen work surface.

Once in the forest, we followed our normal route. Jasper would run into the forest for ten minutes, come back to check that I hadn't disappeared and then shoot off again. While I put the world to rights, Jasper would bound around the long grass and in and out of the trees, without fear of being run over.

I didn't usually check my watch but it seemed to me that on this occasion he'd been gone a fair bit longer than usual so I whistled and called his name. He didn't come back. I spent a further anxious half an hour shouting but there was still no sign of Jasper. If he could hear me, he was ignoring me – not for the first time. I walked back to the car, retracing my steps. I passed several groups of walkers that I stopped but no one had seen him. How could anyone miss a thirty-five kilo, white, golden retriever? Wherever he'd gone he hadn't come back onto the paths. A couple of hours later, I gave up the search and went back to the villa.

'The little shit,' said Debbie when I told her what had happened. 'Leave him there – I would. That dog's always trying to escape – now he's succeeded. Let him get on with it.'

'What am I going to tell Duncan?'

'Nothing, tell him nothing. What good will that do? He can't do anything from where he is.'

'I know but if I don't, Giles probably will. I'd better go back – give it one last try. I don't believe it – he's only been gone a day!'

It was getting dark, so I shone my headlights into the forest. I shouted until my voice was hoarse. I whistled but the only sound that came back belonged to a fox, barking somewhere in the distance.

'I'm going to have to phone him,' I said, toying with my cornflakes. 'Not looking forward to this one. He's going to go fifty shades of ape shit. You know that, don't you?'

'Why will he? What can he say? Look, it's not like you did it on purpose. Besides, there's no more we could have done. We've reported it to the police, we've informed APOT (*Animaux Perdus ou Trouvés*) and we've told the vet. It happens. There's nothing he can say.'

Before I made the call, we sat down for a good hour or so, rehearsing all the answers to every possible question we thought that he could possibly ask. We also decided how best to rebuff any criticisms, should there be any. I made the call.

'Told you,' I said, putting the phone down.

'He can't blame you, surely?' replied Debbie, who was wiping her hands on a tea towel.

'We hadn't thought of this one. You'll like this.'

'I'm listening.'

'What he said was, that because I'd taken him in the car, Jasper had no way of tracing his scent back. So, even if he wanted to come home, he couldn't. So yes, it is my fault apparently. Silly me.'

'So, he'd prefer that Jasper was running round these bloody dangerous roads, waiting to be run over then, would he?'

'Looks that way.'

'Give me strength! The man's a…well you know, one of those.'

Very quickly, Kristina had got involved. Within hours she'd designed an A4 poster, offering a one-thousand-euro reward. We were to print five hundred copies and put them up everywhere. She asked us to supply a list of every vet within a twenty-mile radius and wanted the phone numbers of every local police chief on the Côte D'Azur. Despite reassurance from the lady at APOT that Jasper would be very likely to reappear over the next few days, and that over sixty percent of the dogs that were reported to her as missing were either golden retrievers or Labradors, Kristina wasn't interested. She had radio advertisements planned, had reserved full pages in the local newspaper and wanted to know how much it would cost to hire a helicopter for a morning.

Just as the last poster went up, we got a phone call from a young lad who said that he had found Jasper. He'd wandered out of the woods, the same way that he had gone in and was merrily trotting along the main road towards Gourdon.

We picked him up and took him to the vets to get him checked over, where he was given a clean bill of health. Having told the vet the full story, which he found highly amusing, he advised that we either changed the dog or our job, or better still, both.

Chapter 30

Having been in London for about a week, Duncan sent an email saying that there were what he called two 'dead areas' in the garden. One was on the perimeter of the property next to the front gate and the other was down a bit of a drop to the left of the main lawn, adjacent to the swimming pool. These two pieces of land had been untouched for years and we were asked to come up with some ideas as to how we could improve them. The first and most obvious thought to me was a kitchen garden. A few days before, Debbie and I went to visit Gourdon (without Jasper this time) where, amongst other things, we saw an array of raised beds, out of which grew all manner of fruit and vegetables. This way of growing crops appealed to me for several reasons. Firstly, if sculpted correctly, it would become an extremely attractive part of the garden. Secondly, we would have fresh produce all year round and finally, as there would be no back-breaking digging involved it would be easy to maintain. Debbie suggested that as the other area was quite long and fairly narrow, it would be perfectly suited to a boules court. What could be more French? With Duncan agreeing pretty much immediately, we set about the task of looking for a builder. One after another arrived, most of whom took one look at the villa, assumed the owner had pots of money to spend and without bothering to take any measurements or provide any drawings, followed up with ridiculously priced quotes.

As we were about to admit defeat, a burly chap arrived one evening on a large motorbike. The man parked up, dismounted, offered his hand and muttered something completely unintelligible. I shrugged my shoulders. He nodded, put one thumb up and removed his helmet to reveal a bald head, a button nose and sticky out ears. I was just about to be given a quote by Mr Potato Head.

'Hello, I'm Martin,' he said, struggling to remove his leather jumpsuit, which he'd obviously bought some time before he'd discovered the local bakery. Out of a *panier* he produced a notepad and followed Debbie and I around the garden, furiously writing away. He took measurements by pacing up and down and, for once, there was no sucking air through teeth nor any puffing out of cheeks.

'Are you a qualified builder?' I asked.

'No mate, I'm a chippie but I do a bit of everything – all building work really. I ain't the cheapest but I'm not the dearest either. I'm sure you're getting other quotes but be careful, you get a lot of monkeys round here. See ya.' We left Mr Potato Head wrestling with his leathers and went back up to our apartment.

'He was OK,' I said. 'Seemed pretty efficient.'

'Let's hope his prices are as good,' replied Debbie.

A week later a reasonable quote arrived. Not only was it reasonable, we were also told that both projects should take about eight to ten weeks in total to complete, and that work could be started pretty much immediately. As it was then only the end of September, we felt that we had plenty of time to complete everything before we needed start planting in early March. By the time Duncan and Kristina were due to return for the summer the following year, the kitchen garden would be full of luscious fruit and vegetables and a splendid new boules court would be ready for Duncan and his guests to enjoy while indulging in the odd glass or two of rosé.

And so, Debbie and I began in earnest to clear the dead areas of debris. Unfortunately, it turned out that not everything was quite as dead as we had first thought; consequently, on his first day, Mr Potato Head arrived with a digger, which he used to remove the stumps of some heavy duty trees that had been long since cut down.

All day we worked tirelessly, pulling up the remains of old plants and weeds and burning as much as we could before the annual bonfire ban came into force. By the beginning of November, we had the green, weed-proof matting down and Debbie had carefully marked out with a tin of fluorescent spray paint exactly where the raised beds were to be situated. Mr Potato Head built a very impressive, trellised enclosure and, only a week later, eight tons of soil and five tons of white gravel were deposited in the car park. Debbie drew a plan of the kitchen garden and we spent many an hour deciding what should be planted in each bed as well as which fruit bushes should be growing up the trellis – we couldn't wait for spring to arrive.

The boules court was starting to take shape although, much to my annoyance and frustration, Mr Potato Head was becoming quite unreliable. With Debbie's help I was in possession of quite a meticulous work schedule and had planned much of my week around what our builder was going to do. It began one Wednesday when, as he was packing away his tools he said, 'I'll see you next week then. Either Monday afternoon or Tuesday. I'll give you a ring.'

'We've got you down to be here for the rest of the week,' I replied crossly.

'Yeah, I know but I've got a kitchen to fit. Sorry, didn't I tell ya? It's good money. Anyway look, I'll have it finished by the time your boss gets here. Bye.'

Monday and Tuesday came and went. By the time Wednesday morning arrived I was fuming. 'That bloody man...' I started, and then the phone rang. 'It's him,' I said.

'Hello, mate, it's Martin. I won't be with you today because my daughter's not very well. Won't go to school. Says she's got a sore throat. Not sure I believe her. Personally, I think she's swinging her leg....'

'She's what?' I laughed.

'You know, swinging her leg. She's faking it. You not heard that one before, Brent?'

'Can't say I have, Martin.'

'Really? I thought everyone knew that. Look, should be there tomorrow. Might be a bit late. Got to pick up some four by two on the way in. Got to go.' Still with my ear to the phone, I heard an electric saw start up in the background and then the line went dead.

'What's the excuse this time?' Debbie growled, studying her schedule and shaking her head in frustration.

'His daughter, apparently.'

'What's wrong with her?'

'She's swinging her leg.'

Debbie looked confused. 'She's what?'

'Swinging her leg. Pretending she's ill, when she isn't.' I laughed.

'Oh, for God's sake! Give me strength,' said Debbie as she grabbed the dog's lead from the hook behind our front door. 'I'm going for a walk. The man's a bloody idiot. Come on, Jasper. And you'd better behave yourself.'

Just before lunchtime on Friday Mr Potato Head arrived. He came up to our apartment and, completely oblivious to Debbie's attempt to create a frosty welcome, he smiled and said, 'Something smells good. What have we got?'

'Cold shoulder and hot tongue, I shouldn't wonder,' I replied.

'Really? Sounds nice. Never had that before.'

'Ribs!' shouted Debbie from the kitchen. 'Would you like some Martin?'

'If that's all right, Debbie. That would be lovely. Didn't have time to make my sandwiches this morning. I'll be back in a minute. Just got to go and unload the truck. Ten minutes be OK?'

'I take it you've poisoned his?' I asked Debbie, who was brushing a generous amount of tomato sauce onto some very inviting racks of pork ribs.

'What could I do? Can't bear anybody being hungry. Even him. Set the table would you?'

As we sat down, Debbie said, 'How's your daughter, Martin?'

'Great thanks,' he replied, putting down a bone that he'd just finished chewing. 'Why do ask?' he said, sucking each of his fingers individually at the same time ignoring Debbie's unsubtle hint as she placed a small pile of napkins in front of him.

'I thought she hadn't been well?'

'Don't know where you got that from. Never been better. These are delicious, Debbie,' he said, using a fingernail to extract a small piece of meat from between his teeth.

'Thank you, Martin. Would you like one of these?' asked Debbie, offering him a toothpick.

'No thanks, I'm fine,' he replied, slurping his thumb. With that, Debbie jumped up out of her chair and took her plate out to the kitchen. A few moments later she returned.

'You not hungry, Debbie? Shame, I really enjoyed it. Right, must get on,' Martin said, standing up. 'Shouldn't really have had that. That's another hour wasted. Would've been rude to have refused though, eh Debbie?' he said, smacking his lips.

'Manners of a pig,' I heard her say as she disappeared into the kitchen.

One morning, towards the end of the month, I was painting the trellis in the kitchen garden when I heard a small motorbike pull up outside.

'*Bonjour monsieur,*' said a voice belonging to the local gendarme, who popped his head over the fence. '*Très joli,*' he added, looking at the raised beds, that were waiting to be filled with soil.

'Thank you,' I replied. 'What can I do for you?'

'Would you come here for a moment please?'

As I looked over the fence I could see below that the gendarme had a small, scruffy, ferocious-looking German Shepherd cross something or other, by the collar. It had a big scarf around its neck, was frothing at the mouth and it didn't seem at all pleased to have been stopped from doing whatever it was doing before the policeman had grabbed him.

'Do you know this dog?' he asked.

'No,' I replied, 'and I'm not really sure that I want to, thanks very much,' I replied, pulling up a weed or two from the loose gravel.

'Look, I wonder if you could do me a favour?' asked the gendarme. 'The thing is, you have a car. I wondered if you would take him to the vet for me. I'd do it myself but I only have a *moto* and the people from the stray dog team can't get here for at least an hour. He seems quite friendly. *S'il vous plaît, monsieur.'*

'OK,' I replied, suspiciously looking down at the panting dog.

'Thank you, monsieur. Have a nice day,' said the gendarme, who sped down the road before I had chance to change my mind.

Reluctantly, and wondering again whether rabies still existed in France, I encouraged the dog into the back of the car, grabbed Jasper's lead and headed off to the vet.

'Bonjour, Guss,' the vet said. *'Qu'est ce que tu fais aujourd'hui?'*

'You know this dog then?'

'Absolutely, I know this dog,' replied the vet. 'I operated on him. You see this?' he continued, lifting up the scarf, which revealed a large shaved area on each side of his back. 'This,' he said, pointing at two rows of stitches about a foot long, 'was where he was attacked by two guard dogs. The problem with Guss is that he doesn't like being left alone all day, so he takes himself off for a walk. He's really quite sociable. Unfortunately, he made the mistake one day of visiting the wrong house and was attacked by two Dobermans. He's lucky to be alive. He's also lucky he hasn't been taken to the dog pound. Quite expensive to get a dog back, you know. Often, the owners don't bother to collect them.'

'I see. Tell me something.'

'If I can.'

'Compared to the rest of him, his paws are massive,' I said, looking down at four giant feet. Is that due to his breed?'

'Non, monsieur,' replied the vet. 'It is because he still young. Not very old at all.'

'How old is not very old?'

'Wait a minute, I tell you,' he replied, tapping away on his keyboard. 'He's eight months old,' he said, getting up to retrieve a piece of paper from the printer behind his desk. 'Here is his address,' he continued, patting Guss gently on the head. *'Au revoir, Guss. Au revoir monsieur.'*

Armed with his owners' address, which was only half a mile or so from our house, I made the short journey. There was no reply. As it was a weekday, I surmised that his owners were at work and took Guss back to the villa, where he played all day with Jasper. Early that evening, I returned him to his very apologetic but grateful owners and thought no more about it.

The next morning, at about eight o'clock, Debbie and I were sitting in bed with a cup of coffee and listening to the news when we heard some barking coming from outside. We'd never heard Jasper bark and it certainly wasn't Cocoa.

'I wonder...' I said to Debbie, putting on my dressing gown and picking up a clicker. As the gate partially opened, Guss came belting through wagging his tail and ran straight up our stairs and into our room. Slightly out of breath, he put his chin on the end of the bed.

'What's he doing that for?' I asked.

'I don't know. Maybe he's asking to come up.'

'Come on then,' I said. Not needing to be asked twice, Guss sprang onto the bed. 'A dog with manners. Who knew?' I struggled to say as my ear was being licked furiously.

'I think he likes you,' said Debbie, who was trying in vain to read her book. Moments later, Guss jumped down and headed towards the bedroom door. He turned his head and looked at me as if to say, 'Come on then, about time you got up.'

That morning we made three bowls of food for the dogs, although Guss couldn't have been less interested – he just wanted to have fun. He followed me around all day, stopping from time to time to have a play fight with Jasper on the grass. And when Jasper had had enough, Guss would, every now and again, biff Cocoa on the head with his paw to try and get him to join in. Cocoa, despite his blindness, had a go back.

Every evening for about a week we'd take Guss back to his owners and he'd return the following morning. Soon, he managed to bypass the gates and found his own way in. In a short space of time we became very fond of the little dog and the only time he didn't come to the villa was at the weekends. It amazed Debbie and I how quickly we'd become attached to Guss and how much we missed him. On Monday mornings we would wait, wondering if he would arrive or if his owners had managed to block him in. We weren't disappointed. Usually between eight and nine, we'd see the wire fence next to the gate feverishly moving back and forth and then a small head would pop up out of the grass. Quite often he'd run up to our apartment, jump onto our bed and fall straight asleep.

'What do you reckon that's all about?' I said to Debbie.

'I think he's a little worrier.'

'How do you mean?' I said, stroking him.

'Bet he lies awake at night, fretting about whether he can get out. By the time he gets here, he's exhausted.'

'Never thought of that. Anyway, I'm fed up with always having to take him back,' I said.

'It's their dog – surely it's up to them,' reasoned Debbie, who was reading her book. 'Don't take him back tonight – see what happens.'

That evening we waited nervously for the sound of the intercom but no one came. At nine o'clock we decided enough was enough and turned off the outside lights, shut all the curtains and locked up.

It was three days before one of the owners' sons came to get him. Recognising him immediately, Guss ran straight into the lounge and, trying to make himself as small as possible, hid behind the sofa. With his ears pinned back and shoulders drooping, Guss was bundled into the back of an old white van.

'Why do you open the gates for him?' asked Guss's owner's son accusingly.

'We don't. He finds his own way in and besides, even if we did, it has to better for him than running round these roads? It's not up to us to keep him out, it's up to you to keep him in. Goodbye.'

But they couldn't keep him in. Week after week, Guss arrived, stayed a few days and was then collected. Eventually, I went to see the owners – the situation was becoming ridiculous. I explained that if it carried on much longer, Guss would become very confused as to whom he belonged and that wouldn't be fair on the dog. Despite several assurances, it made no difference.

They just simply couldn't keep him in – Guss had become an expert in escapology. As the weeks went by, he grew very quickly and soon, instead of burrowing under his owner's fences, he was jumping them.

He loved his walks and enjoyed chasing sticks but what he loved most was an old football I'd found in the garage, which I pumped up. I stood in front of Guss and gently threw the ball just above his head. Much to my surprise, he leapt in the air and returned the ball with interest.

'Debbie, Debbie!' I shouted excitedly. 'Look, have you ever seen anything like this?'

'Can't say I have,' she replied with a huge smile running across her face.

'What do you reckon?'

'I reckon we get him signed up and then we retire,' Debbie said before going back into the kitchen.

Chapter 31

'What's wrong with this bloody thing?' I said, staring scornfully at my gleaming new strimmer.

'I don't know, you've only had it five minutes,' replied Debbie. 'Are you sure you've put it together right?'

'Of course I'm sure. How difficult can it be?'

'You and machinery my love. Just saying,' said Debbie, who was watching the strimmer nudge its way across the lawn.

'I'm taking it back. I can feel my whole skeleton shake. Can't be right, surely?'

'Make sure you empty it first though – I'm not having that again,' said Debbie, who was referring to the time when we were at Smythe's and I took the lawnmower in for repair. By the time I arrived at the workshop, the carpet in the back of our car was soaked through with petrol. Not only was it almost impossible to get out, the smell lingered for weeks, so much so that we had to drive along in all weathers with the windows open.

Heeding my wife's warning, I took the strimmer down to the end of the garden, where a couple of days previously we had had a fire. I began to empty the petrol onto the ashes, thinking that this would serve as a good base for the next one. 'Whoosh' was followed very closely by 'Aaaaaargh!' as a huge flame leapt from the ashes, setting light to the plastic petrol reservoir and very nearly me. 'Oh, fuck. Bloody hell. Fuck!' I shouted, desperately looking for a hose. 'Shit, bollocks and arseholes,' I said, as I looked in disbelief at the now black, melted plastic. Not only had I set fire to the reservoir, but swirling around my head, as if to taunt me, were small flakes of orange paint that had peeled away from the strimmer's shaft. Suddenly, the five-hundred-euro piece of machinery that I had purchased, not a week since, was beginning to look as though it would be more at home on a skip. Although it cost me a hundred and fifty euros to put right, I consoled myself that, at least, I wasn't harnessed to the strimmer at the time, it could have been far worse. My biggest mistake was telling Mr Potato Head about my unfortunate mishap, or gross stupidity as Debbie, probably more accurately, had put it. 'Had any nice fires recently?' were, more often than not, Mr Potato Head's first words as he walked through the door.

'What are we going to tell Duncan about Guss?' asked Debbie, who was chopping some leeks. 'He's coming for Christmas in a couple of weeks and we haven't told him. Not exactly easy to miss is he?' she said, tossing some butter into a pan.

'There are already two dogs here – I can't believe that he's going to think that one more's going to make any difference. Anyway, he's here more often than he's with his owners, why don't we see if we can adopt him?'

'Well yes, it's an idea but what if Duncan doesn't like it?'

'I think he'll like it even less if a stray dog keeps turning up unannounced, don't you? Come on,' I said, looking at Guss, who was curled up on the sofa. 'Best take you back. See what they say. Bye.'

Twenty minutes later, I returned to the villa.

'Unfortunately not,' I said, as I threw Guss's lead on the office desk.

'What did they say?' asked Debbie.

'He's quite happy to let Guss go but she isn't. She said that the old dog's not much use these days and she's really worried about security, so they need Guss. That was it really.'

'That's a shame,' replied Debbie, 'but do you think I should send some photos to Duncan anyway, in case Guss comes back when they're here?'

'Can't do any harm.'

By the next morning, Duncan had replied.

'He's really keen to meet him,' said Debbie. 'I sent him a few pictures, including the one of him and Jasper rolling about on the lawn. He loved them.'

'That's something at least. He might not be so bad....'

'Except,' Debbie interrupted.

'Uh, oh.'

'Except, that he says he and Kristina were going to start looking for a new dog soon, for when Cocoa goes, and Guss sounds like the perfect replacement. They can't wait to meet him. Kristina, apparently, has already fallen in love with him and you know how pushy she can be.'

'They think they're going to adopt Guss do they? Over my dead body,' I said. 'He's only here because of us. He doesn't know Duncan or Kristina from a bar of soap. Cheeky bastards.'

'I know, calm down. His owners haven't agreed to let him go to anyone anyway. They told you that yesterday.'

'Yeah, but he's our dog – apart from the paperwork that is.'

'And that, my love, is unfortunately what counts,' said Debbie sadly.

I'd just picked up Duncan and Kristina, who'd arrived for their Christmas break, when Kristina said enthusiastically, 'Can't wait to meet Guss, he looks so adorable. Duncan and I have talked about nothing else,' she went on, turning towards me and smiling. 'Oh, I really want him. He could be perfect.'

'I'm sure we can find a way,' replied Duncan.

'You'll have to get behind me in the queue,' I chipped in from the back seat of the BMW. There was not just no reply – the smile that had, up until now, been written all over Duncan's face quickly turned to stone.

As we drove through the gates, the dogs came to greet the car.

'If you're going to become part of our family, you'll have to get out of that habit Guss,' said Kristina, wagging her finger at Guss, who was jumping up at her with excitement.

'Hello, my boy,' boomed Duncan, who was equally delighted to see him. 'We'll have something to eat and then Kristina and I will take you for a walk. Chance to do a bit of bonding,' he said, at the same time slapping Guss on the side. 'Brent, get the bags. Come on, Guss.'

I took Guss back to his owners the following afternoon to get him out of the way. I thought that he was confused enough already without Duncan and Kristina's input. This, however, didn't put Kristina off as she told Debbie, over coffee, that one of her work colleagues was fluent in French and was in the process of drafting a letter to Guss's owners, begging them to sell him to her.

'Help! Help!' cried a voice that I recognised to be Kristina's, coming from the main road below the rose bed. As I looked over, she was trying to put herself between Jasper and a stray Staffordshire terrier.

'What's going on?' screamed Duncan, who had heard the commotion and was hurrying towards the noise. Running past the garage I grabbed a broom handle and Cocoa's lead. As I sprinted down the road, out of the corner of my eye I caught Duncan, who was glaring demonically over the wall.

'Grab that fucking dog, Brent. Just grab it!' he shouted but by the time I arrived the dogs had given up growling at each other – the fight had sounded a lot more malicious than it actually was. Jasper was wagging his tail and the other dog was now sniffing the grass, oblivious to the mayhem that it had caused.

'You OK, Kristina?' I said as we started to walk back up the hill.

'Yes, fine thanks,' she replied. 'I didn't see it at first. Came out of nowhere. It was a bit of a shock, that's all. Frightened the life out of me. Thanks for coming.'

'You're wel....'

'Brent, will you grab that bloody dog!' screamed Duncan. 'We need to get it checked for rabies. Put the fucking lead on it, will you!'

As we walked through the gates, with the Staffordshire terrier now on a lead, Duncan noticed a tiny scratch on Kristina's index finger. 'How did that happen?' he asked, looking very concerned.

'I'm not sure,' replied Kristina. 'Might have been the dog. Might have been Jasper. Could've been a bush for all I know,' she said dismissively.

Duncan, still furious, fumed, 'Have you called the police, Brent?'

'No, not yet.'

'Why not?'

'I haven't got my phone.'

'Why not?'

'I was too busy trying to rescue Kristina.'

'She could have been killed. It's happened before you know,' he said, wagging his finger in front of my nose.

'Kristina has been killed before? Is that right, Kristina?'

Duncan stormed off, only to return five minutes later to ask again if I'd phoned the police.

'No,' I replied.

'I've already asked ten times.'

'Yes, all in the last five minutes,' I said, firmly. 'I've locked the dog in the laundry room – he can't get out,' although it has to be said that he was trying.

It occurred to me that it was, perhaps, not the first time the dog had been in this situation because, when he wasn't lunging at the laundry room door, he was pulling down the door handle.

Later that afternoon, two very calm police dog handlers came to take the Staffordshire terrier away. The panic was now over for everyone except Duncan, who was convinced that Kristina was shortly going to die of rabies and there would to be no doubt whatsoever as to who would be to blame.

Fortunately for us, Duncan and Kristina had decided to spend Christmas and the New Year with their chums in Saint Tropez so we would only be spending a further two days with them at the villa.

Somehow, late in the afternoon on Christmas Day, Guss managed to escape from his owners and joined us for the festivities – and rather a lot of turkey.

'Could learn a lot from that dog,' I said to Debbie.

'How do you mean?'

'Well, look at him. He doesn't like the life that he's got,' I said, biting into a drumstick and straightening up my party hat. 'He's not happy with the way things are so he's trying to do something about it. This stuffing's nice.'

'Hmmm,' replied Debbie. 'Is this your, not so subtle, way of telling me that you think we should be looking for a new job?'

'Hadn't really thought of it like that but now you come to mention it....'

'It's Christmas Day,' interrupted Debbie. 'Do you mind if we leave this until tomorrow? Or better still until Dunan and Kristina have gone back? Anyway, your turn to do the top-ups. I don't think I can move.'

Chapter 32

'Have you seen this?' Debbie said, waving at me to come and join her at the computer. 'Look, Springsteen's playing in Montpellier in June – he's got a new album out. Can only be two or three hours away, what do you reckon?'

'I reckon if we can afford it, we go. What say you?'

'We can afford it all right – provided you promise not to set fire to any more strimmers, that is!' Debbie laughed.

'Whose side are you on?' I replied, looking quizzically at the screen. 'Give me the number, I'll phone them now,' I said, picking up the handset.

'You don't, apparently,' replied Debbie. 'You get them from your local supermarket.'

'So, how does that work then? Two pints of milk and a ticket to Springsteen please?'

'Some of the bigger shops have got *billeteries*. You know, ticket offices, and there's one about twenty minutes away. Suggest we go now. Where's the keys?' asked Debbie, who was already putting her boots on. 'Come on,' she said, reaching for her coat. 'We'd better get out of here before they're all gone. Grab the bin on the way out would you?'

By the time I'd got down the stairs, the car was in the middle of the courtyard with the engine revving. Debbie put her foot down and before we knew it were at the supermarket entrance.

As we approached the welcome desk there was large black panel, very similar to an old American billboard, that listed every act playing in France from Johnny Hallyday to the local string quartet. There was quite a queue and once we got to the front a very helpful lady shop assistant showed us a plan of the venue and asked us where we would like to sit. Moments later two glossy tickets had been printed out. It couldn't have been simpler – none of the endless, frustrating engaged signals that we'd been used to back home.

Although we weren't actively looking for another job, by February we were starting to be contacted by various agencies and thought that, at least, we should go for some interviews, even if it was just to confirm that maybe we weren't as badly off as we thought. Since arriving in France, we'd become quite adept at separating the mad from the not quite so mad and found ourselves looking for the telltale signs and with Duncan and Kristina not due back at the villa until July, we were in no desperate rush to leave where we were.

'This one looks all right,' I said, 'and not too far away. It's in Biot.'

Within a week of sending off our CV we found ourselves sitting in a bistro on a pretty town square and waiting for our prospective employers to arrive.

'Oh, I can't possibly stay here,' whined Mrs Pilkington on arrival, wiping her brow and pointing to a table a good thirty feet away. 'Look,' she said, 'there are people smoking. This simply won't do. And, look over there darling,' she said to her husband, 'there's a screaming child. Let's go inside.'

Once inside the small bistro, Mr Pilkington talked to me about the garden while the extremely flighty Mrs Pilkington spoke to Debbie about the house. At the end of the conversation the Pilkingtons seeming quite happy and it was agreed that we'd follow them back to their villa to have a look round. With our car being parked further down the road than theirs we agreed to wait for them to pass and then follow them. As I looked in my rear view mirror, instead of passing us, Mr Pilkington screeched to a halt inches from our bumper. He jumped out, ran up to the passenger side door and started banging on the window, which Debbie wound down before he had chance to break it. Slightly out of breath and looking extremely stressed, Pilkington began,

'My wife tells me you don't like cleaning, what have you got to say to that? Come on, what have you got to say to that then? Well?'

Debbie, who was momentarily lost for words, replied, 'What I said was....'

'Yes, yes. Get on with it.'

'What I said was, that cleaning wasn't my favourite part of the job but why would it be? I'm a trained chef – I prefer cooking. That's all I meant.'

'That's all you meant? That's all you meant?' said Pilkington, quite exasperated and gesturing to his wife, who was still sitting in the car behind. He shrugged his shoulders, shook his head and then said, 'I think we all need to think about this. Yes, we definitely need to think about this. No need to follow us back. Good day to you,' and off he scuttled back to his car. Seconds later there was a wheel spin and off the Pilkingtons shot down the road in their bright-orange mini.

It was late February when Mr Potato Head eventually drove through the gates of the villa in a flatbed lorry, on top of which was a mountain of fine gravel. His original estimate of completing the job in eight to twelve weeks had become twenty-two and had we not chased him, almost on a daily basis, the project would have taken a good deal longer.

'Just got to barrow it down there and wacker plate it in,' he said, pointing towards the boules court. 'Looks good, doesn't it? Here's my invoice by the way,' he added, reaching for a coffee-stained piece of paper on the dashboard. 'Any chance you could get it paid today? Only I just got my tax bill. Christ knows how I'm going to pay it,' he said before jumping into the cab.

'Fat chance,' was Debbie's response, who put the invoice straight to the bottom of the pile of bills that were waiting to be paid. 'This should have been completed a couple of months ago,' she said, looking at her schedule, which she'd taped to the wall above the desk. 'What makes him think we owe him any favours? Cheeky bastard.' 'To be fair,' I said with a wry smile, 'he did say when we first met him that there were a lot of monkeys round here.'

'Didn't mention that he was chief ape though, did he?' replied Debbie, who was going through the post.

By March and the garden was coming back to life after a very wet winter. Debbie was loving the kitchen garden and would return from the local garden centre armed with young courgettes, cucumbers, cauliflowers, several varieties of tomato, cabbages, lettuces and sweetcorn, which she would place alongside each bed, ready for us to plant. The trellises were crammed along the edges with blueberry, raspberry, gooseberry and redcurrant bushes. It wasn't long before there was an abundance of ripe fruit and vegetables, ready for eating.

I was just as happy in the garden and was weeding the rose bed one morning when I noticed something wriggling along the ground near a pine tree. Thinking it to be an extremely long but thin snake, I moved back very, very slowly. As I broke into a cold sweat, I could see that the tail of whatever it was, was still coming down the pine tree. After a short while, it became clear that this was actually a long line of very cute-looking furry caterpillars. With my curiosity getting the better of me, and feeling quite relieved that it was nothing sinister after all I went upstairs where I put the kettle on, sat down and typed into Google the words *caterpillar, pine* and *France*.

I turned white. Jumping out of my chair, I rushed into the kitchen and snatched Debbie's blow torch out of the kitchen drawer. I ran down the stairs as fast as my legs would carry me, grabbed Jasper by the collar and threw him into the conservatory just in time to stop him from putting his nose into the middle of the long line. What I had seen, and quickly burned, was a train of processionary pine caterpillars, which can be extremely dangerous to cats and dogs. If they feel threatened, the caterpillars fire out barbed hairs that can penetrate an animal's tongue. If not treated immediately, amputation of the tongue or, worse still, death can follow quite quickly. Jasper had been lucky.

The day of the concert had finally arrived. We took Jasper and Cocoa to very nice kennels and, after much deliberation over what to do with Guss, the three of us headed along the A8 towards Montpellier. Even if we had wanted to, without his paperwork we couldn't leave him with the other two dogs and we figured that if we took Guss back to his owners and he couldn't find us the next day, he'd be very confused and upset. More importantly, so would we.

'Hey look, there it is,' said Debbie, as we drove past the Park & Suites Arena, on our way to the hotel. 'We'll be there in a couple of hours. Excited?'

'You bet,' I replied, still not quite believing that Bruce Springsteen was going to be playing in our neck of the woods. I'd been a huge fan of his for many years and was really looking forward to seeing what the new album, *Wrecking Ball*, was all about.

Our hotel was a good twenty minutes' drive away and thinking it likely that we'd struggle to find a parking space at the arena, we treated ourselves to a taxi. Before leaving, we spoke to an extremely affable night shift manager who volunteered to pop in on Guss at hourly intervals.

Upon arrival at the venue, our suspicions proved to be correct – the car park was gridlocked. Typically, there were no marshals and nothing was moving and so the French resorted to doing what they do best – they sat there honking their horns.

Once inside the arena, we stood in the queue at the bar for a while. We ordered some drinks and although I hadn't drunk much at all, due to my excitement, I must have disappeared to the toilet at least five times before we took our seats. At eight o'clock the lights in the auditorium went down and a voice announced,

'Ladies and gentlemen, *Mesdames et messieurs*, Bruce Springsteen!'

He walked out on stage to huge applause and stood there for a moment or two, raising his guitar to the audience in his trademark fashion. What then happened took me completely by surprise, and to this day I can't really explain it but I was glad that the auditorium, apart from the stage, was completely dark. Without warning, my face just crumpled up with emotion. I turned towards Debbie, who was barely visible in the darkness. Fortunately, she was looking straight ahead and enjoying herself far too much to notice what had happened to me. Was I fifty or fifteen? I thought, wiping a tear from my eye. Just as I thought my emotions were in check, Bruce sang *Jack of all Trades*, a song all about having to reinvent yourself, not through choice but necessity. No song could have been more poignant, nor could have described so accurately what Debbie and I had been through and, once again, I was floored. Up until then I'd never really tried to analyse what we'd been through – we just got on with it and yet, somehow, Bruce Springsteen managed to articulate so much of what I was feeling in one song.

Having cheered up considerably by the end of the three-hour concert, we joined the other fourteen thousand spectators who were milling about in the car park. We were hoping to get a cab but there wasn't one to be seen anywhere, let alone had, so we crossed the road and joined the queue at the bus stop.

After an hour's wait and with the temperature beginning to drop quite rapidly we were quite relieved to see the bus arrive. Ten minutes into the journey and just as Debbie and I had started to get warm and comfortable, the driver announced that the next stop was going to be the last, leaving us with a good two mile walk back to our hotel. What should have been a twenty-minute journey by car turned into a two-hour trek. When we eventually arrived at the hotel we noticed that Guss was curled up on the floor next to the night shift manager.

'I hope you don't mind,' he said, 'but as soon as you left, he started barking, so I brought him down with me. He's been very good company, although he does think it's him and not me who should be greeting the guests. Have a good evening monsieur, dame,' he said, passing us our room keys. 'Goodnight, Guss.'

Chapter 33

Duncan wrote to us saying that he was going to be coming down for a week with Kristina at the end of June and after that we wouldn't be seeing them again until August. By the time they arrived, the house was sparkling clean and the garden was a picture. The boules court, which Duncan had not seen, had been rolled, swept and weeded and a shiny new set of boules was waiting to be played with.

Just before I had to leave to go to the airport I gave the outdoor gym a quick sweep and ran a duster over the exercise bikes and also the television. When I greeted Duncan he was uncharacteristically quiet. He wasn't his usual blustering self, hardly saying a word on the way back to the villa. Once there, he had dinner and almost immediately disappeared up to his room with Kristina.

'How's Duncan this morning?' I asked Debbie, as I returned from the shop with the morning papers.

'He was all right at breakfast. I saw him looking at the kitchen garden – I think you'll have earned some brownie points there,' she said.

'That'll make a change,' I replied, heading towards the door that led to Duncan's office.

'Your papers,' I said, putting them on the desk where he was sitting.

There was no response. Duncan continued to type away on his computer without saying a word. This was a side that I hadn't seen before. I'd become used, though not immune, to Duncan's sudden outbursts of temper – but silence? This had become a whole new ball game, for reasons that I neither knew nor understood.

So, I carried on with my job in the garden and made a point of casually crossing Duncan's path, whenever I saw him, in the hope that he might strike up a conversation about some of the changes that had been made but he said nothing. Surely he'd noticed? Of course he'd noticed – Debbie had seen him.

'Good morning, Kristina,' I said, as I opened the door to the conservatory.

'Good morning, Brent,' she said, toying with her cornflakes. 'Oh, Brent?'

'Yes.'

'I wonder if you could do me a favour?' she said. 'Can you get me the address of Guss's owners please? Duncan's going to offer them five hundred euros,' she added, slurping the milk from her spoon. 'Exciting isn't it? Oh, and I'm really looking forward to seeing the kitchen garden and....'

'They don't want to sell Guss,' I interrupted. 'I asked last week.'

'Look, we'll send the letter and if they still don't want to sell him, Duncan and I are going to go round there. We can be very persuasive you know. Must get on. Byeeeeee,' she said before returning to her laptop.

As I left Kristina, I could feel the anger running through my veins. I'd just got outside when I heard Duncan's very distinctive voice shouting from one of the upper levels.

'Brent! Brent!' he bellowed. As I approached the gym, Duncan was standing by one of the bikes with his hands on his hips and looking very unhappy. 'These machines are fucking filthy,' he growled. 'Look at them!'

'They are not filthy, Duncan,' I retaliated. I was in no mood to tolerate any more of his puerile tantrums, especially in light of what I'd just been told by Kristina. 'They were dusted yesterday and the floor was swept,' I snapped.

'Look, cobwebs on that one, and in the roof,' Duncan replied, wagging his finger furiously in the air.

'It's an outdoor gym, what do you expect?'

'What do I expect? What do I expect?' he snarled in a fit of rage. 'What I expect is for you to come back here with the power washer and sort them out. That's what I expect,' he snapped and stormed off.

'No wonder all of his gym equipment is bloody rusty,' I said to Debbie, who was upstairs in our apartment doing some paperwork. 'He has the bloody stuff hosed down. The man's a twat. Just had a go at me about the state of the gym. The garden and the boules court? Not a word. He's incredible.'

'You said you'd cleaned it yesterday,' replied Debbie.

'I did but I missed a few cobwebs.'

'I don't know what you've done to upset him my love but he really doesn't like you.'

'The feeling's mutual, on that, at least,' I said, putting the kettle on. 'I'm telling you though, if he starts on me again we're out of here. I don't care who he is.'

'You're shaking.'

'I know. Have we got any Calms?'

'In the cupboard, I'll get you some. Have your coffee and then just try and keep out of his way. I'll have a word with Kristina – try and find out what's up with him. Are you sure you haven't said anything?'

'He hasn't said two words to me since he's been here. Well, not until just now, that is. He's got a screw loose that fella, I'm telling you. Thanks,' I said as Debbie passed me a couple of tablets. 'Right, best get back.'

As I dragged the power washer up the several flights of stairs, I could see in the distance that Duncan was waiting for me.

'You don't look very happy,' he said, screwing his beady little eyes up. Surely, he wasn't trying to goad me again? He watched as I attached the hose and plugged the machine in at the mains. Just as I was about to hit the 'on' switch, Duncan, with his hands on his hips, looked up at the roof and said, 'Disgusting, fucking disgusting.'

Without saying a word, I turned on the power washer, aimed, and blasted Duncan from head to foot. I switched it off and headed back to our apartment.

I explained briefly what had just happened, which prompted Debbie to get straight on the computer. Within the space of a few minutes, our letter of resignation was on Duncan's desk.

After lunch, someone knocked on our door.

'Duncan would like to see you at five o'clock to discuss your resignation,' said a sheepish Kristina, who was awkwardly twiddling with her hair.

'I'm sorry this has happened, Kristina,' replied Debbie. 'But he can't carry on treating us like this – we're not here to be bullied,' she added.

'I know, I'm sorry. He's having a tough time in London at the moment. It's difficult for him. He's got a lot on his mind....'

'So he comes down here and takes it out on us,' I interrupted. 'That's nice.'

'Five o'clock then?' said Kristina, who wasn't about to get involved any more than she had to.

As requested, Debbie and I stood in front of Duncan like a couple of naughty children who had been summoned to the headmaster's study. He shuffled a few pieces of paper on his desk and said without looking at us,

'I'll be here on Monday twenty-ninth July. Brent can pick me up from the airport. You will be gone by lunchtime on Tuesday the thirtieth, when I will give you your final pay cheque and you can give me the keys. Now, Kristina has something to say to you. She's working in the chalet – you can see her there. Shut the door behind you. Oh, and Brent, you can leave the garden furniture where it is – it's unlikely we'll be here for the summer.'

'Wow that was quick,' I said as we climbed up to the top level of the garden. 'He doesn't mince his words, does he?'

'No, he doesn't,' Debbie said, as we approached the chalet door. 'Unlikely they'll be coming for the summer? Can't see that, can you? Bet he's got it worked out already.'

'Really?'

'Really. There's no way that Duncan won't be coming here for the summer. I bet you he's got someone in place already. 'The thing is, Brent,' said Kristina, 'we've noticed that you've become very attached to Cocoa, and Duncan and I have been talking about him. He's quite old now and he has no quality of life. He can't see and with his arthritis he can't walk very far and to be honest it's only his heart pills that are keeping him alive – poor thing. Duncan's had him since he was a puppy and really can't face doing it so would you mind, when we're gone, taking him to the vets and you know, well, you know?' she said, picking up her hand mirror. 'Oh, God, have you seen the state of my makeup? I've got a conference call in five minutes. Bloody hell. Could I have some more coffee in about ten minutes please? Byeeeeee.'

'Not on my watch,' I said angrily to Debbie. 'There's nothing wrong with that dog. Not in my eyes anyway.'

'You're not going to take him to the vet?'

'Oh, I'll take him, all right. I'll take him. Trust me, Duncan's met his match on this one.'

We hardly saw or spoke to Duncan or Kristina until the day they left, but once they'd gone, I did exactly as I was asked and took Cocoa to the vet.

'In my opinion, there's nothing majorly wrong with this dog,' I said. 'I would say that there's a good few years left in him yet.'

'So why are you here?' asked the vet.

I sighed. 'Because his owner wants him put to sleep.'

'And, I take it, you don't?'

'No.'

'Well, let's see,' he said thoughtfully. 'The thing is, there are rules. I can't just end a dog's life because someone asks me to. There are four criteria that I have to consider before putting a dog down. For me to even consider carrying out the process, Cocoa must meet at least two of them.'

'And those criteria are?'

'Is he eating?'

'Like a horse,' I replied.

'Is he mobile?'

'He manages to find his way up to our apartment most nights and that's no mean feat.'

'Does he recognise you?'

'Yes, especially at meal times,' I said cheerily, thinking this was going very well.

'And is he in any pain?'

'Not that I'm aware of.'

'Then, I'm not prepared to put Cocoa down.'

'Brilliant!' I said, giving the vet a bear hug, which he clearly wasn't expecting. 'Would you put something in writing for me to that effect?'

'Of course,' he said, readjusting his collar following my over-exuberance. 'You see, Monsieur Tyler, if we buried everyone who was not convenient to us, there would be, quite simply, more people below the ground than above it. I would say he's still got a couple more years left in him, if he's looked after properly. Good day.'

With Guss still arriving on a regular basis and only a day or two to go before Duncan and Kristina were due to return, I thought I'd go and see Guss's owners one last time.

An hour or so later, I was back at the villa.

'We've got him! We've got him!' I shouted triumphantly, waving a red, plastic wallet in the air.

'We've got who?' Debbie asked.

'Guss, who do you think? Look, this is his paperwork. Lists all of his injections – everything that he's ever had done to him. Even got his birthday! I can't believe it – where's the Champagne?' I yelled.

'No way!' said Debbie, laughing.

'Way!' I shouted, bouncing around the room.

'Just calm down and tell me what happened.'

'I went to see his owners and told them that we were leaving, so we could no longer guarantee him a warm welcome if he came to visit.

'And what did they say to that?'

'Nothing to start with. They asked me to hang on, while they went inside for a chat. I was so nervous.'

'And then?'

'And then, after what felt like forever they came out and agreed that, as they couldn't keep him in, he was better off with us. They were obviously disappointed but what could they do?'

'I hope you offered to pay something for him,' said Debbie.

'All they want is the three hundred euros that they had to fork out for his operation when he was attacked by the other dogs. If it wasn't for that, we could have had him for nothing.'

'That's very fair. Did you tell him about Duncan wanting him?'

'Yeah, they went bloody mad. They said they'd never heard of him and why would they let Guss be adopted by someone who was hardly ever there? They might not be able to keep him in but they've still got Guss's welfare at heart. I can't tell you exactly what they said but it translates roughly to bloody cheek.'

'So that's it then, we've got him?'

'Sure is. Right, I'm off to the cashpoint. Come on, Guss.' It was our final day at the villa and, for one last time, we sat opposite Duncan at the conservatory table. We passed over all of the letters and bills that had arrived since his last visit. I had Cocoa's report in my hand, which I began to translate. For a few moments he said nothing but as soon as Duncan could see which way the vet's findings were going, he snatched the piece of paper out of my hand, put it on the pile in front of him and said that Kristina would look at it later.

'One final thing,' Duncan said. 'You'd better give me the address of Guss's owners. Kristina and I are going there this afternoon.'

'We are his owners,' I replied with a broad grin. 'We bought him yesterday.'

Duncan, who had turned a brighter shade of pink, got up from his seat, brushed past us and said, 'I'll open the gates for you on my way to the gym.' With our car packed and Guss happily sitting on the back seat we left. As we turned right out of the gates we noticed an old car parked in the layby opposite. We wouldn't normally have taken any notice but as we passed, the two occupants, somewhat oddly, ducked down in front of the dashboard. 'That was Chloe and Michael,' I said. 'I know.'

261

We'd found a small cottage in Le Rouret, a little village just outside Grasse, where we could stay rent-free for a few weeks in exchange for doing a bit of housework as well as carrying out the odd job or two. There was a sizeable garden, a swimming pool and a television that broadcast all of the UK free channels, which pleased Debbie and I as it meant that we could watch the London Olympics. There were plenty of nice walks for Guss, a local bar-cum-*tabac* and a few nice restaurants close by.

The only problem with the village was that there had been a recent spate of burglaries. According to the barman, every time you closed your windows, there was a good chance you would catch someone's fingers in it! Holidaymakers, especially the British, had unwittingly become a particular target. Opportunist thieves would look out for rental cars or UK number plates and then wait for the right moment. It was quite usual for families, as soon as they arrived, to quickly unpack, fling open the windows and shutters and head straight for the pool, which was often thirty metres or so away. Unfortunately, by the time they returned from their swim they'd find that their wallets, purses, laptops, phones and jewellery had all disappeared and there was nothing the police could do – nobody had seen a thing.

So, Debbie and I took our cue from the French and kept the shutters closed as long as we were outside. Far from being like an oven inside the villa, without the sun beating through the windows, it was really very cool. We spent many a happy hour sitting under the shade of a plane tree, playing scrabble or cards while Guss got great delight in chasing the stray cats, of which there were plenty, for the first few days at least. One afternoon, Guss, who was beside the pool, started barking and wagging his tail. I came out through the kitchen door to see what all the fuss was about. At first, I couldn't see anything but as I looked closer, floating in the middle of the pool was a baby hedgehog that was struggling. I used the pool net to scoop him up and put him down on the paving. Guss went down on all fours, where he stayed nose to nose with the hedgehog.

'Come and look at this,' I said to Debbie, who was hanging out some washing. 'Guss's new best pal.'

'I don't believe it,' she said, looking at Guss, who was motionless apart from a wagging tail. He stayed there for a good half an hour until the hedgehog, fully recovered, went scuttling off into the sanctuary of the bushes.

'That was Mandy from the agency,' said Debbie as I was crunching into a piece of toast. 'She's got us an interview in La Garde-Freinet.'

'That's nice. Never heard of it.'

'Me neither,' replied Debbie, who was looking on the computer for directions. 'Apparently it's just above Saint Tropez and is, hang on a minute, about an hour and a half from here, according to the AA.'

'When is it?'

'Tomorrow.'

'And they want someone to start when?'

'As soon as. She said that that the new owner bought the property about six months ago and the guardians have already left but there is a management couple, Sally and Michel who come in most days. Not sure I like the sound of that but they do need someone straightaway.'

'Why so?'

'You'll like this – there's a film shoot starting in September.'

'Ooh, sounds interesting,' my interest awakened all of a sudden. 'Anyone famous?'

'No idea, didn't ask.'

'You didn't ask? What do you mean, you didn't ask? By this time next year....'

'I'm off to the shops. See you later,' replied Debbie, who clearly had no interest in my newly found aspiration to become an actor.

'This is a bit remote,' I said as we bumbled along some windy roads that meandered through the middle of a dense forest. 'Looks like real tractor country.'

We drove through the two imposing stone pillars that guarded the château and carried on down an unpaved track for about half a mile, passing a small cottage on our right hand side. We parked, let Guss out and walked towards the very impressive stone fountain that was in the middle of a manicured lawn just in front of the château. We were, we thought, suitably attired in casual shirts, three-quarter-length trousers and summer shoes until we saw the lady who came to greet us. Dressed in a full-length skirt, formal blouse and a brooch, she wouldn't have been out of place in a lavish costume drama.

'Hello, I'm Sally,' said the dark-haired woman in her fifties. 'Mr Johns will be with you in a minute,' she continued, leading us to a cast iron table and chairs on the front terrace. 'Sit yourselves down. Would you like a coffee?' she asked in a heavy Yorkshire accent. 'Excellent, won't be a minute. Aren't you lovely?' she said, patting Guss on the head before going back into the villa.

'This is beautiful,' I said, taking in our elegant surroundings.

'Sure is,' replied Debbie.

'Are you sure we're in the right place?'

'How do you mean?' asked Debbie.

'Well, this is more like a stately home.' I laughed. 'Looks like we've come dressed for the beach.'

To the right of the huge, pale-blue shuttered château was an undulating lawn, on which a miniature train track had been built. There was a station, a station master, a platform and twenty or so waiting passengers but no train – it so reminded me of home. To our left was a croquet lawn surrounded by shoulder-high earthenware urns and, from where we were sitting, we could see a meadow that stretched for a mile or two, beyond which there was a large forest.

I was just beginning to fully relax in the morning sunshine when a jolly-looking chap with long hair and a floral shirt appeared from the front of the house.

'Hello, I'm Adrian. Glorious isn't it?' he said, offering his hand.

For a good hour, in between taking phone calls, he told us the story of the property, how it had once been owned by a famous French actress and more latterly by a renowned interior designer. He went on to tell us how he felt that he didn't really own the property at all – he was just the custodian. This, we were to find out later, was apparently not quite how his wife had seen it. She was more concerned that the estate had cost in excess of six million euros and our jovial host hadn't bothered to tell her about the purchase until two months after he'd bought it.

Thanking us very much for our time and keen to know when we could start, he left it to Sally to show us the rest of the property. Once inside the house, it became clear that nothing had been spent on the upkeep for a very long time. Paint peeled away from the walls, floor tiles were cracked, banisters wobbled and the kitchen was from a bygone age. On our tour, Sally told us that the previous owners had run out of money but was hopeful that Mr Johns would be able to transform the place to its former glory.

Once back outside, Sally took us through an archway at the end of the croquet lawn where there were some steps leading down to a very long swimming pool that had a wooden footbridge going across it. Beyond the pool we saw an olive grove and although there was no orchard as such, around the grounds there was an abundance of fig, cherry, pear and apple trees. There was a small greenhouse that housed a few potted citrus trees that had been taken in for protection against the winter frost.

'I used to live here with my husband, François,' mused Sally, who was showing us around an empty apartment a little way up the drive. 'We brought our kids up here. Got some great memories.'

'So, why did you leave?' asked Debbie.

'The trouble was, François would never leave the place – still can't really,' Sally said disappointedly. 'He'd find something to do from the minute he got up 'til the minute he went to bed. He was married to the job, not me. In the end, I had to persuade him to get us a place in the village, so we could spend some time together. That's why I'm so glad you're here, I think he's addicted to the place,' she said. 'He was on his own here before I met him. There was no decoration in the apartment. He used to have a pitchfork above the door that he slung a blanket over – that was it. That and a bed. Took me a long time to change him. He's a proper country lad, is François. You'll meet him next time, that's if you start. You are going to start aren't you?' she nodded eagerly.

We hadn't got to the top of the drive before Debbie said, 'I don't like it. It's way too remote. Not only that, after Christmas I reckon it's going to become a building site. If they want to rent it out, they can't leave it looking like that. And as for that apartment, it's so cold and depressing. Did you see all the damp running down the wall? It's worse than Duncan's and that's saying something,' she said as we turned onto the main road.

'I know but what choice do we have? It's September. Where else are we going to get something this time of year? Money's not going to last forever. Anyway, might be fun being on a film set. Bet we'll meet all sorts of interesting characters.'

'I suppose. It's just so not us, that's all. And, I hate the thought of having to work for managers. I'm not a team player – you know that. Pass me the water, would you?'

Early one Sunday morning in October we said goodbye to Le Rouret and, a couple of hours later, were heading back down the long drive in La Garde-Freinet to start our new job. About half way down I noticed in the rear view mirror that an old, white pick-up truck was coming up quite quickly behind us. Very soon, I lost sight of it as a cloud of dust that the wheel-spinning idiot behind us had created covered the back of our car. The tune *Duelling Banjos* started playing in my head. A little further on, there was an electric fence that straddled the driveway. A sullen-faced man, who I presumed to be François, got out of the truck, walked past us without looking in our window and unhooked the three cables.

As we pulled up outside our new apartment, Sally leapt out of the truck's passenger seat.

'You made it then? So glad you're here. Come on, François, come and say hello to Brent and Debbie.'

Reluctantly, and with no change of expression, he jumped out the truck, looked at us and nodded his head. As quickly as he had got out, he got back in and sped off, narrowly missing Guss, who was busy investigating all the new smells. Debbie and I looked at each other, not knowing at all what to make of this.

'Don't worry about François, he's not upset because you're here, his sister's not well, that's all,' said Sally unconvincingly. 'You get yourselves settled in then and we'll see you tomorrow. Eight o'clock all right? Oh, and if you do go out for lunch or something, make sure you put the electric fence across won't you? There are loads of *sangliers*, wild boar, round here – they can tear up a lawn in seconds.
Anything you need, you've got my number. Now where's that husband of mine? Bye.'

'What a very odd thing to say,' said Debbie.

'What was?' I replied.

'That her husband isn't upset because we're here. That's the first thing she said. Sounds to me as if that's exactly why he's upset.'

'Bloody hope not.'

'Come on, let's unload the car,' said Debbie, who was looking very worried. Our previously undecorated apartment now boasted a washing machine, a well-used fridge, an old sofa and a double bed with a heavily stained mattress.

'Maybe he sees us as a threat, thinks we're going to take his job,' I said as I stood in the kitchen with a cup of coffee. 'I mean, it wouldn't surprise me. The place has got new owners. Happens all the time.'

At a quarter to eight the following morning there was a knock on our front door.

'Sorry, we're a bit early,' apologised Sally. François, or Clampit as we had christened him the night before over a glass of rosé, barged through with an armful of dustsheets. He went back to his truck, which he had left running, and returned with tins of paint, paintbrushes, rollers, ladders and indoor scaffolding.

'Would you like a coffee?' I asked.

'Haven't got time for that lad – need to get on,' replied Sally. 'Maybe about eleven o'clock. Adrian's wife has got a list as long as your arm for us to do. Where's Debbie?'

'Doing her teeth.'

'That's good, she won't be long then. Now then,' Sally said, 'where do you think we should start?' she asked, quickly going from one room to the other.

'Start what?' I replied, aggrieved at my morning coffee having been interrupted by the whirlwind that was Sally and her very grumpy husband.

'Didn't I tell you? We're all painting the apartment this morning. Meant to do it before you arrived – didn't have time. Right, you two start in the bedroom, me and François will start in the living room. How long did you say Debbie was going to be? Is she usually up this late?' asked Sally, who was changing out of her metal-heeled boots and into a pair of old trainers.

With bleary eyes, Debbie and I began painting the bedroom. Next door there was a lot of banging about and swearing. '*Merde*' and '*putain!*' were often followed by something or other, usually a paint pot, crashing to the floor.

When he'd finished painting, François smeared a good deal of sealant around the rotting window frames to stop our apartment from becoming even damper.

At the end of two physically demanding days, our apartment, painted brilliant white, was finished.

'Got to start the proper work now,' announced Sally, looking at her watch on the Wednesday morning. 'Brent will be helping François and Debbie…where is Debbie? She can't still be cleaning her teeth,' she said, 'it's almost eight o'clock!' she went on, shaking her head in disbelief. 'Where was I? Oh, yes.

Debbie will be sorting the house out. François's got the same list as I have so we can cross them off as we go. He's up at the guest house so you can meet him there.'

I was tasked with helping move a lot of furniture, some of which was extremely heavy. François and I huffed and puffed our way through the next few days, hardly exchanging a word. Then, one afternoon, an email arrived from Adrian saying that I was to look after the pretty bits in the garden so that it would all look good for the film, while François was to strim the meadow and cut back the trees that were overhanging the drive so that the crew could get down in their lorries. As I mowed the croquet lawn, weeded the beds and added some extra plants, Guss, who was in his element, would appear from time to time with a pine cone that he'd drop, stare at and expect me to throw. He used to do the same to François but there's only so many times that even the very persistent Guss was prepared to be ignored. With François's and my paths not crossing very much, everything seemed quite harmonious.

One Friday morning Debbie and I made the short trip to the village market, which was pretty much the same as any other French market, with one major difference. In amongst the usual array of fruit and vegetable stalls was a vendor in his mid-sixties dressed as a woman. He had the full regalia, all the way from a pearl necklace to high-heeled shoes. For moments we stood there mesmerised while he continued to sell his cooked chickens to his customers, who didn't bat an eyelid. It wasn't so much the fact that the man was a crossdresser but more about the location that he was in. It wasn't quite what we were expecting to see in a small parochial village in the middle of nowhere. Feeling guilty for having stared at him for so long we felt obliged to buy one of his chickens, which we tucked into at lunch with a salad and a glass of wine.

'Who would have thought it?' said Debbie, smiling and raising her glass. 'Good for him.'

'Here's to the chicken man,' I replied. 'Just when you thought that France couldn't surprise you anymore. The man can cook too,' I said, picking up another drumstick.

Chapter 35

We were woken up at seven-thirty by someone banging very loudly on the front door. I put on my dressing gown and slippers and went to see what the fuss was all about.

'Where's the fire?' I asked a very distraught Sally, who was waving a piece of paper in her hand.

'She's coming next week, she's coming next week,' she replied, looking around for any sign of Debbie.

'Who is?' I yawned.

'Annabelle, Adrian's wife, and she wants to know if you can drive a seven-and-a-half-ton truck. There's a load of furniture she wants bringing down and thinks it a good idea if you could fly to England and drive it back here.'

'No.'

'What do you mean, no?'

'No means I can't a drive a seven-and-a-half-ton truck. It also means I'm not doing it. Would you like a coffee?' I asked, reaching for the kettle.

'You don't need a special licence.'

'Then get Clampit to do it.'

'Who's Clampit? Hang on, phone's going. Suggest you hurry and get dressed lad, there's a lot to be done before she gets here. Hello....' Sally went outside and returned five minutes later. 'Don't worry, it was her. She's found someone else but we do need some help with some other stuff. This friend of yours, Clampit, could you give him a ring for us? I think we're going to be really busy. What a funny name. You still not dressed yet? I don't know...' and away she ran, slamming the door behind her.

In preparation for Annabelle's arrival, Debbie spent many hours planning menus for the three days that she and a small entourage were to be staying. For the first evening, she made a velouté using mushrooms that had been picked from the estate, she prepared a main course of pan-fried sea bass and to finish she'd baked a lemon tart dessert.

Just after six o'clock François returned from the airport with our new boss's wife, three young women who were fussing after her and a mountain of luggage. Annabelle, a woman in her late thirties, tall, rake-thin with very sharp features and elegantly dressed in a flowing black designer trouser suit and scarf, swept across the courtyard and disappeared through the front door.

As it was warm enough to eat outside, a table next to the fountain was set for dinner. Guss turned on the charm and when the food came out he lay down quietly several feet away from the diners. As I wasn't needed at the house, I sat in front of the television in our apartment and opened a bottle of beer. Seconds later the intercom buzzed.

'Annabelle wants you to come and get Guss. She doesn't want a dog anywhere near the table,' said Debbie. 'Please be quick.'

I grabbed his lead and ran to the villa. When I got there the entourage all smiled and said hello. Annabelle just glared.

'What an absolute cow,' said Debbie, throwing her chef's whites onto the bed.

'Who is?'

'That bitch of a wife of his. Won't be a minute, just going to get changed. Do the beers, would you?'

'Do tell,' I said, as we sat down on the sofa.

'She waited until the end of the meal and then called me over. She started by saying that the sea bass was way too much for her and really wasn't her thing. Wouldn't mind but she cleared her plate.'

'OK.'

'The dessert apparently was too rich and the mushroom velouté was totally inappropriate.'

'How can it be inappropriate? Mushrooms are in season. Did you happen to mention that they were picked here this morning?'

'Didn't get chance. Once she finished what she was saying, she turned her back on me and started talking to the others.'

'Didn't occur to her to tell you in private?'

'Doubt it, the woman has no manners.'

'Clearly.'

'Anyway, apparently, she's on a macrobiotic diet, which she said she'd already told Sally to tell me.'

'And Sally didn't speak up.'

'No, Sally didn't,' replied Debbie, quite angrily. 'She just sat there looking rather sheepish.'

'You should've said something.'

'What's the point? That would only have got Sally into trouble. Besides, I don't actually care – every single plate came back clean and that tells me everything, regardless of the crap madam comes out with. Get me a top-up, would you? Can't move. Spineless bitch,' Debbie muttered as I went to the kitchen.

Over the coming days, we scarcely saw Sally at all – she was far too busy hurrying around after Annabelle. François would sometimes arrive and the three of them could quite often be seen in a huddle in the courtyard. Up until that time, we hadn't seen François smile, let alone laugh out loud. For someone who appeared to us to be so miserable, he certainly knew how to turn on the charm when it came to his bosses. One evening we were sitting in the lounge, when Debbie looked up from her new Philippa Gregory book and said,

'You know how some kings and queens have names like *Louis the Sun King* and *Napoleon the Great*?'

'Yes.'

'Perhaps we should rename him *François the Obsequious Little Shit*. Just a thought.'

I was on my way to the villa one morning when I spotted someone that I didn't recognise peering through the windows. There was a silver Porsche 911 in the car park and a red briefcase had been placed on the table where Debbie and I were interviewed when we first arrived. Hearing my footsteps, the man, dressed in a casual suit, open-necked shirt and suede shoes swivelled round.

'Hello, I'm John,' he said with a warm smile. 'I'm one of the film's producers.'

'Brent,' I replied, offering my hand. 'I'm the new guardian. Would you like a coffee?'

'Great, could I have it out here?' he asked, while picking up his phone, which over the coming days seemed to be almost permanently glued to his ear. 'Black, no sugar, thanks.'

As I returned five minutes later, I noticed that the lid of the briefcase was open and inside was a script with the words *Dom Hemingway* emblazoned on the front. As John was pacing up and down the lawn talking to someone or other, I thought to take a closer look. With the help of a gentle breeze and a small nudge from me, the front page turned. In front of me was the cast list that began with Jude Law and Richard E Grant. I left John to his coffee and went in search of Debbie, whose interest in the film suddenly increased, quite noticeably.

Although initially there was no sign of the two principal actors, as the days went past all sorts of people connected with the film arrived to transform the villa. Overnight the front door was changed from racing green to lilac, the chimney breast in the lounge was painted bright-red and two or three enormous pictures of some very angry-looking monkeys filled the walls. The Art department appeared with all manner of weird and wonderful props, including an extraordinarily heavy safe that somehow had to be taken upstairs. Camera trucks full of equipment slid down the dusty driveway, bouncing off the grass verges as they went. A makeshift production office was set up in the small hut next to the swimming pool and chaos ensued as several cars began to block the driveway, meaning that no one could get either in or out of the property. While some people were milling about and not doing very much, others were rushing round with walkie-talkies in an attempt to bring order to what was beginning to appear a complete shambles. Complaints started to come from all directions as there was precious little Internet access, meaning that communication with the outside world had become extremely limited. The managers in the office asked the rest of the crew to cut down their usage unless absolutely necessary. The request was completely ignored until it was pointed out that one of the most important employees on the set was actually based in the hut. It wasn't the director, the producer or even Jude Law. It was someone who wielded much more power – the cheery lady in charge of payroll. Once she'd politely but assertively explained to the masses the implications of her not being able to do her job, phones were switched off immediately and as a consequence, several people could be seen wandering about the grounds, looking a bit lost for something to do.

In amongst the pandemonium, we'd organised for all of our worldly goods to be brought over from the UK. Sally had impressed upon us that getting our things here would be seen as a very positive move as it would demonstrate a certain amount of commitment to the job. One evening, just as it was getting dark and raining quite heavily, our fruitwood dining room table, chairs with matching mirror and console, as well as crockery, cutlery, paintings, DVDs, CDs and over three hundred cookery books arrived.

As the nights drew in we watched back-to-back episodes of our favourite sitcom, *Outside Edge*. For a while we forgot about François's and Annabelle's hostility and replaced it with cheerily saying, 'All right, love you, fair enough,' at each other and, on the odd occasion when something went right, instead of saying, 'Well done!' we'd shout, 'Well played Bernard.' This cheered us up so much that I wrote to Robert Daws to thank him and the rest of the cast for the laughs. Much to my delight and surprise he replied, in character, with a very sweet email. Thank you Skip.

Debbie took great delight in reacquainting herself with her cookery books and I, when not watching the TV, played games on the computer. Through all the madness that surrounded us we were beginning to feel that, at last, we were getting settled.

'Oh look, that's Jude Law,' said a very excited Debbie, who had been asked to cook lunch during rehearsals.

'And that's 'Richard E Grant,' who was striding through the car park towards us.

'I'm so nervous. I hope they'll be OK,' said Debbie. 'Is my hair all right?'

She needn't have worried. Every lunchtime the two actors would bound into the kitchen and give Debbie a huge hug – something that really made her day. They also adored Debbie's cooking, so much so that one day before the rest of the crew arrived, Richard E Grant triumphantly announced, 'I appear to have eaten all of the beef,' and fell about in fits of laughter. The atmosphere had become fun and relaxed. Any preconceived notions that we had had of prima donnas arriving on the set were completely ill-founded.

'Bitch doesn't know what she's talking about when it comes to food,' I said to Debbie as I watched her bring out platter after platter onto the kitchen table.

'Which bitch is that?' she replied.

'Annabelle, taste of an onion that woman.'

'Forget her,' said Debbie, who was watching her food disappear at a rate of knots. 'She can go boil her head. I just hope I've made enough,' she said worriedly, as she watched another four or five people that she hadn't been told about come through the door.

Although Debbie wasn't due to cook once the filming started as caterers had been hired, her cooking had gone down a storm with the twenty or so crew that used to come for lunch during rehearsals. Whether just for coffee, lunch or a chat, the kitchen soon became the place for all and sundry to gravitate. Jude Law, when not rehearsing or learning his lines, could often be seen sitting at the long wooden dining table, surrounded by a group of women from the Costume or Makeup department, who seemed to hang on his every word. We met Richard Shepard, the Director, a very charming man who I used to see strolling along the lawn, deep in thought.

'Hello, I'm Arwel,' said a jolly chap with a Welsh accent. 'I'm from the Art department. Are you all right my lover?' he said, giving me a kiss on either cheek. Seeing I was looking less than comfortable with this greeting, he walked over to Debbie, shook her by the hand and said, 'How are you, darling? I've heard all about your cooking. Sorry I wasn't here earlier. Anyway, must get on,' he added before grabbing a sandwich and disappearing out of the door.

'That was a bit friendly,' I said nervously to Debbie, who had found the whole episode very amusing.

'He obviously likes you,' she replied. 'If there's anything you ever want to tell me....'

'Oh, very funny.'

In the mornings after finishing the garden, I'd help with the preparation for the lunches. Arwel would pop back from time to time and massage my shoulders. As soon as I started to squirm, which wasn't usually very long, he'd whisper in my ear, 'See you later my lover,' wink and off he'd go.

When rehearsals were over and filming started, Guss stayed with us until around midday, at which point he'd run down to the helicopter hangar at the bottom of the meadow, where he would join the fifty or so cast and crew members, who were tucking into their lunch. Far from being interested in the food, Guss just wanted to play. He'd pick up a pine cone, drop it at someone's feet and wait for it to be thrown. Very quickly, almost everyone had developed a soft spot for Guss – everyone, that is, apart from François, who when seeing Guss stare intently at his prize, would mutter '*Maladie de balle*,' and walk past.

As I walked around the grounds with my secateurs and watering can, I'd often hear someone shout, 'Turning over, quiet please!' Like the many others who were not involved in the upcoming scene, I stood still, said nothing and waited for the command, 'cut!' This seemed to work pretty well for everyone – everyone except Debbie, who was in a world of her own. With ideas for recipes, as well as all things laundry buzzing around her head, she was completely oblivious to the film or anyone associated with it. She'd suddenly pop up out of nowhere, ask herself why there was a small crowd of ten or eleven people huddled together seemingly not saying or doing very much, reason that it must be a tea break or some such and disappear again.

'How did you get here my love?' Arwel asked her one day.

'I just walked here like anyone else,' Debbie replied, somewhat bemused by the question.

'You didn't hear anyone shout, "Turning over"?'

'Apparently not,' she giggled, as did the rest of the group that she'd found herself in the middle of.

And that wasn't to be the last time that Arwel and Debbie were to meet on set. One evening, she was coming out of the villa when she noticed that there was a scene being shot on the croquet lawn. Seeing a nice white sofa at the far end that was empty, she sat down, put her laundry on her lap and waited for the action to begin. All of a sudden, Arwel gently took Debbie by the arm and whispered in her ear,

'I don't remember you being on the cast list, Debbie, my love. You see that camera there?' he said with a big grin. 'I know it looks a bit far away but it's about to pan round in this direction and you and your washing will become famous. Come on, my love,' he said, leading her towards the kitchen, much to the amusement of the rest of the crew.

'I'm sorry about that,' apologised Debbie, looking very embarrassed.

'Don't you worry about that my love,' said Arwel, putting his arm around her, 'they hadn't started filming. Actually, I'm quite glad you're here because I've got a small favour to ask you.'

'Really?' said Debbie, sitting down, very relieved not to have become the centre of attention.

'There's a scene see, with a cooked rabbit. It needs to be nicely presented on a silver platter. Do you think you could do that for us? You would really be helping me out.'

'Me? Are you sure?' replied Debbie, surprised.

'Of course you. Why not you? Your food's lovely – should be a walk in the park. Would you do it?'

'I'd love to.'

'Thank you, Debbie. I'll speak to you about it later. I'm needed on set now. Thanks again,' he said before closing the door gently behind him.

Being in the middle of the countryside, where hunters' gunshots were often heard, we assumed that getting hold of a rabbit would be an easy task – it proved to be anything but.

The people who weren't at the time needed on the film were given the address of every butcher within a ten-mile radius and set off. At about five o'clock they'd all given up and went in search of alcohol – a far simpler and much more enjoyable task. On the way back they stopped at the local supermarket, where they picked up six cases of beer and two rabbits. One of the rabbits was given to Debbie, which she cooked and then placed on a bed of Dauphinoise potatoes, garnished with a few sprigs of rosemary.

The scene was due to be shot at about eleven o'clock that night but as we were to discover, timings for many reasons can change and this was no exception. At one o'clock in the morning Arwel came into the kitchen and said to Debbie, who had been waiting both nervously and patiently, 'Sorry, my love, it's going to be tomorrow.'

'That's OK,' replied Debbie, who began to consign her third batch of potatoes to the bin. 'Goodnight Arwel.'

At eight o'clock the following evening, from a distance and with her arm round Arwel, Debbie watched proudly as the rabbit scene was filmed.

About an hour later, I wandered down to the set, leaving Debbie and Guss at the apartment. 'Do you know how to turn this fountain off, Brent?' asked John, the producer. 'We're about to shoot right beside it and we don't want the sound of the water drowning out the actors' voices.'

'Sorry, I don't but I'll phone François.'

'Thanks.'

'You want me to come back?' asked François, with a heavy sigh. In the background, I could hear the clattering of cutlery and someone slurping a drink.

'No, François, I don't need you to come back. Just tell me where the switch is.'

François said that the tap was in amongst some bushes below the steps that led down to the meadow. Soon, I found myself lying down in the long, wet grass and brambles, looking for a metal tap that I, after a while, was beginning to think didn't exist. Even François had admitted it was quite well concealed. 'It's got to be here somewhere,' I whispered, shining the torch towards my increasingly cold, wet and now scratched hands. I was on the verge of giving up and had just turned off my torch when my body froze as I felt something warm, wet and slimy crawl over my wrist. A cold sweat ran down my spine. Shaking like a leaf, I managed to turn on my torch.

'Bloody hell, Guss, you little shit, what are you doing here?'

A lick on the ear and a wag of the tail was his response.

Having failed dismally in my quest to find the elusive tap, I made my way back through the woods to the apartment, closely followed by a, very pleased with himself, dog.

Chapter 36

'What are they?' I asked John, who was supervising the delivery of two massive machines that were carefully being unloaded from the back of a white truck.

'Rain makers,' he replied.

'Rain makers? Sounds interesting.'

'Would be, if it wasn't for the weather forecast. Apparently, it's absolutely going to chuck it down tonight,' he added, looking suspiciously at the sky.

'And the problem is?'

'The problem is that I've just paid fourteen grand for two machines and we might not need them at all,' John said with a sigh.

'Wow!'

'Yeah, wow! See you later.'

Unfortunately for John, that evening his worst fears were realised – I had never seen it rain so hard in all of my life. Within seconds, the croquet lawn was waterlogged, the outbuildings were starting to flood and the rain machines had been rendered useless. Debbie, who had been serving sandwiches and coffee to the crew, was back at the apartment while I, in a moment of complete madness, had volunteered to stay behind and do the washing up. I was minding my own business, drying up a few cups and thinking about nothing in particular, when François, dressed from head to toe in waterproofs, came bursting through the back door.

'Pelle!' he shouted.

I had never come across the word before, or at least if I had, I didn't remember it.

'Pelle?' I asked. 'Sorry, François, I have no idea what....'

'Pelle, pelle!' he said angrily, raising his arms with frustration.

'No, still haven't got it. In English, perhaps?'

For a few seconds we stood in silence, racking our brains and then came the lightbulb moment. François put his index finger in the air and said triumphantly, 'Spud.'

'Spud?' I replied, trying not to laugh. 'I don't see how one of those is going to help this situation much – I think I'd better go and get Sally.'

'Why, what is spud?'

'This, François,' I began, reaching for a bag of potatoes, 'is….'

'*Merde, merde*! Where is my wife?'

'I'm guessing at our apartment with Debbie. They were going have a drink this evening.'

'Tell her *pelle, pelle* urgent,' replied François, who ran out of the back door, cursing me as he went. Moments later, I left via the front door and within seconds was soaked through. My only protection from the rain was a thick, woollen fleece which, by the time I got back to our apartment, felt as heavy as I was. As I walked through the door, Debbie and Sally, who were in the kitchen relaxing with a glass of wine, shrieked with laughter.

'You look a bit wet lad. Not raining outside by any chance is it?' Sally quipped.

'Just a tad,' I replied, looking down at the pool of water below me that was beginning to spread across the kitchen floor. 'I've got a message for you from François. He tried to ask me first but, unfortunately, I'd got no idea what he was on about.'

'Go on then lad – spit it out. What did he say?'

'He said, *pelle*, urgent. What's a….'

'Oh shit!' said Sally, putting her glass down and snatching her coat from behind the front door. 'A spade. He wanted you to get a spade.'

'Oh I see,' I replied, kicking off my sodden trainers.

'He must be in the barn. Always floods and the tapestries are on the floor. Shit, should've moved them earlier! François must be going ape.'

'He is an ape,' I muttered under my breath.

'You'd better get changed and quick,' Sally ordered, putting up the hood on her coat and rushing outside. I watched her as she splashed as fast as her legs would carry her through the puddles along the drive, before disappearing into the night.

I had a quick shower, put on some fresh clothes and hoped that the rain would have stopped by the time I left to go back down to the villa. As I looked glumly through the kitchen window, I could see that, if anything, it had got worse. The once dusty drive had turned into a fast flowing river and it wouldn't have surprised me at all if I'd seen Jude Law and Richard E Grant come whizzing past our front door on a raft. Reluctantly, with the aid of Debbie's pink umbrella (complete with bunny ears) and a pair of cowboy boots that I hadn't worn for years, I set off for the barn.

By the time I got there, the tapestries were off the floor and the mopping-up operation was all but over. As François hadn't noticed me when I peered through the door, I thought it best to return to the kitchen. There was nobody at the table but there were a few people milling around in the back kitchen. There was some water on the floor and, to my right, I noticed that Sally's backside was going up and down like a piston as she shovelled out spade after spade of unwelcome water. Not only that, her metronomic bottom had gained quite an audience so I offered to take over, which cleared the room immediately.

With the rain having died down, and with nothing more to be done, I left the villa just before two in the morning.

The next morning after breakfast, at about eight o'clock, I was able to fully see the extent of the damage caused by the previous night's flood. The croquet lawn, which luckily was no longer needed for the film, had become a mud bath, the plain trees had been stripped of their leaves and the previously pristine terrace was covered in mud. It was impossible for any of the trucks to make it up the driveway and many of the cars that attempted the climb only managed part of the way before sliding back down again. With much more immediate problems to think about, no one had remembered to pull the electric fence cables across before leaving. This was not lost on the *sangliers*, who at some point during the night had made it onto the lush lawn that housed the miniature railway and completely turned it over. François, who up until then used to grunt at me as he walked past, just glared. Clearly, in his mind at least, I was to blame.

The time for one of the most talked about scenes in the film had arrived – Jude Law was about to run naked through the olive grove. Only a select few people were allowed on set and several of the crew had been posted around the perimeter of the estate to ward off any opportunist paparazzi that might have camped out in the shrubbery. Everybody not involved in the shoot was forbidden from going within a hundred metres of the guesthouse until the all- clear had been given. I was on my way back to our apartment when I heard some footsteps quickening behind me. As I turned round, Debbie, who could hardly contain herself, came running up and grabbed me by the arm.

'Brent, Brent,' she said. 'You won't believe what I just saw!' Debbie went on excitedly, with a smile as big as I'd ever seen.

Oh no, I thought, she's done it again. Surely, she hadn't managed to get past all of the security?

'Well, I was taking some sheets up to the guesthouse and I'd just got to the front door when I saw Jude Law's peachy bum running through the olive grove. I couldn't believe it. Woo hoo. That's made my day, my year in fact!' Debbie laughed and then said quite thoughtfully, 'Mind you, you'd think they'd have a bit better security wouldn't you?'

'Didn't anyone tell you?'

'Tell me what?'

'It was a closed set.'

'I have no idea what one of those is but too late now anyway. I saw Jude Law's peachy bum, I saw Jude Law's peachy bum,' she chanted as she turned round and skipped back down the driveway. For days I heard about nothing else and nor for that matter did most of the crew, who found Debbie's delight and the whole episode very amusing.

It was the last day of the film and just as the final scene was being shot Arwel came to our apartment to say goodbye. With him he brought a box, out of which he took five bottles of Moët et Chandon that he placed on the coffee table.

'I just wanted to say thank you for everything Debbie, especially the rabbit. I've had a look at the footage and it looks wonderful. Couldn't have asked for more.'

'My pleasure,' replied Debbie, who was visibly moved by both Arwel's words and generosity. 'Where do you go from here, Arwel?' she asked.

'Back to Wales. I spend Christmas with my wife and kids and then back to work in January, and....'

'You do what?' I interrupted. 'With your wife and kids! What do you mean, your wife and kids? Am I missing something here?' I said, looking very confused.

'I do that rather well, don't I, my love?' Arwel replied with a smile. 'Kept you on your toes though, didn't it? Give us a hug, Debbie, I'd best be off. Thanks again. Hope you have a lovely Christmas, bye-bye.'

Debbie and I were sad to see the film crew go but at least they had left us with some great memories, one in particular which Debbie was to share time and time again.

We were talking about Arwel and his friends over breakfast the following morning when a very glum Sally arrived.

'Do you mind if I sit down?' she asked nervously.

'Go ahead,' I said. 'Coffee?'

'No thanks. Look, there's no easy way to say this but they've decided not to keep you on.'

'You don't say,' I replied, looking at Debbie, who had put her head in her hands. 'And the reason they've decided this is what exactly?' I asked.

'The garden,' replied Sally.

'The garden? The garden! What's up with bloody garden?' I said, angrily

'I don't know,' replied Sally. 'They just said the garden.'

'First I've heard of it. It's winter, what do they want, Kew Gardens? The film crew were happy enough so what's wrong with Adrian and Annabelle? Actually, I'll tell you what's wrong with Adrian and Annabelle shall I? It's what your husband's told them. He hasn't wanted us here from day one.'

'I'm not sure about that,' replied Sally, who was beginning to fidget uncomfortably.

'We do. He's stitched us right up – snake!' I said, pacing up and down the living room. 'Anyway, it's not important now, so what's the plan?'

'They'll pay you until the end of January. They said you can stay until then if you like.'

'And what about our stuff?' asked Debbie, who was looking despondently around the room.

'What about your stuff?'

'You asked us to bring it over from the UK,' said Debbie, shaking her head. 'Cost us a small fortune to get it here, are they going to pay for that?'

'I'll see what I can do.'

'I think you'd better.'

Sally was getting up to go when François appeared.

'I'm sorry to hear you're going,' he said with a broad grin.

'Don't give me that crap, François. This is your doing!' I said angrily. He didn't reply. 'Oh and Sally,' I added, 'you know it's illegal to evict people in France in winter do you? We can stay as long….'

'This is your trial period,' she interrupted. 'Doesn't apply to you.'

'Anyway,' said François, making no attempt to conceal his delight, 'if you don't go when we say, I just cut off your electricity. I don't want to have to do that. Come on Sally.'

Christmas was upon us before we knew it and, far from being at all upset about leaving La Garde-Freinet, we were looking forward to getting away from the isolation. Christmas Day was one of the best ever. We opened one of the bottles of Champagne given to us by Arwel for breakfast, enjoyed a fabulous turkey courtesy of our loyalty points gained at the local supermarket and then popped the cork of another bottle at lunch.

'That was a bit extravagant,' said Debbie.

'I know. Cheers, Arwel. Is there any pud?'

'You couldn't.'

'So say you. Where's the brandy butter?'

Chapter 37

By the beginning of February, we'd found a cheap place to rent in Théoule Sur Mer, a small seaside town about half an hour from Cannes, and had put everything back into storage, though this time in France. As it was out of season, our two-bedroom apartment, which overlooked the Mediterranean, only cost four hundred euros for the month.

'Normally,' said our genial landlord, who led us from room to room, 'it goes for fifteen hundred euros – rented out by yacht crews in the summer. They get up to eight people in here. It's a bit cramped but they're used to that, being on boats,' he said.

'We'll take it,' said Debbie, almost immediately.

'You don't want to think about it?' replied our host, looking quite stunned by the speed of the decision.

'No,' she said, glancing towards me.

'OK, right you are then. When do you want to move in?'

'Now all right? We've got all of our stuff in the car.'

'That's fine by me,' our new landlord replied hesitantly. 'You OK to pay up front?'

'Sure,' I replied, producing some notes from my wallet.

'That was quick,' I said to Debbie as we went down to the car to unload.

'I know. I'm just so happy to be out of that place – be somewhere normal, somewhere where I can relax. I've had enough. I want a holiday and I want to get settled.'

Our apartment was extremely cosy. There was a log burner that could heat the lounge-cum-dining room within minutes and when the sun shone it was warm enough to sit outside on the balcony and read the paper with a cup of coffee. Guss was very happy as, because it was winter, the rules about forbidding dogs on the beach weren't enforced and he could chase seagulls to his heart's content. There were shops, all within walking distance, cafés to sit in while watching the world go by and there was a very good hypermarket only ten minutes away by car.

Soon, we began to feel part of civilisation and were loving every minute of it. Our quirky landlord, James, who we got to know quite well, would often phone us on his way back from one of the local bars and, moments later, would appear at the front door with a bottle of wine.

'I've checked you out. You're OK,' he slurred one evening, before slumping into a comfy chair.

'You've done what?' I asked.

'The registration on your car, I've checked it out. You can never be too careful. Hope you don't mind,' he said, lighting a cigarette with the end of one that he was about to put out. 'Anyway, never mind all that – have I mentioned Fernanda?'

'Can't say you have,' replied Debbie, who was still clearly confused as to why our car had come under scrutiny in the first place.

'She's Brazilian and completely nuts. We have an on–off relationship, more off than on to be honest. People say I should get rid of her. I don't know. I'll show you some pictures but I warn you she is a bit wild,' he said. 'We were out in a restaurant one night when she suddenly got up on the table and started shouting at everyone. She thought that we were being ignored because the waiters were racist. They weren't, the restaurant was just crap. Gotta love her. Where's the corkscrew, Brent?' James continued, staggering towards the kitchen. About one o'clock and two bottles of wine later, he said goodnight, singing all the way up to his apartment.
At breakfast, as Debbie was putting on the toast she said, 'Why don't we invite him for dinner tonight? He seems nice enough and maybe a bit lonely?'

'Hang on,' I said as I opened the door to our terrace, 'I'll see if his car's outside. Yes, it's down there. I'll go now.'

A very weary James answered the front door in his dressing gown. 'You all right?' he asked.

'Fine thanks. Look, Debbie's asked if you'd like to have dinner with us tonight.'

'That's very kind but the thing is I've got a terrible cold, might even be the flu,' he said, reaching for a tissue and blowing his nose. 'I've cancelled work today. I think I'd best go back to bed. Thanks anyway.'

That evening Debbie and I decided to get a takeaway pizza. As we were about to walk into the restaurant, James waved at us from the bar on the opposite side of the road and persuaded us to join him for a glass of rosé while we waited. His cold had, miraculously, cleared up.

The day before we left, I was just about to get into our car to go to the shops when I noticed that an orange line had been painted on the tarmac around it. As I began to examine the scene, James appeared on the top balcony and looked down.

'Hope you don't mind, Brent, only I've got my boat arriving tomorrow on a trailer and I want to make sure no one nicks the space. The paint should be dry in about an hour, do you think you could hold on until then? Thanks very much.'

Our last evening in Théoule was upon us, so we invited James for one last drink, which he declined but turned up for anyway.

'You will be gone by ten won't you?' he said as he got up to leave. 'I won't be here. I need to be gone by six – taking a boat to Cannes and my mate Chris will need your space.'

'Of, course,' replied Debbie, as she opened the door. 'Night, James.'

'And don't forget to put the keys….'

'We won't,' I said, just before hearing the lock click into place.

At nine-thirty the following morning, as I dropped our keys through the letterbox upstairs I could hear the sound of someone gently snoring in the background. We never did get to meet Chris or James's eccentric Brazilian girlfriend but we did find our time in Théoule extremely enjoyable, entertaining and bizarrely, quite therapeutic.

We were hoping to stay in the south but as it was the beginning of March we were coming out of low season and the low prices associated with it were no longer available. Everyone was asking much more than we could afford. So we made the four-hour journey west to Villeneuve-Minervois, a small town fifteen miles north of Carcassonne. A young English builder and his girlfriend were renovating some apartments and, as long as we didn't mind putting up with the occasional bit of noise, we could stay there for five hundred euros per month, which was about half what we were being asked on the south coast. Our one-bedroomed house was in the middle of the town centre opposite a family butcher's and only a few doors along was a bakery. There was also a *tabac*, a small restaurant and a convenience store. Being in the heart of the French countryside, we were pleased to have plenty of walks to take Guss on. There was something, however, a little strange about how information from the *Mairie* was disseminated to the residents. They didn't seem to bother with local newspapers or fliers in Villeneuve-Minervois. Instead, we'd be woken by the crackling of a speaker somewhere outside, which was followed by a very tinny announcement.

'Bloody hell,' I said, 'it's like a Japanese prisoner of war camp. Are you sure we're on holiday?'

'Castres's not too far away,' said Debbie, poring over a map of the local area. 'What do you reckon?'

'What do I reckon? Are you mad, woman?' I replied, nearly spitting my coffee out. 'Have you completely taken leave of your senses? We couldn't wait to get away from there and now you want to back? What on earth makes you think that's a good idea?'

'Just to be nosey. Find out what Smythe's up to.'

'Who cares what he's up to? For all we know, our replacements could've killed him by now. Anyway, what if he's there?'

'We'll drive past,' replied Debbie, who was busily writing down the route.

'So, let me get this straight. We drive an hour and a half to Castres. We get there, look through the gates and if we see either of those two idiots, we drive straight past?'

'Yes. What else have we got to do?'

'No, no and no. I'm putting my foot down on this one, Debbie. We are absolutely not going to Castres.'

Half an hour later we were in the car, heading in the direction of our former employer.

As we approached *Rose des Vents*, we could see a couple of a similar age to ourselves in the courtyard. After a short while, and deciding it was safe, I called through the gates. Richard and Julie, who we were to discover had been our fourth replacements since our departure, invited us in for coffee.

'Is it OK to let our dog out?' I asked.

'Of course,' replied Richard. 'This is Alfie,' he said, putting out his hand to stroke an elderly crossbreed who had come to see what was going on. 'He's quite...' but before he had chance to finish, he and Guss had run off into the woods at the back of the villa, wagging their tails as they went.

'Where's Herbie?' I asked.

'Back in the Cayman. They take him everywhere they go these days.'

'So, how's it going?' Debbie said.

'Not well, if I'm honest,' replied Richard. 'The thing is, I don't really get it. Xander spent nearly two years trying to persuade us to come here and as soon as we arrive he treats us like rubbish.'

'Sounds familiar,' I said.

'I told him I wasn't a gardener, so what did he do? Spent all summer criticising me about it. And all she ever did was moan.'

'It was exactly the same with us,' said Debbie. 'What are you going to do?'

'Leave, I'm sad to say,' replied Julie, who was putting down a tray on the wall beside us. 'We've given in our notice. Shame, we thought we might be really happy here. Never mind.'

'Sorry to hear that. When do you go?' I asked.

'Well, that's the only downside,' said Richard. 'He's asked us to give four months' notice but at least he won't be here.'

'Not all bad then?' I said.

'Suppose not,' replied Julie. 'Anyway, we've had enough of him and they've had enough of France, so it might work out for the best.'

'They've had enough of France? Really, they're selling?' asked Debbie, who looked quite shocked.

'Let's say they've been trying,' replied Richard, picking up his coffee. 'As usual, it hasn't been straightforward – nothing ever is with those two.'

'Do tell,' I said, eager to hear what had happened this time.

'Well,' began Richard, 'you know how Xander thinks this place is the be-all and end-all of properties in the south west of France?'

'Yes,' I said.

'The thing is,' said Richard, biting into a chocolate biscuit, 'Xander tried to persuade a top estate agent in Montpellier to put *Rose des Vents* on their books. Someone came round, had a quick look and buggered off – wasn't exclusive enough apparently. Xander went mad and bombarded them with emails and phone calls. All credit to them, they ignored both to start with.' Richard laughed.

'So, what happened?' I asked.

'In the end they passed on the details to someone else, just to get rid of him. Anyway, the bloke turned up one morning and was kept here for a good four or five hours.'

'Four or five hours? What the hell was he doing here for four or five hours?' I asked.

'You know what he's like,' said Julie. 'He goes into every minute detail and doesn't let you go until you ask for some aspirin.'

'Tell me about it,' agreed Debbie. 'One day I'll tell you about our last day here, you wouldn't believe it.'

'Anyway,' continued Richard, 'just as the poor man was about to leave, Xander asked him for his card. He ferreted about in his pockets but couldn't find one. "Don't worry," said Xander, "I'll get the details from your website." "I don't have one of those either," the chap replied. "I'm just starting up." You should have seen Xander's face.'

'No!' I said, quite astonished.

'Seriously,' Julie added. 'Xander didn't let him finish. He just opened the gates and told him to get out and that was that.'

'Turns out he was the brother-in-law of the estate agent. Never sold a property in his life,' Richard said as a broad grin ran across his face. 'Well, he wouldn't have would he?'

'Why so?' asked Debbie.

'He's a plumber. Lives in Castres. Bumped into him last week. Is there any more coffee Julie?'

For a good while the four of us swapped stories. It seemed that nothing had changed and that, one way or another, we were all better off without Xander Smythe.

'So glad we're out of there,' I said to Debbie as we drove back out of the Gates of Hell, waving as we went. 'Fancy some lunch?'

When we got back to Villeneuve-Minervois we'd been sent details about a job working in a château just outside Carpentras, a small town fifteen miles north of Avignon. According to the agency, the fifteen-acre estate was owned by a titled lady who was also a distant relative of the Queen and although it was more remote than we'd have liked, the property was hardly occupied. Apart from the summer, our time would be very much our own and, as the gardens had fallen into disrepair over the years, there was an opportunity to make a noticeable difference quite quickly.

'I've got a good feeling about this one,' I said optimistically, as we drove through the château's gates later on that week.

'Me too,' Debbie replied. 'I so hope you're right.'

We were welcomed by Geraldine, a very well-spoken lady in her fifties. She walked towards us in her tweed suit and wellington boots, at the same time trying to hold down her long scarf that was flapping in the wind.

'Best go inside,' she said. 'Can't hear a damn thing out here. This way,' she beckoned. 'Come on, I'll show you round. Sorry about the wind,' she apologised, while wrestling with a shutter that was banging against the outside wall. 'Why don't you give yourselves a bit of a tour? I'll be with you as soon as I've sorted out this little sod.'

It seemed that the agency was right about the château hardly being used, as a very musty smell filled every room – no one had opened a window in a very long time. A big, sweeping staircase led up to the bedrooms. Thick floral wallpaper, full-length, dark, heavy curtains and classic paintings covered the walls.

When we finished upstairs we went down to the kitchen, where we met Geraldine, who explained that a refurbishment had been promised for many years but so far nothing had been done. Inside, many of the handles from the store cupboards were either hanging by a thread or missing. The red floor tiles were cracked and the walls hadn't been painted for many a year. An old range cooker sat in the corner, alongside a small dishwasher and butler sink. Just a few yards away from the château was a brick-built barn that housed a washing machine and tumble dryer.

'Fabulous, isn't it?' beamed Geraldine. 'Proper, French countryside. What do you think?'

'I think it's really nice,' said Debbie, nodding in my direction.

'Me too,' I agreed.

'And you can start pretty much immediately? Fantastic, I'll speak to the agency. Shit, that's another shutter. Bye!' Geraldine shouted as she ran into wind, waving as she went. We watched her disappear round the back of the château before we headed off.

'What are you up to?' asked Debbie the next morning, as I was sitting at the computer.

'Writing.'

'I can see that. I could hear you thumping away at the keyboard from the bedroom. Who are you writing to?'

'I'm not writing to anybody. I'm writing a book I'll have you know.'

'You're writing a book? That's different. What's it about?' said Debbie, who was peering over my shoulder.

293

'I'll read you the first few lines shall I?'

'Go on then.'

'*Our little business had collapsed and we, that's my wife Debbie and I, were sitting in our local pub, spending money that we could ill afford. It somehow....*'

'You're writing about us? she interrupted. 'Blimey. What makes you think anyone's going to want to read about us?' said Debbie, brushing her hair.

'Well, you couldn't make it up – what's happened to us since we've been in France. One minute we're virtually homeless and the next we're offered a job working for royalty. How bonkers is that? And there's everything in between. Loads of people will want to read it.'

'I suppose you might be right,' said Debbie thoughtfully. 'Though, you'd better not write anything that makes me look a complete fool.'

'Would I?'

'Knowing you, yes you probably would. Anyway, I'm not sure I want my dirty linen aired in public. Speaking of which, give me a hand, would you?'

'Why? Where are we going?'

'Launderette – washing machine's on the blink,' Debbie said, putting on her coat. 'Come on, Shakespeare.'

'Come on, Shakespeare? Come on, Shakespeare!' I replied. 'Bet Anne Hathaway never spoke to him like that.'

'Who?'

'See, you know nothing,' I said, slowly getting up from my chair and stretching.

'This much I do know my love – if you don't hurry up, the launderette will be shut and you and Anne Hathaway won't have a clean pair of underwear between you and then where will you be? And don't forget to take the tissues out of your trouser pockets!' she shouted as I sauntered into the bedroom. 'Come on, Guss, let's get your collar on.'

Made in the USA
Middletown, DE
17 March 2018